Luke Lea
of
Tennessee

Luke Lea
of
Tennessee

Mary Louise Lea Tidwell

Bowling Green State University Popular Press
Bowling Green, OH 43403

To the memory of my husband
Doctor Cromwell Tidwell,
whose conviction that this book should be written
and his never-failing encouragement and assistance
contributed greatly to making it a reality;
and to my children
Percie, Lea, and Crom,
and to my grandchildren
in the hope that in its pages they will come to know
my father

Contents

Preface

This is the first biography of Luke Lea. Based on my intimate knowledge of the man and his personal papers to which previously only a few persons have had limited access, it presents his story from his perspective which at times differs considerably from opinions heretofore advanced.

It makes no pretense of being a scholarly nor definitive history of the period, nor a final settlement of complicated and controversial matters. However, it strives to present Lea's life within the context of the early third of twentieth century Tennessee. Further, it attempts to address some of the issues relative to him raised by the scholarship of that period, primary among which are his relationship with Rogers Caldwell, the loss of state funds in their joint enterprises, and his conviction of banking law violations.

Luke Lea and Rogers Caldwell were political allies, personal friends, and business associates. The most important of the several enterprises in which they were connected were their joint ownership of Southern Publishers, holding company of the Memphis *Commercial Appeal* and the *Knoxville Journal*, and a large block of stock in the Holston-Union National Bank in Knoxville. Because of several mutual interests they became indissolubly linked in the public mind with all of each of their enterprises being lumped together.

Concurring with opinions about Lea and Caldwell of political opponents and the opposition press, John Berry McFerrin set the tone in *Caldwell and Company*, first published in 1939 and reissued by the Vanderbilt University Press in 1969, which has been almost uniformly followed, often uncritically. Although McFerrin, the foremost authority on Rogers Caldwell's financial

1

enterprises, was careful to point out that Lea was never connected at any time with Caldwell and Company nor the Bank of Tennessee, neither in their ownership nor management, and that Caldwell never had any connection financially nor editorially with Lea's newspaper, *The Nashville Tennessean*, the misconception of Lea-Caldwell interests being one entity has persisted.

When Caldwell's financial empire collapsed in 1930, the state of Tennessee lost more than six million dollars in various failed banks. The thesis of much of the scholarship of that period is that Lea and Caldwell were in league for mutual profit. It has been charged by some that they manipulated state funds in an effort to bolster their sagging finances.

I assume Lea was influential in securing state deposits for banks in which he was a stockholder, but the state also lost money in banks in which he owned no stock. He stood to gain no monetary profit from political measures he supported such as women's suffrage. He strongly advocated building roads and schools, but he had no company that sold materials, services, or insurance to the state, its officials, or employees. Sometimes his political convictions actually cost him money such as the loss of all national tobacco advertising in Lea newspapers after he supported in the mid-1920s a state tax on tobacco.

Luke Lea's total assets at the time of his death in 1945 were $35,000 of life insurance. Instead of taking bankruptcy, he was still struggling to repay with interest his large personal debts and the indebtedness of companies he owned. His family did not have an automobile and their home had been purchased in 1936 after his release from prison with the $15,000 life insurance his son Percy had left to the three younger Lea children.

In the general hysteria following the widespread bank failures of the 1930s it was not uncommon for persons connected with financial institutions to be indicted. However, the fact that Lea was convicted of banking law violations and served nearly two years in the North Carolina state prison was proof to many that he engaged in illegal activities. I am unable from firsthand knowledge to comment on his modus operandi in business or politics. However, from the intimate father-daughter relationship that we shared for nearly 23 years—from my birth until his death it is impossible not to know the kind of person he was. The fact that he saved all records, every letter, and that he waived extradition and voluntarily went to North Carolina to stand trial indicate a man who did not believe he had broken any law.

While he was in prison the highly respected A.M. Pullen & Company, certified public accountants with which he had had no previous connection, made an audit of all Lea interests' transactions with the Central Bank. That audit cleared him of any wrongdoing on the charges on which he was convicted. Thereby is strengthened his often repeated assertion that his imprisonment was a miscarriage of justice instigated by his political enemies in Tennessee to strip him of his influence.

The axiom, "power corrupts," is almost universally accepted. Luke Lea unquestionably was powerful for a time in political affairs. There appears to be no doubt that he enjoyed politics and relished being at the center of action. The motivation of another can seldom be determined with absolute certainty because it is usually comprised of a number of factors. However, Lea's political agenda and his civic activities support his classification as a progressive and tend to lend credence to his assertion, stated in his letter to Governor Henry Horton declining the appointment to the United States Senate in 1929, that his primary interest was the advancement of the state.

In addition to researching Lea's considerable body of papers, I have had: ongoing discussions through the years with my mother and my brother; innumerable conversations with my father's private secretary, Winifred Hagerty, and his lifelong intimate friend, David A. Shepherd of Sewanee; and interviews with many of Lea's key associates. I have consulted newspapers, court records, and papers of some of his contemporaries, and I am familiar with much of the literature about the period.

I have attempted to integrate the sources cited to form what I believe to have been Lea's point of view. His papers set forth his thoughts, his opinions, facts as he understood them. Since this is

Luke Lea's story, statements expressed in his papers, are neither corroborated nor refuted by other sources. The perspective of his contemporaries and the secondary literature are outside its scope. As he had no connection with Caldwell and Company nor the Bank of Tennessee, commentary on Rogers Caldwell and the transactions of those institutions are not addressed, as they are not applicable to Lea. However, I have tried to narrate as objectively as possible the events that happened and to include opinions of the opposing political faction.

The recounting of my father's life has posed several serious considerations for me. One of the most difficult has been how to tell what actually happened without stirring up old bitternesses better forgotten. It is not my purpose to discredit any individual. Therefore, persons have been included only to the extent that a knowledge of their actions is pertinent to an understanding of what happened.

Another problem has been how, without legal or fiscal training, to make complex affairs simple enough to be understood and concise enough to be readable and yet recount Lea's involvement accurately.

In spite of my limitations, I believe my first-hand intimate knowledge of the man himself, my grasp of his affairs gained through careful perusal of his personal papers, and my deep interest in his side of the story being presented, currently qualify me better than anyone else to write a personal account of Luke Lea's life. In a sense I believe he commissioned me to do so. At various times he wrote some of his experiences. Once when I urged him to record all the events of his life, he replied that he intended to but that, if he did not get around to it, maybe I would.

Although I take full responsibility for this book and any errors it contains, it could never have been written without the help and encouragement of many persons. I shall be eternally grateful: to my mother, my brother, Luke, Winifred Hagerty, and David Shepherd not only for the important information I gleaned from our many conversations but for their ever-willingness to talk with me; to author James Summerville who helped me edit the first draft and who has continued to be generous with his time, his expertise, and his encouragement in all phases of the preparation and marketing of the manuscript; to eminent historian Doctor Dewey Grantham and renowned economist Doctor Rendigs Fels for reading the first draft and their invaluable comments; to writer and newspaper editor Laffitte Howard who read the early manuscript as well as a later draft, making excellent suggestions for improvement; to Virginia Shoulders Youngblood who spent much time in my home when we were in school and who made pertinent comments on the embryonic manuscript; to noted attorney Jack W. Robinson for his careful reading of the completed manuscript; to John Poindexter, editor of the Vanderbilt University Press for his advice and assistance through the years; to my sisters-in-law Betty Lea, for her thoughtful suggestions, and Anne Lea, for reading the original draft; to editor Candace Floyd who did a masterful job in helping me compress a too lengthy manuscript; and to my sister and brother-in-law, Laura and Bill Knox, for their careful reading and invaluable comments on the almost-final draft.

I am most appreciative of the assistance of the staffs of the libraries in which I have done research: Marshall Stewart of the Nashville Public Library, the Tennessee and North Carolina state archives, the University of North Carolina Library at Chapel Hill, the University of the South library at Sewanee, the public libraries in Knoxville, Memphis, Chicago, and New York, and the Library of Congress in Washington.

I want to thank again the many persons who through the years have typed portions of the manuscript, not only for their skill but for their encouragement, especially my niece, Elizabeth Knox, and her husband, Alex Gentle, Betty Jean Taylor, who typed the manuscript and its revisions onto computer discs, Cathy Falconberry, Michelle Wilson, Kelly Clark and her mother, Sue Clark, and Sandra Stone.

Mary Louise Lea Tidwell

June 1993

Chapter One
A Life Bright with Promise

The men's voices, urgent and excited, became louder, interrupting one another while I stood quietly outside the library door. I heard my father speaking and noticed the others had stopped.

He glanced toward the door, and I beckoned. He nodded and went on talking. When he finished, he stood up, excusing himself, and came to find out what I wanted. He smiled as I slipped my hand into his, and we walked through the hall and into the living room where we could talk in private.

"How much longer will it be?" I asked.

"Not very long," he replied. "We are almost through. Call Mr. Branham and ask him to have the horses saddled in half an hour."

I gave my father a quick hug. With a trace of a smile still at the corners of his lips, Luke Lea returned to the men in the library.

My mother heard my conversation on the telephone. Knowing that her husband always took time to find out what the children wanted, she called her seven-and-a-half year-old daughter to her.

"Darling, you know not to bother Daddy when he is in conference," she said, "particularly now, when he is quite worried about business matters due to the depression."

I paused a moment, then replied, "I thought a lot of men had been coming to see Daddy lately. He'll get the depression fixed like he does everything else."

The son of Ella Cocke and Overton Lea, Luke was born at his family's home, Lealand, on April 12, 1879. He was named for his father's brother, who had died while a student at Bethany College, and for his great grandfather Luke Lea, soldier, banker,

Congressman, and Indian agent.

In 1879 the South was emerging from the depression which followed the devastation of war and Reconstruction. Middle Tennesseans enjoyed a more favorable economic position than many Southerners, and the Leas fared better than most of their neighbors. The bulk of the Leas' wealth was in land in downtown Nashville and in the business section of Memphis, in addition to rich farmland in Davidson and Shelby counties and timber acreage in Polk County. Luke Lea's paternal grandmother, Elizabeth Overton Lea, had inherited those properties from her father, Judge John Overton, a noted jurist and the law partner of Andrew Jackson. When Elizabeth married John M. Lea, in 1845, who as a young man had come from the eastern section of the state to Middle Tennessee, they were given 1,000 of the 10,000 acres of Judge Overton's farm, Travellers Rest, in Nashville. This tract, known henceforth as Lealand, lay between Granny White and Franklin Pike. There General John B. Hood had his headquarters on part of the second day of the fierce Battle of Nashville, December 16, 1864.

John M. Lea, mayor of Nashville in 1849 and later judge of the Davidson County circuit court, was a Union man. His integrity commanded the confidence of both Northerners and Southerners, and therefore he was able to be of much service during the War between the States and Reconstruction. Partially because he had assured President Lincoln that Tennessee would voluntarily abolish slavery, the state had been exempted from the Emancipation Proclamation (*Nashville American,* June 1910). Lea prevailed upon Andrew Johnson, military governor of Tennessee, to submit to the Tennessee General Assembly an amendment for voluntary emancipation. Tennessee thereby became the only state in the South to free all slaves within its borders.

Judge Lea's wife, Elizabeth Overton Lea, was a semi-invalid from the birth of their youngest son in 1849 until her death in 1890.[1] Her poor health was the reason Lea refused a more active public role, including a seat on the Tennessee Supreme Court and the post of attorney general in President Andrew Johnson's cabinet. Blessed with a good disposition and common sense, she managed, however, to make a happy home for her family.[2] Lea increased the value of her inheritance and accumulated sufficient money so that their two sons could retire after practicing law only a few years.

Overton, the eldest, attended Bethany College in West Virginia, and after graduation from the University of Virginia Law School, he traveled abroad for several months before returning to Nashville and opening his practice. A man of intelligence and principle, with courtly manners, he was tall and well built, with fair skin and blue eyes whose gaze was serene.

In September 1869, at a ball celebrating the opening of the Maxwell House Hotel,[3] he met Ella Cocke of Knoxville. They married less than a year later, on August 18, 1870, at St. John's Episcopal Church in Knoxville. Slender, with a regal carriage, translucent skin, and luxuriant brown hair, Ella's demure smile and gentle voice cloaked an unbending will.

In downtown Nashville, Judge Lea built for his son and his bride a large red brick house next door to his own home on Vine Street. Adamantly opposed to gambling, the Judge promised his son that later he would build him a house on the site of the summer house at Lealand if he would promise never to breed racehorses.[4] The promise was carried out, and a mile-long driveway led from Granny White Pike to the handsome red brick structure with brown sandstone facing, reminiscent of a French chateau.

Overton Lea gave promise of a notable legal career, but after ten years his health became poor, and fearing tuberculosis, he and Mrs. Lea began to travel. Upon their return to Nashville, he decided to give up his practice and to farm Lealand.

He became interested in Sussex cattle and in 1884 imported the first of his herd. They thrived on the acres of bluegrass at Lealand, and each year on trips abroad he would buy additional choice heifers or a bull. By 1888 the herd had increased to over 100 head and was valued at $50,000, making it one of the three largest Sussex herds in the world, and the only one of consequence in the United States.

To the Overton Leas' four children Lealand was an island unto itself, where they were secure, at liberty to roam, barely touched by the outside world. When they were young, they seldom left Lealand except for an occasional trip into the city or to go with their parents to their house at Monteagle, a summer resort on the nearby Cumberland Plateau. Instead of attending school, they were taught at home by governesses.

There was only 20 months difference in the ages of Luke and his elder brother, Overton, and they were inseparable. Luke would be the larger of the two when his heavier-set frame filled out, and both would be well over six feet tall. Luke's hair was almost black while Overton's was blond. Both had fair skin, blue eyes, straight noses, and rather sensitive mouths. Strong-willed and charming, Luke was a natural-born leader. Amenable and placid, Overton had inherited his father's nature.

The eldest child, Laura, at a young age evidenced an interest in music, painting, and literature. Being the baby, and somewhat dependent by nature, Elizabeth, a sweet child with a merry disposition, had been indulged since birth, not only by her parents but by her brothers as well.

The tranquil life of Lealand was interrupted one cold January morning of 1888. Only half-awake, Luke became conscious of voices and hurried footsteps. Then he smelled smoke.

Small puffs were visible through the floor of the front hall, but there was no immediate danger. A bucket brigade of the farm workers proved of little help. When the flames, running along the parquet floor, reached the stairwell, they leapt with a roar toward the roof.

The interior of the house was gutted, but the thick walls remained. Numb from the shock of the fire and with the children wrapped in blankets, the Leas left the smoldering ruins late that morning and drove into town to Judge Lea's home.

Plans soon got underway for a new house, but it was more than two years before the Leas could again live at Lealand. On a hillock in a 40-acre wooded park, the house of mellowed red brick faced with sandstone had 35 rooms on three floors. The long, narrow windows under the mansard roof were capped with arched stone, and a stair tower and two bay window turrets reached farther skyward. Graceful iron work outlining the roof was connected into an elaborate lightning rod system. Lealand had a tennis court, and during the mid-1890s Overton Lea began building one of the earliest golf courses in the state. Beyond the shady lawn stretched pastures and 750 acres under cultivation.

Viewed from the present day's hectic pace, life at Lealand appears almost idyllic. Certainly it was pleasant, but it contained little conviviality, as Ella and Overton Lea viewed life as filled with pitfalls, which it was one's duty to guard against.

An inverterate letter writer, Overton Lea's correspondence depicted a man who handled financial matters with an exactness characteristic of his precise attention to detail. Unceasingly he endeavored to make life pleasant for his family. He considered his first duty to be to to his wife and children but, with his brother Robert and his family living in Europe, the responsibility of his father weighed heavily upon him as Judge Lea advanced in years.

A highly refined but austere person with little sense of humor, Ella Lea had a deep interest in literature and music. She considered Nashville woefully lacking in culture,[5] and busy with her family and living nine miles from town, she did not take part in the daily activities of the city. Constantly alert against sickness, she anxiously watched the weather, because when it was bad it could cause illness. Once when the McGavock Dickinsons came to call, she feared they might have brought germs from the city and would not allow her children to go outside and play with their cousins. She permitted them only to go to the windows and tap on the glass at their visitors.

Luke came to believe that had economic necessity been present, or had his parents not been unduly concerned about health, his mother might not have persuaded his father to retire and live the life of a country gentleman.

Despite their protectiveness of their children, Ella and Overton Lea in 1892 allowed their daughter, Laura, to go to Germany, where she studied music for more than three years. She had been in Dresden only a few months, however, when Mrs. Lea and her son Overton sailed to spend a month with her, and during those years before one visit to her was concluded, another was planned. As Luke did not enjoy the trips to Europe, he stayed at home whenever he could.

Overton Lea decided in the autumn of 1893 that a tutor was needed for his sons. William Clendenin Robertson, a Texan who had just graduated from the University of the South at Sewanee as valedictorian of his class, was chosen, and he was to be associated with the Leas the rest of his life.

Luke had an unusually quick mind and retentive memory. His native reasoning ability became sharpened through practice, and he learned to devote his entire attention to the matter at hand. The boys progressed sufficiently in their studies to be ready for college in two years, and they were enrolled at Sewanee on March 19, 1896.

A small liberal arts college of high academic standing, the University of the South is owned and operated by the Southern Dioceses of the Episcopal Church. The domain covers roughly 10,000 acres atop the Cumberland Plateau in Tennessee. The campus with Gothic buildings of sandstone is in the little town of Sewanee, just six miles from Monteagle where the Leas had a summer home. Sewanee rather aptly has been described as a state of mind—a place in which the code of gentlemen prevailed and the outside world was held at bay. In a faculty home the two Lea brothers secured a room provided with a grate fire and cleaning, at a cost of $24.00-$26.00 a month including dinner.

Elizabeth was enrolled at Fairmont, a school for young ladies at Monteagle, where the Leas had always spent much time. During the years that their children were in schools on the mountain, the Leas were in residence at their home there most of the time.

Of his first class at Sewanee, Luke later wrote:

...The fates were against me. I was the first one called upon by the professsor to translate—it was a Latin class....and not knowing whether to sit or stand when reciting in a classroom, I squatted. The amusement of the classroom, loudly expressed, resulted in my such utter confusion that I could not have given my name much less have translated Ovid into English.[6]

Sewanee boasted several fraternities, and Luke and Overton were promptly pledged Alpha Tau Omega. Challenged by the stimulation of sound instruction and competition with other students, they learned to accommodate the demands of the totally new situation. In time Luke became president of his class and a member and finally head of all the most prestigious student organizations.

Many of the friendships Luke and Overton made at Sewanee were close and enduring, but no ties were stronger than the bonds between the Lea brothers and David Shepherd. When David, an only child, was ready for college, the widowed Mrs. Shepherd had also moved to Sewanee.

Luke was awarded his B.A. degree in August 1899, a term earlier than the regular four-year period. However, he remained at Sewanee another year and immediately started work on his M.A.

Although he participated in many college activities, it was in connection with football that he made a name for himself that has never been forgotten at Sewanee (1900 Sewanee *Cap and Gown*). He was manager of the fabled 1899 team whose remarkable exploits are still recounted when talk turns to football of yesteryear.

Several years previously Sewanee had decided to enter big-time football, so a certain amount of preparation preceded the miracle performed by the team of 1899 in setting a record that would almost positively never be equalled. In six glorious days that small Episcopal college in the mountains of Tennessee won five big football games on a 2,600-mile road trip (*Sports Illustrated* 16 October 1961).

Sewanee had opened its season by defeating the University of Georgia 12-0. The next team to bow to the Sewanee Tigers was Georgia Tech 32-0, followed by the University of Tennessee 46-0, and Southwestern 54-0. In high spirits over their success on the gridiron thus far, the squad of 21 men, Coach Herman Suter, and Manager Lea boarded the train on November 6 for that memorable trip. The team had a special sleeper, and to guard against possible gastric upsets caused by drinking water to which they were not accustomed, Lea had two barrels of Sewanee spring water put aboard.

A few miles past Cowan, a small town at the foot of the mountain, Lea discovered that the trunks containing the team's uniforms were not aboard. In the excitement of farewells, they had been left behind on the station platform. So as not to alarm the players, no mention was made of this oversight. The young manager went into a huddle with the conductor, made a few notes on train schedules, telegraphed back to Sewanee and had the trunks shipped on the next train.

With calamity thus narrowly averted, the Tigers defeated the University of Texas in Austin 12-0. The next day in Houston, they beat Texas A & M 10-0. On to Louisiana, they trounced Tulane 23-0 and beat LSU 34-0. Next they played Ole Miss in Memphis and scored 12 points to Ole Miss's 0. Returning to Sewanee, the team clobbered Cumberland University 71-0. On Thanksgiving, Sewanee played Auburn in Montgomery and was leading 11-10 when the game was called due to darkness. All 11 scheduled games won, Sewanee challenged the University of North Carolina and defeated it 5-0 on a field goal, which in those days counted for five points (*Sports Illustrated 16* October 1961).

Sewanee was then the undisputed champion of the South. That small school had amassed a phenomenal record: an undefeated season against 12 rugged opponents, scoring 322 points to 10. Furthermore, under Luke's management, all team expenses had been paid and no debt incurred.

Luke was awarded his M.A. and Overton his B.A. degree in August 1900. Following commencement both boys joined the family in New York where they sailed for Europe. After being abroad a month Luke and Overton returned in time to register at the Law School of Columbia University.

They secured an apartment in Harlem, then a choice location

for students, and quickly learned their way around the city. They had their younger sister, Elizabeth, who again that winter was a student at Miss Huger's boarding school at 725 Fifth Avenue, with them a good part of every weekend.

Luke was elected president of the second-year law class by a vote of 65 to 31,[7] and he was editor his senior year of the *Columbia Law Review*. The editorship, in addition to his classes, kept him extremely busy, but he thrived on the challenging demands.

He and Overton studied quite hard that spring. Only 28 members of the class passed all subjects, and the Lea brothers were among that number.[8] Following the Columbia examinations, they both passed the New York bar examination on June 9. Neither of them had any intention of practicing in New York, but at that time being a member of the New York bar entitled a lawyer to practice in almost every state in the union. Their school days concluded, the Lea brothers stood on the threshold of careers bright with promise.

Chapter Two
Publisher and Politician

Within the next few years, Luke Lea's interests propelled him into business, politics, the newspaper field, and real estate development. Changes that come to most young men—death, marriage, birth—also were his.

His grandfather and brother both died in 1903. Judge Lea, since the death of his wife 13 years previously, had lived with the Overton Leas. The judge was suddenly taken ill at Monteagle on September 17 and died two days later from uremia. On Christmas Eve, Overton, Jr. developed a severe cold, which quickly went into pneumonia. Never robust, he sank rapidly and in five days was dead. His death was a devastating blow to his parents. His room at Lealand remained unchanged and his clothes were aired by the servants twice a year and carefully rehung in the closet.

Luke, anxious to begin his law practice, had not gone abroad with his family in the summer of 1903 and had opened an office in downtown Nashville in the Cole Building. Vice-chancellor B.L. Wiggins wanted Luke to teach in the law department at Sewanee, but had only $1,000 that could be used for salaries.[1] Luke went to Sewanee and after thoroughly discussing the offer agreed to teach some classes that autumn and during the following spring.

After his graduation from Columbia, it did not take Luke long to become acquainted with Nashville's younger set. Overton Lea, fearing that his son's health would suffer from the demands of an increasing law practice and a busy social life, thought it would be wise for Luke to spend at least one year at Sewanee, abandoning for the present his law practice. Luke also realized he should either give up teaching or practicing law, but was far too engrossed in his activities in Nashville to consider leaving. Therefore, he requested to be relieved of his teaching duties at the beginning of the term in March 1905.[2]

Shortly after he began practicing law, an enterprising young boy presented himself at Lea's office with a message that the lawyer's cousin, Memphis attorney William A. Percy, was sending him the best office boy in the United States. Thus began an enduring association between Luke Lea and Walter Seigenthaler, an independent, impish boy in whom the young lawyer took a protective interest.[3]

One of Lea's first clients was the Long Distance Telephone and Telegraph Company. This company provided service to the subscribers of independent plants, because at that time the Bell Telephone Companies of the Telephone Trust would not furnish long distance service to subscribers of independent telephone companies. The authority to grant or to reject franchises was vested in the mayor and city council, and the Telephone Trust had succeeded for several years in keeping independent telephone companies from obtaining permission to establish an exchange in Nashville.[4] Lea's papers indicate he was opposed to monopolies which he thought usually had high rates and provided poor services. Thus his first cases, as well as his natural inclination, thrust Luke Lea immediately into politics.

The practice of law also led Lea into business. One of his first enterprises was the Home Telegraph Company, organized January 26, 1906, to construct a telegraph line from Franklin to Goodlettsville. In the litigation that followed its organization, the Home Telegraph Company alleged that its charter rights were interfered with by Nashville's mayor and city council in order to protect a contract the local government had entered into with the Cumberland Telephone and Telegraph Company on December 14, 1905. A provision of the contract stipulated that the Cumberland Telephone and Telegraph Company was to pay to the City of Nashville three percent of the company's gross earnings from its Nashville exchange, which sum was not to be less than $10,000 per year. In return the mayor and city council would not grant a franchise to any competing company in Nashville.[5]

In this case, Lea challenged the entrenched order that kept out competition through political influence. The court of chancery appeals on February 23, 1907, decided in favor of the Home Telegraph Company. The verdict was appealed, and it soon became recognized that the telephone was inherently a monopoly, but one that needed regulation.[6]

As stimulating as business and law were, Lea found politics even more heady. The United States was forced to cope during the turbulent early years of the twentieth century with many new problems created by rapid change as the country became industrialized and urbanized. During the period that came to be known as the Progressive Era, organized interest groups evolved to promote efficiency in government, social justice, better schools and roads, equality of women, prison reform, public health, and to regulate business, child labor, and alcoholic beverages. The common thread running through the agitation for change and reform was a search for solutions to problems for which there were no familiar answers, and to make the political system responsive to the new needs of its citizens (Shahan, "Reform and Politics in Tennessee" 1, 9, 31-32, 34, 59-60, 94).

When Lea entered politics, prohibition was the dominant issue of the day in Tennessee, and he was an ardent advocate of temperance. Most prohibitionist leaders were reformers who sincerely believed that the evils caused by alcohol could be abolished by outlawing liquor. As the movement gained momentum, the temperance goal advanced from moral suasion to local option to absolute prohibition. The temperance crusade in Tennessee was in no way an isolated phenomenon, but it was a political force there and in other states, long before it became a national issue.[7] Liquor control was more a disruptive force in Tennessee politics perhaps than anywhere else in the nation.

The Four Mile Law, enacted in 1877, prohibited the retail sale of liquor within four miles of a chartered school outside an incorporated town. The Tennessee Anti-Saloon League, organized in 1899, had been influential in having temperance majorities returned to both houses of the General Assembly in the election of

1900. The League in 1903 secured the passage of the Adams Bill, which extended the provisions of the Four Mile Law to towns of under 5,000 population that reincorporated after the passage of the bill (Isaac, *Prohibition and Politics* 97). In order to protect their hard-won gains, the temperance forces became increasingly involved in politics. However, temperance reform could not succeed in Tennessee unless the election laws were also reformed (Knoxville, *Journal and Tribune* 30 November 1902).

When the legislature convened in 1905, it showed no great enthusiasm for extending prohibition, but it was reluctant to take any backward step. So long as the Democratic party remained reasonably united, it appeared unlikely that any major change would be made in the liquor laws. However, the death of United States Senator William B. Bate on March 9, 1905, shortly after he had been reelected for a six-year term, had a tremendous influence on the prohibition movement.

The incumbent governor, James B. Frazier, and two former governors, Benton McMillin and Robert L. Taylor, all three leading members of the Democratic party, aspired to the Senate seat thus vacated. A Democratic legislative caucus, afterwards branded the "snap" caucus, met March 16, overruled Taylor's and McMillin's efforts to secure a delay, and by acclamation nominated Frazier, who was easily elected the following week by the Democratic majority in the legislature. The speaker of the state senate, John I. Cox, a well-known East Tennessee Democrat, automatically succeeded to the governorship.

Taylor was angered by his defeat, and he held Tennessee's other United States senator, Edward Ward Carmack, a political ally of Frazier and Cox, responsible for the "snap" caucus. Taylor challenged Carmack in his bid for reelection, and it was during that campaign that Carmack emerged as the great champion of the temperance cause.

Although temperance was not the principal issue in the senatorial primary held in May 1906, Carmack attributed his defeat to opposition by the liquor interests.

Malcolm R. Patterson, at that time one of prohibition's greatest opponents in Tennessee, announced in 1905 that he would be a candidate for the Democratic gubernatorial nomination against the incumbent Cox. It was unusual for a Tennessee governor after having served only one term to be challenged by a leader of his own party. Patterson attacked Cox for machine politics thereby making election law reforms, rather than prohibition, the principal issue of the campaign. The people, he said, had the right to decide for themselves about the sale of liquor. His platform contained a rather comprehensive plan for reform of the state government, including repeal of the governor's power to appoint election commissioners, adoption of a uniform system of party nominations, revision of the revenue laws, and better schools and roads (Shahan, "Reform and Politics in Tennessee" 82).

Luke Lea was convinced of the need for reform of the election laws and strongly advocated the direct primary. The gains made by the temperance movement appeared safe-guarded by Patterson's endorsement of the Adams Act. Hence, Lea favored his candidacy and became a member of the Patterson delegation from Davidson County.

Interest in the political contest mounted throughout the spring until it crackled at white heat when the Democratic convention convened in Nashville at noon on Tuesday, May 29, 1906, at the Ryman Auditorium.[8] Approximately 5,000 delegates overflowed the first floor into the galleries.

The nomination depended on contests in Davidson, Shelby, Dickson, Williamson, and Giles counties. If these five counties went to Patterson, he would easily be the nominee; otherwise he would be defeated. Under party precedent, if a contest was filed, the delegation from that county was temporarily disfranchised until its status was resolved. An attempt to enforce this rule precipitated the wild disorder that reduced the opening session from a deliberative body to a noisy mob. Because of the intra-party struggle, there were more counties in which two delegations appeared than ever before in the history of the state.

The battle was joined at once over the selection of the temporary chairman. After much confusion, temporary secretary

Edward B. Martin, clerk of the House of Representatives, was directed to call the roll of counties. When Davidson County was reached, both E.R. Richardson, chairman of the regular delegation, and William O. Vertrees, chairman of the contesting delegation, answered. Pandemonium stopped the proceedings.

When order finally was somewhat restored, Richardson presented his delegation's credentials, which he demanded be read. He charged that the other delegation was not entitled to seats and stated that he did not recognize its contest. As the chair next recognized Vertrees, Luke Lea jumped to his feet and raised the point of order that Vertrees was not a member of the Davidson County delegation. Confusion and excitement increased as the shouting of the delegates became a roar. The chair ruled that in instances in which a county was contested, the chair could not determine which was the rightful delegation, that being a matter for the credentials committee to decide after the temporary organization was concluded.

Lea appealed that ruling and the chair ordered another roll call. When Davidson County was reached, Vertrees yelled that county cast its 77 votes "aye," and E.H. McNeilly, representing the Patterson forces, roared that county's 77 votes were cast "no." In the bedlam that followed, the secretaries of the convention, not knowing how to record Davidson's double vote, did not record it either way. Lea loudly protested this action, as a free-for-all fight erupted on the other side of the platform. In the middle of this turmoil, William K. Abernathy gave up trying to preside and left the platform.

A delegate from Shelby County moved that Luke Lea, who had emerged that afternoon as the leader of the Patterson forces, take the chair and preside. The motion received several seconds and was adopted. The tall young man, who had relentlessly raised point after point of order, strode to the platform and picked up the gavel.

Abernathy changed his mind and returned to the platform to resume his position as acting chairman, but the crowd continued to chant for Lea and Patterson. In vain, Lea appealed through a megaphone for quiet. His motion to adjourn lost by a voice vote. For the remaining three hours, there were two presiding officers, Lea and Abernathy. An agreement was finally reached between the leaders of the various factions that the convention be adjourned until ten o'clock the following morning and that a committee of four representatives of each candidate meet to select a temporary chairman.

By his quick and forceful action in seizing the gavel as the stormy convention threatened to disintegrate, Luke Lea burst onto the turbulent political scene, and for the next quarter century he would be a factor to be reckoned with.

Patterson was nominated later in the week. Lea was a member of the committee that drafted the party's platform which, in harmony with Patterson's statements on the liquor issue, not only opposed any change in the Adams Act but approved its extension, provided that the people affected consented. Thus the objectives urged by the Anti-Saloon League for several years seemed to be incorporated officially into the Democratic platform.

With the cause of Prohibition advanced, Lea turned his attention to the local press. Newspapers had always fascinated him. While a student at Columbia Law School, he would watch the papers roll off the press, and for at least a year he had contemplated starting another newspaper in Nashville. He believed that the local papers were under the domination of the railroad and the whiskey interests and that the public was not getting unbiased news.

Overton Lea agreed with his son that a newspaper conducted along the lines he proposed would be good for the city and the state. Nevertheless he did all in his power to keep Luke from undertaking the project because he thought his son did not have the capital nor could he obtain sufficient funds to make it a success, but Luke was not to be dissuaded.

The Tennessean Company was organized on March 28, 1907. Overton Lea refused to be an officer or director of the company or to take any stock, but he lent his son $15,000.

The press and stereotyping outfit of the old *Nashville News* were bought, and seven linotype machines were purchased. The Currey Building, on the north corner of Church and Eighth Avenue, was leased and an experienced staff was assembled with Herman M. Suter, coach of Sewanee's fabled 1899 football team, as editor at $75 a week.

The first issue of *The Nashville Tennessean* rolled off the presses on Sunday, May 12, 1907. Its two competitors and its avowed enemy, the "wets," were variously blamed for the power failure during the press run that caused the new paper not to be delivered that first day until late afternoon.[9] *The Tennessean's* morning competitor, *The Nashville American,* was then under the control of Major E.C. Lewis, who opposed prohibition and was a high ranking official of the Louisville and Nashville Railroad. The evening paper, the *Nashville Banner*, reflected the personality and convictions of its owner and publisher, Major E.B. Stahlman, formidable, colorful, and passionately interested in politics (McGill, *The South and the Southerner* 90).

The Tennessean at first operated at a deficit. After a few weeks Overton Lea advised letting the paper die. That Luke was not willing to do, and his father became surety for another $15,000. By July the elder Lea thought that not only was continued publication impossible, but that Luke had gotten his financial affairs into a deplorable condition. To prevent involuntary bankruptcy and to give Luke an opportunity to sell the newspaper under the most favorable terms possible, Overton Lea lent him an additional $28,000.[10]

No purchaser was readily available, however, and Luke did not look upon his financial problems with the same alarm as did his father. Overton Lea in October 1908 executed two mortgages on property he owned in downtown Nashville to secure funds to lend his son to pay debts contracted for *The Tennessean*. With the paper thereby on a more secure financial basis, Luke planned to devote himself to his law practice. However, the following month an event occurred that not only changed the course of his life but also altered the political history of Tennessee.

Lea had been instrumental in the election of Malcolm

Patterson but before long he had broken with the governor and became one of his severest critics. Deeply committed to the temperance cause, Lea thought Patterson had become allied with the whiskey interests. Lea also believed the governor had betrayed the trust of the people who had elected him by not keeping his campaign promises to reform election laws.

At the urging of Anti-Saloon League leaders who had also become opposed to Patterson, Edward Ward Carmack announced in September 1907 that he would seek the Democratic nomination for governor the following year.[11] Carmack's campaign on a prohibition platform caused a serious split in the Democratic party, which was further widened by differing opinions on the kind of primary to be held. In addition to the temperance question, the two candidates held sharply differing attitudes toward big business, especially the railroads.

In the primary held in June, Patterson won the Democratic nomination by a clear margin of 85,000 to 79,000. Luke Lea employed Carmack as editor of *The Tennessean* in August. Reluctantly advising his readers to vote for Democratic candidates in the coming general election, Carmack bitterly denounced the machine politics of Patterson, alleging he had packed the state convention with whiskey and railroad delegates thereby making it impossible for prohibition Democrats to write their views into the platform.

After Patterson won the governorship over his Republican opponent, Carmack continued his scathing editorials in *The Tennessean*. He denounced the liquor forces in hopes of lining up members of the legislature for the approaching session. All the resources of the reelected governor were focused on the same objective—control of the legislature (Hooper, *The Unwanted Boy* 49).

In his vitriolic editorials on the Patterson organization, Carmack made several sarcastic references to Colonel Duncan B. Cooper, a prominent advisor of Patterson. Carmack was particularly critical of the part Cooper had played in the reconciliation between Patterson and former Governor Cox, whom

Patterson had defeated in 1906. Angered by those insinuations, Cooper warned Carmack "that Nashville was becoming too small to hold both of them" (Isaac, *Prohibition and Politics* 157) and that his name must not be used again in the editorial columns of *The Tennessean.*

Carmack was not in the habit of carrying arms. His friends, however, fearing for his safety, forced on him a pistol for his protection until Colonel Cooper's ire had cooled.[12]

As Carmack was going from the newspaper to his lodgings on November 9, 1908, he met Colonel Cooper and his son, Robin, and Nashville businessman John D. Sharp. Duncan Cooper started across the street. He later claimed he was going to demand that Carmack desist from use of his name in the newspaper in the future.

Mrs. Charles H. Eastman, an eyewitness, stated that Carmack had just raised his hat to speak to her when she heard someone say, "We've got you, all right, sir. We've got the drop on you" (*The Nashville Tennessean* 10 November 1908).

Pistol shots exploded. Carmack lay on the street, killed instantly by three shots fired in rapid succession by Robin Cooper, who was wounded by one of the two shots fired by Carmack.

A message, reputedly from the political faction that was bitterly opposed to Carmack,

...boldly and blatantly threatened to kill the succeeding publisher if he called the killing "murder" instead of that southern euphemism "a street duel." The owners of the paper were also warned not to demand the prosecution of the Coopers.[13]

The Nashville Tennessean did both.

Duncan and Robin Cooper and John D. Sharp were indicted on November 13 in the criminal court of Davidson County for first-degree murder. The slaying of Carmack caused an uproar across the state and brought about an abrupt change in Luke Lea's career. No qualified person could be found to take charge of the paper at that tense time, so Lea gave up his promising law practice to assume its active day to day management.[14]

The Democratic members of the incoming legislature were sharply divided between local optionists and statewide prohibitionists led by Lea. Total prohibition was favored by a large majority of the Republican legislators. An alliance of prohibitionist Democrats and Republicans elected William Kinney, speaker of the Senate, and Hillsman Taylor, speaker of the House. Immediately bills to extend the Four Mile Law to the whole state and to outlaw distilleries were passed despite the governor's veto. A bill giving the General Assembly power to name the state election board was passed, was vetoed by the governor, and then promptly passed over his veto. With the reform of the election laws and the enactment of prohibition by the 1909 legislature, the goals of the prohibitionist faction of the Democratic party were achieved, and Tennessee took its place in the mainstream of progressive reform. However, the price paid was high: the state Democratic party had been split asunder.

Along with politics and the newspaper, Luke Lea was deeply involved in real estate development. He thought the fashionable residential area of the city would continue to move westward and that the most choice land for future development was the 5,000-acre Belle Meade farm approximately six miles from the heart of downtown.[15]

Jacob McGavock Dickinson had conceived the idea of converting this magnificent plantation into suburban home sites and had chartered the Belle Meade Land Company in 1906. Luke Lea formed the Belle Meade Company in the spring of 1910 to develop a 1,255-acre tract.

Lots were advertised for sale that summer, but none was sold. Nevertheless, the Belle Meade Company purchased an adjoining 624 acres, known as the High Pasture, from Mrs. Howell E. Jackson for $43,000, bringing the land owned by the company to 1,879 acres.

Luke Lea proposed to the Nashville Railway and Light Company that it construct a single line cartrack from the terminus of its West End line for approximately four miles through the property owned by the Belle Meade Company, three miles to be flanked by a macadam road.[16] Thus was laid out Belle Meade Boulevard, land facing which is still more than three-quarters of a century later the most expensive residential property per foot in Davidson County.

Lea's Belle Meade Company donated 144 acres to the Nashville Golf and Country club; J.O. Leake gave 25 acres; and J.W. Forsythe gave 50 acres. In accepting the gift of land, the club, which later changed its name to Belle Meade Country Club, agreed to build a clubhouse costing not less than $25,000, construct a standard 18-hole golf course on the Belle Meade Company property and maintain it for 25 years.[17]

In contrast to the rough and tumble of politics and the keen competitiveness of business was the domestic happiness enjoyed by Luke Lea and his devoted young wife.

George Frazer, who shared offices with Luke in the Cole Building, first introduced him to Mary Louise Warner and took him to Renraw, the 60-acre estate of the Percy Warners on Gallatin Pike.

President of the Nashville Railway and Light Company and with interests in utility companies throughout the South, Percy Warner was esteemed, philanthropic, and a teetotaler. He was married to Margaret Lindsley, daughter of John Berrien Lindsley, and granddaughter of Philip Lindsley, both of whom served as president of the University of Nashville and were ordained Presbyterian ministers.

The two eldest Warner daughters, Sadie and Mary Louise, just eighteen months apart in age and dressing alike, were often mistaken as twins as both were of medium height, and had reddish hair and brown eyes. They were formally presented to society at a ball at Renraw on November 18, 1904, and a year later, Sadie and George Frazer were married.

The more Luke saw of Mary Louise, and he had seen a great deal of her after her debut, the more he became smitten. By nature the quietest and most gentle of the five Warner girls, she had an innate dignity and reserve combined with a sunny disposition, a pure heart, and a kind tongue.

From the first moment Percie, the youngest sister, saw Luke she adored him, and he had a special affection for that long-legged young girl. Seventeen years older than Percie, he treated her as an adult, even as a co-conspirator in his courtship of her older sister.

Confident his love was reciprocated, Luke talked with Mary Louise's father in the spring of 1906 and was granted permission to press his suit. This he did with characteristic ardor, and plans were soon under way for an autumn wedding. After looking at several houses they decided upon an attractive two-story residence on Twenty-first Avenue.

Several hundred guests gathered on November 1, 1906, at Renraw for the wedding. After the ceremony a bountiful supper was served the guests seated at small tables on the canvassed-in porch. Later that evening Luke and his bride left by train on a wedding trip to the East.

Mary Louise, in her calm, unassuming way, created a happy home and kept their household on an even keel although her buoyant husband allowed so many demands to be made upon his time that he was never able to adhere to a fixed schedule. Her letters evidence her unbounded love for him and her complete confidence that whatever course of action he took was right.

Mary Louise presented Luke with a son and namesake on March 24, 1908. This young baby, the image of his father, immediately took possession of a special place in his father's heart.

Luke became increasingly concerned about Mary Louise in the spring of 1909. She had developed a persistent cough. Baby Luke had had whooping cough, and naturally Mary Louise had been exposed. When the cough continued, she consulted their family physician, who said that although she had not contracted the child's disease, she had developed a sympathetic cough. This explanation did not satisfy Luke, but he did not want to alarm Mary Louise, who was again with child. Finally, he determined that another physician's opinion was needed. Tests confirmed his worst fears. His beautiful young wife, who looked the picture of health, had developed tuberculosis.

High altitude was thought to be beneficial to persons with that disease so it was decided that she should go to Denver, with its dry, bracing climate. On their arrival in the summer of 1909, they at once saw Doctor Walter M. Dake, who confirmed the diagnosis. Luke knew that at best Mary Louise's recovery would take several months, so plans were made to close their Nashville house.

Mary Louise gave birth to a second son on Halloween, October 31, 1909. She survived the pregnancy and delivery amazingly well and the baby showed no sign of lung weakness. Named for his maternal grandfather, baby Percy, as he grew, was to take after Percy Warner in many ways.

Chapter Three
The Youngest Member of the Club

In contrast with Luke Lea's joy over the birth of his second son was his dissatisfaction over the poor enforcement of the prohibition laws—a dissatisfaction he shared with many Tennesseans. It was still legal to ship liquor into and out of the state, and some saloons had been converted into locker clubs where members' liquor could be stored and served to them. Mayors Edward H. Crump of Memphis and Hilary E. Howse of Nashville both openly declared that public sentiment made it impossible to enforce prohibition in their cities.

Believing it could be enforced, prohibitionist members of the Democratic party set up a "state-wide" organization within the party. Leaders of this group included Jeff McCarn, Chancellor Edward L. Bullock, Benjamin A. Enloe, William Kinney, speaker of the Senate, and Luke Lea who presided at the large convention in Nashville, September 21, 1909.

That convention urged the enforcement of prohibition, endorsed the new primary law, and approved the "state-widers" entering the Democratic primary in 1910. In the following months prohibitionists waged vigorous campaigns to wrest control of the Democratic party from Governor Patterson. Luke Lea's name was frequently mentioned in connection with the forthcoming race for governor, but he made it clear he was not a candidate.

The dramatic Cooper trial began January 20, 1909. After two months of sensational testimony, John D. Sharp was acquitted, and both Coopers were found guilty of second-degree murder and were sentenced to 20 years each in the state penitentiary. The defendants appealed the verdict, and on April 13, 1910, the Tennessee supreme court reversed the lower court's conviction of

Robin, who had fired the shots that killed Carmack, and granted him a new trial. The court sustained the conviction of Duncan Cooper, who had not fired at all. Governor Patterson had already prepared a full pardon for the elder Cooper, which he dispatched by messenger as soon as the decision was made public. Within the hour Duncan Cooper was free (Hooper, *The Unwanted Boy* 56).

The public was outraged by the governor's hasty setting aside of the court's verdict in behalf of his close political friend who had been convicted of murdering the governor's most outspoken critic. When Robin Cooper's new trial was called in criminal court in November 1910, Judge A.B. Neil, sitting by appointment of Governor Patterson, impaneled a jury, then directed a verdict of acquittal.

In addition to Governor Patterson's pardoning of Duncan Cooper, several other developments in the spring of 1910 deepened the conflict within the Democratic party and brought allies to the prohibitionists in their battle against the governor. The compulsory primary law of 1909 had been declared unconstitutional by the Tennessee Supreme Court. The Democratic executive committee, dominated by Patterson, decreed that a county-unit primary should be held to nominate candidates not only for governor and United States senator, but also for the Supreme Court, the court of appeals, and sundry other offices. The governor's opponents severely criticized this plan as an effort to perpetuate the Patterson machine. Prohibitionist leaders, along with Senator James B. Frazier, a candidate for reelection, refused to participate in such a primary.

The greatest objections to the proposed primary were leveled against the nomination of judicial candidates in a general primary instead of in the customary special convention. Chief Justice John K. Shields and two other Supreme Court justices refused to enter the primary, making the startling charge that the governor had attempted to coerce the court to acquit Duncan Cooper.

In this seething cauldron Governor Patterson announced his candidacy for a third term. The burning issue of Patterson's attempt to control the judiciary took precedence over the prohibition question. The term "Pattersonism" became synonymous with all the evils and corruption of machine politics, dominated by whiskey and railroad interests.

Luke Lea assisted in raising funds to finance the prohibition movement, and in April he sent to key men across the state calls for a state convention to consider the vital questions of judiciary and election reforms.[1] When the primary campaign got under way, he was in great demand as a speaker.

The anti-Patterson faction, who labeled themselves independent Democrats, held a convention attended by more than 5,000 persons in May 1910 in Nashville. They set up a separate party organization, headed by William O. Vertrees, and endorsed the judicial candidates who had refused to enter the primary called by Patterson. However, so many anti-Patterson men were also anti-prohibitionists that no declaration was made on liquor or law enforcement.

Qualifications of the judicial nominees received little attention in the bitter campaign waged on Patterson's record. The Independents charged that the governor had created a ruthless machine, had attempted to coerce the Supreme Court, had opposed the election reforms of 1909, had misused his pardoning power, and had a corruption fund from the whiskey interests of $100,000 at his disposal.

In the Democratic primary in August, the Independents' judiciary ticket was elected by a large majority—a severe defeat for Patterson. He was successful, however, in gaining his party's nomination for a third term as governor.

The Republican strategy, capitalizing upon the dissension in the Democratic party, stressed enforcement of prohibition and preservation of a free judiciary. Ben W. Hooper, an able young attorney from East Tennessee and an ardent prohibitionist, was the Republican nominee for governor, and B.A. Enloe, an independent Democrat, was endorsed for railroad commissioner, then an important state office (Isaac, *Prohibition and Politics* 188).

Governor Patterson, cognizant of his almost certain defeat by the coalition of independent Democrats and Republicans, abruptly withdrew from the gubernatorial race on September 11. The Independents, in their state convention four days after Patterson's withdrawal, nevertheless carried out their agreement with the Republicans to nominate Hooper for governor and Enloe for railroad commissioner. The coalition of independent Democrats and Republicans, called Fusionists, claimed they were continuing the struggle waged by Carmack against the forces of evil and disorder.

The regular Democrats, hopelessly divided on the liquor question, ignored it, and drafted popular Senator Robert L. Taylor to run for governor.

In the midst of the chaotic campaign, Luke Lea, by a stunning coup, dealt a severe blow to the waning fortunes of the Patterson machine. The *Nashville Tennessean* on September 25, 1910, absorbed its morning competitor, *The American*, which had strongly supported the governor and advocated party loyalty. The morning Associated Press franchise was secured with the merger and *The Nashville Tennessean and the Nashville American* became the only local morning newspaper as well as one of the largest dailies in the South.[2]

Following a hard-fought campaign, Hooper gained enough Democratic votes in Middle and West Tennessee, as well as carrying the traditional Republican areas, to be elected. With a Republican governor, the Fusionists in control of the House, and the regular Democrats in control of the Senate, the climate was anything but harmonious when the 1911 General Assembly convened on the first Monday in January.

No sooner was the House officially organized, than the legislature became embroiled in the election of a United States senator. James B. Frazier had served only a few months of his second term as governor when he was chosen by the legislature to fill the unexpired term of Senator W.B. Bate and was a candidate to succeed himself.

Due to the unusual composition of the legislature, there was no Democratic caucus. The election was thrown immediately on January 11 into the general assembly (Hooper, *The Unwanted Boy*

89-92). The regular Democratic candidate was Benton McMillin, twice governor of Tennessee and for 20 years a member of the United States House of Representatives. The Independents at first were not agreed on a candidate. The Republicans cast complimentary votes for various members of their party while waiting for the nomination of an Independent who, with the aid of Republican backing, could muster the necessary 66 votes to be elected.

On the first ballot McMillin received 57 votes; Newell Sanders, a well-known Republican, 32; Guston T. Fitzhugh, a prominent Memphis attorney who had served as prosecutor of the Coopers, 22; and Senator Frazier, 19. Fitzhugh, who showed the greatest strength among the Independents as the balloting began, withdrew after the third ballot because of the death of his young daughter (Qualls, "The Fusion Victory and the Tennessee Senatorship" 90).

It soon became apparent that it was going to be difficult for any candidate to be acceptable to enough legislators to be elected. Ballot after ballot was taken by members of the general assembly meeting daily in joint sessions,[3] with McMillin getting as many as 62 votes on January 17. The regular Democrats, failing to get McMillin nominated, finally tendered the senate seat to Governor Hooper, who promptly rejected the offer.

Senator Frazier withdrew from the race on January 18, and B.A. Enloe, who had been elected railroad commissioner on the ticket with Governor Hooper, was nominated as the Fusion candidate. That day the vote was McMillin, 64; Enloe, 62; but on subsequent ballots neither could acquire enough votes to be elected.

Luke Lea was willing to run only if he were confident of winning. He had quietly been receiving pledges of enough votes from the Memphis delegation that, combined with Fusion votes, would be sufficient to elect him. He went to Governor Hooper on January 23 and announced that he had the necessary votes from the Memphis delegation. The one obstacle was Enloe. Only Governor Hooper, a good friend of Enloe, could persuade him to stand aside.

Hurriedly, Hooper arranged a conference and told Enloe that Lea wanted a chance at the senate seat and that he believed, with Enloe's votes, he could be elected. Lea pledged that if he were not elected on the first ballot on which his name appeared, he would withdraw and Enloe could resume his candidacy. Finally, after much discussion Enloe reluctantly agreed.

Word spread that something new would be tried that day to break the deadlock, but not until an hour and a half before the balloting began did it become known that the Fusionists had agreed to support Luke Lea. In a desperate effort to stem the tide, the Regulars decided to nominate Colonel L.D. Tyson of Knoxville. Excitement mounted as the session was called to order, but the chamber became quiet as the roll call of the Senate proceeded with few changes of votes by the Independents and Regulars from the previous ballot.

The roll call of the House began. As each of several Shelby County delegates cast his vote for Lea, it was greeted with a loud cheer. For a moment or two after the last name was called, no one spoke as the vote was hastily totaled and passed from hand to hand. A buzz of whispers then arose that Lea was elected. The official confirmation came as the clerk announced the figures: Lea, 68; McMillin, 48; Tyson, 11, Wooldridge, 2; Raine, 2. Lea's supporters yelled their joy as they tossed their hats into the air and slapped one another on the back. Ladies waved their handkerchiefs and applauded. The new senator-elect's timing had been perfect; he made his bid when everyone was anxious to break the long stalemate.

Informed of his election, Luke Lea strode into the chamber. Shaking the outstretched hands of supporters, he made his way to the podium. The demonstration reached its crescendo as the young man bowed his acknowledgment and waved to the crowd.

In a loud voice filled with emotion he said,

I hardly think you can expect me to make a speech at this time, after spending many nights in dreams of roll calls. I fully appreciate the vote of every man who voted for me; and for those who voted against me, I will be glad to represent them, too. Any energy I have, or vigor, I now propose to consecrate and dedicate to Tennessee. (*The Nashville Tennessean and the Nashville American* 24 January 1911)

The election to the Senate of a 32-year-old man—only Henry Clay had been younger when elected—caused widespread newspaper comment. His opponents decried his lack of experience and blamed him for having contributed to the bitter division that existed within the state Democratic party. His supporters considered his election a triumph for good government and believed he had an unusual opportunity to heal party factionalism and serve his state and nation.

The independent Democrats and the Republicans both considered Fusion to be purely a state matter. Conditions in Tennessee demanded their banding together to achieve election law reforms and to maintain the temperance statutes, but on the national level they continued allegiance to their respective parties. While a Republican had been elected governor in 1910, Democrats, either Independents or Regulars, were elected to Congress from all the districts traditionally Democratic.

Lea was a Democrat. No man, however, represented all Tennessee Democrats. The overthrow of Pattersonism and the attendant reforms had not been achieved without a bitter struggle, which had left the Democratic party with many deep divisions. As long as the party remained split, the Democratic members of the Tennessee congressional delegation would be in a difficult position on the national level, particularly the new senator who owed his election to the Fusionists.

The spirit of reform throughout the nation reached into the United States Senate. Many of the "old guard" were not returned, their places being taken in the 62nd Congress by younger men of more progressive views. Luke Lea, a product of his time, was, according to political columnist Gilson Gardner, one of the eight new Progressives elected bringing the total to 22.[4]

Progressivism coupled a nostalgic look backward to a smaller, less restrained America with a look forward to a more centralized government. These concepts, united with the ideas espoused by Jefferson, Jackson, Lincoln, and the Populists, set the Progressive apart from the more conservative and more liberal. Progressivism had a strong base in the Middle West where the emergence of local reform had rekindled that section's interest in railroad rate regulation, which by 1905 had become a major national issue (Mowry, *The Era of Theodore Roosevelt* 36, 58, 104-05, 132, 198, 263).

After his election to the Senate, Lea, as was the custom at that time, was given a pass by the Louisville and Nashville Railroad. He promptly returned it. The railroad was thereby put on notice that he could not be controlled.

Some of the first matters to claim the attention of the new senator were the location of a national summer capital and the establishment of a new army camp. He proposed Lookout Mountain in Chattanooga as the site of the summer White House, but the federal government decided not to proceed with plans for a summer presidential residence. Two months after he was sworn in, Lea introduced a resolution that directed the Secretary of War to accept title to approximately 5,000 acres of land in the vicinity of Tullahoma, which had been offered to the federal government to establish a camp for troop maneuvers and artillery ranges. This land continued to be so used in World War II and beyond.

A major issue that session was the renewed investigation of the election of Senator William Lorimer of Illinois. About a year after his election, the *Chicago Tribune* published on April 30, 1910, an exposé of corruption in the Illinois legislature. Charles A. White, a member of that body, stated he had been bribed to vote for Lorimer. Indignantly Lorimer arose in the Senate shortly thereafter and demanded an investigation. The Senate committee took testimony in Chicago and Washington from September to December 1910, and a report exonerating the senator was submitted. Senator Albert J. Beverage of Indiana, however, presented a minority report sustaining the charges against Lorimer. The majority report was adopted by the Senate, March 1, 1911, by a vote of 46 to 40 with five abstaining.

Much dissatisfaction had resulted from the perfunctory methods employed by the Senate investigating committee. When an Illinois resident stated that he had been asked to donate $10,000 to a $100,000 campaign fund for Lorimer,[5] the Senate voted to have another investigation, to be conducted by a subcommittee of the Committee on Privileges and Elections to which Lea had already been appointed. Lea gained national exposure through his service on that new subcommittee of eight which was organized immediately and began daily sessions to hear testimony.

By early January 1912 counsel for the committee was ready to submit several recommendations before further hearings opened.[6] As they sat in the small room on the second floor of the Senate Office Building, it soon became apparent that the majority of the committee were unimpressed with the testimony presented against the "blond boss," as Lorimer was called. However, to the three new members of this subcommittee, Lea, John W. Kern of Indiana, and William S. Kenyon of Iowa, all freshman senators, the evidence pointed inescapably to the fact that several members of the Illinois legislature had accepted bribes for electing Lorimer to the United States Senate (Bowers, *The Life of John Worth Kern* 238-42, 247-51).

The hearings closed on February 9. When the committee met March 27 to vote on a report, it split five to three on all proposed resolutions and amendments. The majority report continued the previous whitewash, and the minority report recommended that Lorimer be expelled.

Lea, Kern, and Kenyon met night after night to review the evidence and prepare the minority report, which they determined should be limited to presenting evidence that showed votes for Lorimer had been bought.

It concluded:

...we have no hesitancy in stating that the investigation establishes beyond contradiction that the election of William Lorimer was obtained by corrupt means and was therefore invalid, and we submit the following resolution:

"Resolved, That corrupt methods and practices were employed in the election of William Lorimer to the senate of the United States from the state of Illinois, and that his election was therefore invalid." (Congressional Record 1912; 6790)

The Senate debate began June 4, and for four consecutive days Kern reviewed in detail the evidence on which that report was based.

Nearly a month elapsed before the debate resumed. Lea, who had introduced the resolution embodied in the minority report, spoke for forty minutes in its support on July 11. He stated the matter consisted of two questions: had the Senate the right to consider the case, and had the investigation of the committee appointed by the Senate proved corrupt methods had been used in the election of Lorimer? The answer to both, he concluded, was affirmative.[7]

Lorimer made an eloquent plea in his behalf and a defiant attack upon his detractors, particularly the three signers of the minority report. Lea, Kern, and Kenyon decided not to answer Lorimer's attacks but to proceed with the vote. The roll was called on the pending Lea resolution. The minority report was adopted 55 to 28, a surprisingly large margin by which the Senate reversed its own vote of the preceding year.

Another contested election came to the attention of the Senate after Lea became a member of that body. Senator Issac Stephenson of Wisconsin admitted spending $108,000 in his campaign. At that time such a sum was considered inordinate, so the burden of proof was on him to show that the expenditure was legitimate. The explanation was unsatisfactory to many of his colleagues.

The Senate investigating committee, of which Lea was a member, tried vigorously though unsuccessfully to have Stephenson's election declared void. Its efforts coupled with its success in the Lorimer case, however, were a warning to special interests against attempting to purchase seats in the United States Senate.[8]

Many claims resulting from the Civil War still remained

unsettled when Lea was elected to the Senate. A total of 213 claims from Tennessee, consisting of 149 private, 49 church, eight educational, and seven fraternal, and which amounted to more than $400,000, approximately one-fourth of the aggregate amount, were included in the omnibus bill before the Congress. Toward the end of the summer 1911 session Lea took charge of the Omnibus Claims bill, which had been handed down by each Congress to the succeeding one for the past 16 years. It was passed in the final week of that session, and Lea was gaining a reputation among his colleagues of being able to get things done.

A proponent of fiscal responsibility, Lea kept close watch on federal expenditures. He voted against the blanket Sherwood Pension bill, which in the first year would increase pension appropriations $75 million,[9] and he moved to reconsider three bills that were strongly supported by the senator from Wyoming, Francis W. Warren, chairman of the powerful Appropriations Committee, allotting $207,500 for the construction of public buildings in three small towns in Wyoming. Lea and several other senators believed there was no justification for these particular appropriations in view of the size of the population of the localities. Lea's motion antagonized not only the Wyoming senators, two of the most influential Republican members, but also a number of long-time leaders who perceived the motion as an interference with prevalent pork barrel practices. Lea was subjected to great pressure to withdraw the motion. However, he remained firm in the stand he had taken.[10] Even though the Republicans were still in control of the Senate, Lea and other Progressives were able to defeat those measures he considered looting the treasury.[11] As he was opposed to subsidies, Lea was also steadfast in his support of the Panama Canal tolls repeal bill.

The senior senator from Tennessee, Robert L. Taylor, died on March 31, 1912. Lea requested appointment to the vacancy thus created on the Post Office and Post Roads committee and to be excused from further service on the Naval Affairs committee, whose work was not of great interest to the people of Tennessee. Both requests were granted, and in accordance with his wishes he was also relieved from service on the District of Columbia committee and appointed to Military Affairs (*Congressional Record* 1912; 4574).

During Lea's first few months in the Senate, Mary Louise was well enough to visit him in Washington. However, she had not been there a month until she was stricken with internal hemorrhages. It was discovered that she was pregnant but that the fetus was in the Fallopian tube. It was necessary to operate, and the surgery was performed Saturday, June 17, at Georgetown Hospital. She withstood the operation, but the doctors did not attempt to conceal that she was gravely ill. The bleeding had stopped the next day but she had lost so much blood she could not rally. Her condition became alarming as her vital signs weakened.

Luke urged the doctors to give Mary Louise a transfusion and offered his own blood.[12] At that time few doctors in the country had performed the procedure. The doctors yielded to his urgent pleas but stated that it would be necessary to test both his and his wife's blood because if they were not the same type the transfusion would be fatal to her. Before the tests were completed, her condition deteriorated to the point that her life was despaired of. Luke implored the doctors to go ahead with the transfusion. Since his wife was dying, the transfusion could do no harm and was in fact her only chance of survival. The doctors acceded to his logic, but with little hope of saving her life.

At half past two that Sunday afternoon, the transfusion began. The technique consisted of connecting by a glass tube the main artery in Luke's arm, which had been severed and taken out for four inches, with a large vein in his wife's arm. Just before the flow of blood began the report from the tests was received indicating their bloods were fusible.

The transfusion lasted for over three hours. From the onset Mary Louise responded to the procedure, and gradually color returned to her cheeks and lips. As it did so, the healthy glow was drained from her husband's face. When the transfusion was terminated, Lea arose from the cot and walked unassisted from the room but fell in a dead faint outside the door. For the next ten days he was also a patient in the hospital suffering from loss of blood.

The following year his father, Overton Lea, was stricken with bronchial pneumonia. At his bedside when he died June 10, 1912, at age 66, at Chestnut Hill Hospital in Philadelphia were his wife and three children. Following funeral services at Lealand and interment at Mount Olivet Cemetery, Luke immediately went to Denver, where Mary Louise was recovering from a mild heart attack.

Chapter Four
A Progressive in State and National Politics, 1911-1914

Luke Lea had barely been sworn into the United States Senate in 1911 before a fight erupted in the Tennessee legislature.[1] The Regulars, who had a majority in the state Senate introduced a bill purporting to provide them proper representation, which in reality completely revamped the laws the independent Democrats and Republicans had enacted in the 1909 session (Hooper, *The Unwanted Boy* 108). In that age before the advent of voting machines, the personnel of the state and county election commissions was crucial. Whoever controlled the election machinery usually won the election.

The bill passed both the House and the Senate in the spring of 1911, but Governor Hooper promptly vetoed the measure. The bill was returned to the Senate, whose members overrode the veto. When the roll was called in the House the following morning, 34 Fusionist representatives were absent, having purposely broken the quorum and going to Decatur, Alabama.

Lea, still regarded the leader of the Fusionists, was urged to return to insure that their hard-won gains were not lost. He hated to leave Washington when the Senate was being organized. However, the split in the state Democratic party had created so much distrust among its members that he considered it his duty to return to Nashville in April to try to settle the controversy.

The immediate problem to be solved was the legislative deadlock, but the long-range concern was to create a plan for reuniting the Democratic party without sacrificing election law reforms or state-wide prohibition. Lea proposed a compromise by which the election law would remain in force, no action would be taken on the prohibition laws, and a direct primary law would be enacted, administered by commissioners representing both factions of the Democratic and the Republican parties.[2] He believed that direct primaries, protected by law as were regular elections, would go a long way toward solving political friction.[3]

Several Fusionist leaders, recognizing the Shelby County delegation as the key to the deadlock, began negotiating an alliance. Memphis had long had a reputation as a wide-open river town in which vice and political corruption flourished. Following the city's adoption of the commission form of government, Edward Hull Crump had emerged as a powerful political leader and was elected mayor in 1909 and again in 1911.

In return for a representative on the State Board of Elections and control of the election commission in Shelby County, the Crump organization agreed to end the legislative deadlock. The Shelby County representatives were instructed to vote with the Fusionists in order to prevent the House from passing any new election law over the governor's veto, and on June 23 the 34 Fusionist legislators who had succeeded in maintaining the election and prohibition laws, were back in their seats. The quorum restored, essential appropriation measures were passed.

No sooner was the legislature adjourned than Senator Lea and other Independents, concerned about the 1912 presidential election, again began trying to restore harmony to the Democratic party in the state. Lea concluded in an editorial in the September 25, 1911, issue of *The Nashville Tennessean and the Nashville American*:

> Let us remember the rank and file of the party are asking the question, not why we are divided, but what is preventing our reunion?
> And finally let us remember that division means defeat, and that union means success, and in so remembering forget our differences.

After the Regulars rejected three overtures by the Independents, the two factions agreed to call a convention for

May 16 to elect delegates to the national Democratic convention in Baltimore in July. The proposed unified primary plan was denounced by three extremist Independents, Jeff McCarn, Gus W. Dyer, and E.B. Stahlman, as a return to Pattersonism, and Lea was labeled a traitor to the temperance cause. To unite with the liquor interests would be an abandonment of principle, they charged. Many Independents, believing they would be out-voted by the Wets, refused to participate in an unified primary so the harmony movement collapsed (Isaac, *Prohibition and Politics* 199).

Something had to be done quickly in order for Tennessee to be duly represented at the Baltimore convention. Approximately 30 editors representing independent and regular Democratic newspapers met with leaders of both factions and worked out another harmony proposal. The convention scheduled for May 16 to elect delegates to the national convention would be held. On that date a new state executive committee also would be elected. That committee later ordered two primaries with no poll tax in which all Democrats not only were eligible but were urged to vote. Nominees for governor and railroad commissioner would be elected on August 1; nominees for positions to be filled by the legislature, including a United States senator, would be chosen on November 1 (*Nashville Banner* 16, 27 May 1912).

In the tide of progressivism and reform sweeping the nation, new leaders were coming to prominence in the Democratic party, and new issues—especially the tariff—demanded attention. In the same year that Ben Hooper was elected governor of the Volunteer State, Woodrow Wilson was elected governor of New Jersey. Before the campaign ended, Wilson, repudiating the bosses who had been influential in nominating him, came out in favor of a far-reaching program of reform (Link, "Democratic Politics and the Presidential Campaign in Tennessee" 109).

At the May 16 state convention to select delegates to the national convention Lea was assigned to Wilson, but one of his most active workers, K.T. McConnico, stated that Lea, despite his interest in the New Jersey governor's candidacy, considered himself bound for personal reasons to cast a complimentary vote for Oscar W. Underwood, congressman from Alabama.[4]

From the perspective of three-quarters of a century later, Lea's preferring to go to the convention instructed for Underwood rather than for Wilson seems inconsistent. His reasons can only be surmised. The representative from Alabama was the ranking Democratic member of the powerful House Ways and Means committee. His candidacy had great sentimental appeal in the South. He entered the campaign hoping not only to win the nomination, but also to put an end to any factional feeling remaining in this country (*The Nashville Tennessean and the Nashville American* 3 July 1912). Never a professional Southerner, Lea nonetheless had a loyalty to his region, and senatorial courtesy compelled him to support the elder statesman of the same party from an adjoining state.

Not only would it have been awkward for him to have been instructed for any candidate other than Underwood, but Lea had reservations about Wilson's commitment to progressivism. Lea's primary objective was for a progressive to be nominated and for a progressive platform to be adopted. Underwood might very well hold the balance of power. Wilson was the second choice of most Underwood delegates, so together could block the nomination of front runner Champ Clark of Missouri, speaker of the House of Representatives. The other major candidate was Judson Harmon, governor of Ohio, considered a conservative. However, William Jennings Bryan, who had been three times the Democratic standard bearer, was still a powerful force, and could again become the party's choice.

The convention hall in Baltimore was crowded when Norman E. Mack, chairman of the Democratic national committee, rapped the opening session to order on June 25.[5] The first battle entailed the election of a temporary chairman. After much debate, in which Luke Lea's name was mentioned as a possible candidate, Alton B. Parker won the position. Increasingly the convention became viewed as a struggle between progressive and reactionary forces. Lea soon became convinced that Wilson would make an excellent president and had the best chance of any of the leading candidates of being elected in November, so became one of his most enthusiastic supporters.

Speeches droned on in the sweltering heat at the second day's session as members of the credentials committee struggled over the seating of contested delegates. In one extremely important contest, Luke Lea negotiated an agreement that as much as any other single incident at Baltimore determined the outcome of the nomination (Link, "Democratic Politics and the Presidential Campaign in Tennessee" 124). In return for Roger Sullivan's committing the Illinois delegation to support the Wilson men when they took the South Dakota contest to the floor of the convention, the Wilson representatives on the credentials committee pledged their support to Sullivan in the Illinois contest, which gave his faction enough votes on the credentials committee to be seated as the rightful Illinois delegation. Thereby ten votes were immediately added to Wilson's growing strength, and Lea proved himself one of the most resourceful of Wilson's managers.

The oppressive weather and explosive tempers combined to make the auditorium almost unbearably hot for the evening session June 27. It was nearly midnight when chairman Ollie M. James, senator from Kentucky, banged his gavel and declared the floor open for presidential nominations. As each major candidate was nominated, wild demonstrations erupted, the one for Wilson lasting over an hour. It was nearly seven o'clock the next morning when the first ballot was taken and the weary delegates left the hall. On that ballot Clark received 440-1/2 votes; Wilson, 324; Harmon, 148; and Underwood, 117-1/2.

As all the candidates had far less than two-thirds of the votes required for nomination, a long hard fight ensued. Lea attended several meetings to try to break the prolonged deadlock. Finally after the twenty-sixth ballot, the tired delegates adjourned until Monday (*The Nashville Tennessean Magazine* 25 August 1968, "Those Long Hot Days in Baltimore").

As Lea, William F. McCombs, Wilson's campaign manager, Representative A. Mitchell Palmer of Pennsylvania, and Representative Albert Sidney Burleson of Texas emerged Sunday night from a long conference, they were immediately surrounded by reporters. Smiling broadly, Lea pointed to the steady gain made by their candidate and the corresponding weakening of Clark (*Washington Post* 1 July 1912).

The Cleveland *Press,* reporting highlights of the convention, stated on July 1:

> The statesman at Baltimore who, next to Bryan, has immersed himself in most glory is young Luke Lea, the boyish faced Senator from Tennessee, who has been one of the leaders in the Wilson camp. He has made friends among all factions by his vigor, fairness and parliamentary skill, but nowhere has his stock ascended higher than among the thousand newspaper men.
>
> "What's the matter with Lea as a compromise candidate?" asked a newspaper man among a group of a dozen who were talking with Lea in the lobby of the Belvedere last night.
>
> A poll showed he was the unanimous choice—and the proposal wouldn't be as wild as it sounds, either, except for one fact: Lea was born in 1879. To be eligible for the presidency he must be 35 instead of 33 years old....

Monday Wilson gained nearly 100 votes, passing the 500 mark on the 39th ballot. On the 46th he received the nomination.

The remaining order of business was selecting the vice-presidential candidate. Lea was among the small group that immediately went into conference to consider the matter. (McCombs, *Making Woodrow Wilson President* 179). The Tennessee senator had been one of a handful acceptable to Wilson, but Lea's age barred him from the ticket, and Governor Thomas R. Marshall of Indiana got the nod.

In the November election, Wilson defeated the incumbent Republican president, William Howard Taft, and the Bull Moose candidate, former President Theodore Roosevelt, who also had considered Lea as his running mate.

As pleased as Lea was with Wilson's victory, the 1912 Tennessee elections were most unfortunate for the senator. Two days after the May 16 convention in Nashville in which both Independents and Regulars participated to elect delegates to the Baltimore convention, the hope of the unification of the state

Democratic party was shattered. Former Governor Patterson announced he would be a candidate for the Senate seat (*The Nashville Tennessean and the Nashville American* 19 May 1912) vacated when Senator Robert Love Taylor died and to which Governor Hooper had appointed Newell Sanders to serve until the legislature elected Taylor's successor.

James B. Frazier, whose seat in the Senate Lea had taken, announced he was a candidate for governor. Former Governor Benton McMillin also decided to run, as did Thomas J. Tyne of Nashville and Thomas R. Preston of Chattanooga. The gubernatorial primary in August proved that the party was still deeply divided on the question of prohibition. Despite urging from Senator Lea and other leading Independents, a large number of that group refused to cooperate with wet Democrats, which accounted, in Lea's opinion, for Benton McMillin being nominated.[6]

The convention in May had decreed that the Democratic senatorial primary would be held at the same time as the general election for governor in November. Two of the three candidates who had announced for the senate seat withdrew, leaving anti-prohibitionist Malcolm Patterson with no opponent. The state Democratic committee, although besieged with requests to cancel the primary because Patterson was an anathema to several elements within the party, carried out the agreed upon plan (Isaac, *Prohibition and Politics* 204).

A large number of Independents could not support Patterson. Furthermore, the platform adopted by the Democrats was considered by many as a betrayal of the plan advanced by the Democratic editors representing both factions, and Lea did not believe it could be binding upon members of the legislature.[7] He and several party leaders decided their best course was to support candidates for the legislature who would not send Patterson to the Senate even though he had, albeit through default, the nomination of the state Democratic party.

The fight between the Independents and Regulars was not understood nationally, and the brunt of this misunderstanding was suffered by Senator Lea, who was sometimes viewed as a man with a foot in both camps, espousing one side in Washington and the other in Tennessee. A Fort Worth newspaper predicted on September 11 that should the Regulars regain control of the municipal offices, Lea would be a man without a party.

The Republicans nominated Hooper for a second term, and in the November general election he defeated McMillin in a race that was admittedly complicated by the senatorial primary. On the national level the Independents endorsed Woodrow Wilson, but on the state level they supported Hooper, prohibition, and law enforcement (Isaac, *Prohibition and Politics* 210).

After a hard fought contest across the state the Regulars won, by a narrow margin, control of both houses of the legislature provided the Shelby County delegation remained within their ranks. Hence, the balance of power was once again determined by Crump and Shelby County.

Crump was resentful toward the regular Democratic machine because of the back-tax harassment of Memphis citizens. Together with the Fusionists he wanted a thorough legislative investigation of back-tax graft. On the other hand, the repeal of the 1909 election law, sought by the Regulars, was not of vital importance to Crump because he already had control of the election machinery in Shelby County. The big issues on which he opposed the Fusionists was how prohibition applied to Memphis and the enactment of additional enforcement laws.

Immediately after the general election in November 1912, Lea met with a group interested in the organization of the legislature by members opposed to the Patterson-Dibrell faction. Agreement was reached to try: to defeat Patterson for the Senate; to oppose reelection of Frank Dibrell as state comptroller and to investigate his office; to overhaul the tax system; to outlaw free railroad passes; and to enact no further law enforcement legislation (Isaac, *Prohibition and Politics* 210).

Lea's papers indicate that he believed it was quite important to the incoming national Democratic administration that the junior senator from Tennessee be a progressive and that Attorney General

Charles T. Cates, Jr. was the most progressive man that could be elected. John K. Shields, chief justice of the Tennessee Supreme Court, had expressed an interest in going to the Senate, but he had refused to be a candidate prior to the November 1912 general election.

Facing certain defeat, Patterson withdrew from the race. Shields became a candidate without resigning from the bench and was opposed by the independent Democrats because they wanted him to continue on the state Supreme Court. Within four days after the balloting by the legislature had begun, he became the choice of the Regulars and by their backing was elected over the strenuous opposition of Lea, Stahlman, Crump, George Fort Milton, and Jonas Amis who supported Cates. Thus the junior senator became aligned with the same machine and interests that the Independents had challenged in three great battles for political supremacy in Tennessee (*Columbia Herald* 25 August 1913). The day after Shields' election, the legislature, in a complimentary appointment, named revered schoolmaster W.E. (Old Sawney) Webb to fill the remaining six weeks of Taylor's unexpired term.

In an effort to hold together the 1913 legislative coalition that had again been formed by the Fusionists and the Shelby County delegation, Lea asked the governor not to press for passage of further enforcement laws that might make Crump return to the Regulars. Hooper stated he had never agreed to give up on enforcement laws (Isaac, *Prohibition and Politics* 212), and, in a special message concerning prohibition, he said that his cooperation with anti-prohibitionists on certain other matters was not a compromise on temperance legislation (Isaac, *Prohibition and Politics* 214).

Crump kept his part of the agreement and voted with the Fusionists during the first part of the legislative session. Aware of the sensitive spot in the Hooper-Crump alliance, the Regulars began to push for the enforcement of the governor's stringent enforcement laws. The majority of Fusionists in the legislature having been elected on law enforcement platforms could not vote against those laws.

Lea's objective was to maintain the prohibition laws and election reforms enacted in 1909. He believed Hooper had not kept the agreement the Fusionists had made with Crump not to change the liquor laws in return for Shelby County's vote with them on other measures, and so stated in a front page editorial, "A Breach of Good Faith," in the *Nashville Tennessean and the Nashville American* on March 3, 1913. The agreement had been made, Lea maintained, to keep Crump from joining with the Regulars to repeal existing prohibition laws. It was at this point that Lea ceased to support Hooper.

When the legislature reconvened after the mid-season recess an agreement had been worked out between Crump and the Regulars. Hence no enforcement bills were enacted. Even though Crump thereby breached his agreement with the Fusionists, Lea was reluctant to do anything that could be construed as a betrayal of faith on his part (*Columbia Herald* 20 September 1913).

He believed Hooper had precipitated the collapse of the agreement between the Fusionists and the Shelby County delegation by insisting on the passage of the force laws, and he considered Crump his friend both personally and politically[8] and refused to heed warnings about him. This inability to recognize anything he did not want to see in one he regarded as his friend was a costly mistake Lea was to make time and again. Deeply concerned about his alignment with Crump, David Shepherd had written to Lea a year previously:

Luke, pardon me if I venture from my inexperience and ignorance, but from my deep affection for you to offer some advice. I don't believe you can afford to be allied with Crump. From what is being commonly said down here [Memphis], I believe his crowd made a crooked count in a number of wards here and carried ring politics into the election of a Board of Education—surely that is one set of men that ought to be elected regardless of politics. Furthermore, leaving principle for expediency, I have heard more criticism over the state in regard to your affiliation with Crump than about anything else. It is really hurting you.[9]

Tennessee, where in politics the amazing was commonplace,

was rocked in July by former Governor Malcolm R. Patterson's being arrested intoxicated in a house of ill-repute in Nashville. The arrest took place during a bitter mayoralty race in the city, and only that one house was raided. After hearing the evidence, the judge declared, "There is something behind all of this, and I dismiss every case" (*The Nashville Tennessean and the Nashville American* 26 July 1913).

A short time later Tennesseans were electrified when Patterson announced that he had undergone a conversion and had espoused the cause of temperance. His reversal on the liquor issue knocked the props from under Hooper's position as the defender of temperance and was the greatest blow since Carmack's death to the whiskey interests. The *Lewisburg Tribune* stated on October 31 that Patterson left little doubt that he expected to be forced to run for public office and to be elected by the very element that he had for years opposed.

Even though Lea was a staunch advocate of statewide prohibition, he was, however, of the opinion that the enforcement bills went too far. Hence, he was in the strange position of opposing law enforcement measures, which had always had his strong support, while Patterson, who had always opposed them, was speaking in behalf of their passage.

Lea thought that liquor would continue to disrupt the Democratic party in Tennessee as long as the party continued to take a stand on the matter. His papers express his belief that the best way to maintain prohibition was to elect legislators who favored temperance and would not repeal prohibition statutes.

Governor Hooper, determined to finish the fight on open saloons, issued a call for a second special session to consider the enforcement bills. To make certain that their long struggled-for goals were not thwarted, Prohibitionists organized mass meetings across the state. Finally convinced that public sentiment was overwhelmingly in favor of law enforcement measures, the Regulars abandoned the fight against their enactment.

The threat to the election laws, however, was the most serious crisis the 1913 General Assembly had to face. The Regulars, with the help of three Republicans, passed a bill that gave them the absolute control over election machinery they had enjoyed prior to 1909 (Hooper, *The Unwanted Boy* 147; Isaac, *Prohibition and Politics* 217). Governor Hooper promptly vetoed the measure.

Once again the Fusionists resorted to breaking the quorum in the House in order to keep the election law reforms intact. The Regulars then passed a bill making it a crime willfully to break a legislative quorum. That measure Hooper also vetoed. The Fusionists returned in June to enact a funding bill in order to maintain the state's credit. Armed guards appeared to prevent anyone from leaving the chamber. While a quorum was present, the Regulars repassed over the governor's veto, the election law passed earlier in the session, (Isaac, *Prohibition and Politics* 219) which was a serious set-back for the Fusionists and reform-minded progressives.

The disagreements between the Fusionists and the Regulars could not be confined to state matters. Shortly after Wilson's inauguration, in April 1913, the Democratic members of Tennessee's congressional delegation had met in Lea's office to discuss patronage.[10] Since a Democratic administration had taken over the government in Washington, many jobs in Tennessee, filled by federal appointment and then held by Republicans, would become vacant. The state's Democratic congressmen having been elected by various combinations of Independents and Regulars, were aligned with different factions within the party. With nearly every county having at least two Democratic party organizations, it was extremely difficult to agree on who should be appointed to what position.

Lea's papers evidence his belief that Senator John K. Shields, by becoming allied with the old Patterson machine, by whose support he had been elected, had deserted the principles for which they had both struggled. The friendly relations between the two men ended. Shields stated that since Fusion was no longer needed, he would endorse no one for federal office who endeavored to maintain the Fusionist movement (*Chattanooga News* 16 August 1913).

Lea had always believed that Fusion was a state matter and that Tennessee should be represented nationally by Democrats. His papers indicate that he believed he had demonstrated time and time again his willingness to be fair and to compromise in order to achieve harmony within the Democratic party. He could not, however, sanction appointment to public office persons who held beliefs that he had fought ever since he had been in public life.

Predictably federal appointments became tied up. Finally President Wilson announced that the two senators must reach agreement before any appointments could be made (*Chattanooga News* 14 September 1913). Lea and Shields then evolved a working arrangement by dividing available positions as equally as possible. Both senators agreed not to oppose the other's nomination for a post in return for the other's consent to his choice for a comparable appointment.

Although a key factor in Wilson's being nominated, Lea never received recognition nor patronage for the vital service he performed at Baltimore. His having gone to the convention as an Underwood delegate minimized, in the eyes of Wilson's cabinet-to-be, the importance of the role he had played.[11] Moreover, his credentials were questioned by some Democrats on the national level because he had been elected to the Senate with the aid of Republican votes.

Even before his inauguration Wilson had to decide whether to be the leader of a coalition of progressive Democrats, the great majority of whom had supported his candidacy, and insurgent Republicans, or whether to work entirely through his party and its congressional machinery. He chose the latter. It was his intention to reform the Democratic party by assisting the progressives, who in nearly every state were battling the conservatives for control. However, in many states the conservatives wielded much power and held many seats in Congress. Soon the realities of public life forced him to sacrifice party reform in order to put through his legislative program.

Key elements of his plan, termed the "New Freedom," were honest government, destruction of financial and industrial monopolies, and the repeal of special interest legislation. He proposed limited federal regulation as opposed to federal intervention in economic and social issues (Link, *Wilson and the New Freedom* 241). His policies were often denounced by the conservatives as going too far and by the progressives as not going far enough. Unfortunately the administration's patronage policy resulted in increased segregation in government offices and throughout the Democratic party in the South (Link, *Wilson and the New Freedom* 147-48).

Wilson's leadership was strengthened by unusual conditions in Congress. There was no rival leader in either house, and because of the disarray of the Republican party, the Democrats had a large majority in the House and a workable one in the Senate. Out of 290 Democrats in the House, 114 were serving their first term and eagerly supported the president's policies. Southerners of long tenure in both houses were aware that the future of the Democratic party depended upon their success in translating the public's demand for reform into legislation (Link, *Wilson and the New Freedom* 153).

Two years earlier the Democratic progressive senators, including Luke Lea, had served notice on their conservative colleagues that they must be given consideration in committee assignments. Their ranks had been swelled by the recent election so that not only would the Senate in the 63rd Congress be reorganized under Democratic leadership, but the progressives would be the largest group of Democrats in that body. John W. Kern of Indiana was selected as floor leader, and Lea was elected by the Democratic caucus of the Senate to the committee on committees (usually called the steering committee), which made committee assignments and had virtually entire charge of the organization of the Democratic Senate. This assignment gave the first-term senator increased influence.

The progressives brought about many changes in the reorganization of the Senate. Even though their innovations were not destined to endure forever, the importance of their revolt against the seniority system should not be minimized.

The 63rd Congress convened in special session on April 7, 1913, for the purpose of revising the tariff downward in accordance with public demand and the pledge of the Democratic party. Senator Lea was appointed for that Congress to the standing committees of Appropriations; Military Affairs; Privileges and Elections; Post Offices and Post Roads; and the Library, of which he was chairman (*Congressional Record* 1913; 20, 25).

A progressive Southerner, rooted in the anti-monopolistic tradition stretching back to Andrew Jackson, Lea helped bring about far-reaching changes during this decisive time in American political history. Public opinion, regardless of party affiliation, demanded reform of the tax and currency structures, and enactment of social legislation, including women's suffrage, prohibition, and safeguards for labor.

The first objective of President Wilson's New Freedom—tariff reform—was approved by the House on May 13. The Underwood bill provided for a graduated income tax to offset the anticipated loss in custom receipts. The bill then went to the Senate, which twice before had defeated tariff reform (Link, *Wilson and the New Freedom* 181). Lea actively supported the Underwood tariff, pointing out that although a genuine revision downward, the measure still contained much protectionism.[12] The measure as finally passed by the Senate contained lower tariffs and higher taxes on income than the bill it had received from the House.

No sooner had tariff revision been accomplished than Congress became embroiled in Wilson's second and more far-reaching objective, the overhauling of the nation's outdated banking and currency systems (Holt, *Congressional Insurgents and the Party System* 106-08). The administration bill foundered on the afternoon of August 19, 1913, at a meeting of the Democratic members of the Senate committee on banking and currency who repudiated the principal of a system of regional reserve banks on which it was based. Lea's recently introduced amendment to the Vreeland emergency currency act offered a compromise as it broadened that measure "by providing that five instead of ten banks with a capital of $1,000,000 instead of $5,000,000 may form an association for the issuance of emergency currency" (*Inter Ocean* 20 August 1913), and by affording relief in the rate of interest. After a long struggle the federal reserve bill was passed in December. Lea hailed it as the most constructive piece of legislation that any Congress had enacted since the Civil War, not excepting the Sherman antitrust act.

Wilson's third objective was an antitrust program. When he took office there were several pending antitrust suits, among which was the control by the Union Pacific Railroad of its competitor, the Southern Pacific (Link, *Wilson and the New Freedom* 418-27). Lea strongly supported the Clayton antitrust bill, which made interlocking directorates of corporations unlawful. He also was in favor of the trade commission bill, which authorized federal supervision of giant corporations.[13]

In the mainstream of the reform movement that had swept across the continent, the measures Lea continued to support were indicative of his socially progressive but fiscally solvent philosophy. He believed that women should be given the ballot and that all citizens should be encouraged to vote as special interests could and did control a minority of voters but could not control the majority. He was in favor of senators being elected by direct vote and of a constitutional amendment providing for the direct election of presidents (*Montgomery Advertiser* 13 December 1916). He also thought that expenditures of and contributions to presidential and vice-presidential campaigns should be made public.[14]

Having fought for prohibition on the state level, he supported the Webb-Kenyon bill which allowed dry states to exclude the shipment of liquor into their territory. He also advocated the question of prohibition being submitted to the voters of the nation in a constitutional amendment.

He voted for the Vardaman amendment which permitted the states to determine enfranchisement without restrictions as to color or sex,[15] and for the La Follette seaman's bill which freed seamen from the virtual bondage by which they were bound.

He approved the principle of an eight-hour work day for all

laborers, with safeguards to protect the rights of women and children, and the establishment of the children's bureau.

He considered the stamp tax on patent medicines just and therefore voted for it, even if by so doing *The Tennessean* were to lose every patent medicine advertisement.

Measures that would directly affect his constituents included an amendment he introduced authorizing the necessary expenditure to establish immediately maneuvering grounds for United States soldiers on the 5,000-acre tract of land offered to the federal government by the city of Tullahoma (*The Nashville Tennessean and the Nashville American* 22 March 1914). He also supported the establishment of a brigade post at Chattanooga and the acceptance of national cemeteries and battlefields at Murfreesboro, Franklin, and Nashville into a park system to be maintained by the federal government. He was interested in farm relief, the Tennessee and Cumberland rivers being made more navigable and the flooding of the Mississippi being better controlled. He introduced bills to provide a district judge for Middle and for East Tennessee.

The latter part of September 1914, Lea was contacted by the comptroller and treasurer of the State of Tennessee. They had been in New York for several days trying to sell short-term notes of the state to obtain the funds necessary for financing maturities due October 1, but had been unable to secure a loan with less than eight percent interest.[16]

Gaining the assistance of Treasury Secretary William Gibbs McAdoo, Lea went to New York and conferred with several leading banks including the National Park which had previously flatly refused to make the loan. Lea thereupon proposed to the Treasury department that it cooperate by making a deposit of gold with the National Park Bank. That bank then made the loan at six percent, which was two percent below the rate New York City had been obliged to pay a few days earlier (*The World* 26 September 1914).

Perhaps Lea's most ambitious undertaking during his tenure in the Senate was his attempt to have the railroads investigated. The enormity of the power of the major lines both in stifling competition and in their alleged corrupting influence on state government had made their regulation a major public issue.

Ever since he entered public life in 1906, Lea had heard that Tennessee politics was dominated by the Louisville & Nashville Railroad and the Nashville, Chattanooga & St. Louis Railway.[17] Coming to believe those reports, he determined to try to strike off the railroad shackles by which he believed Tennessee was bound. In so doing he was aware that he was jeopardizing not only his political career but also perhaps his life, because he believed that the railroads had attempted to destroy every man in public life who dared to make them, like any other corporation or citizen, conform to the laws of the land.

He started to assemble data that he believed would dissolve the ownership of the N C & St. L Railway by the L & N and sever their powerful hold on the state. Lea's decision to propose an investigation of the railroad became known in the summer of 1913. Milton H. Smith, president of the L & N, sent a promise of political backing to Lea on the condition that he desist in his efforts. Lea was not to be dissuaded and on August 6 he introduced Senate Resolution No. S. 153 calling for the investigation.

Only days after its introduction, Winston Baird, acting on behalf of the L & N Railroad, whose identity was at first hidden, offered to purchase part of Lealand. Lea was informed several weeks later that the railroad wanted a right-of-way for a pipeline across the family estate.

The month following Lea's introduction of the Senate resolution, he was advised that if he would agree not to press the inquiry, Milton Smith would have Major E.C. Lewis cease publication of the *Democrat*, the morning competition of *The Nashville Tennessean and the Nashville American*. Lea replied that he intended to continue to push the resolution and it passed the Senate on November 6, 1913. The Interstate Commerce Commission on November 10 ordered an investigation of the financial relations, rates, and practices of the L & N, the NC & St.

L, and other carriers. Thereafter the ICC, an administrative body, quasi-judicial in character, had complete control of the inquiry.

Men representing themselves as railroad engineers began in January surveying the property Lea owned in Belle Meade. The real estate development would be almost completely ruined as an investment if railroad tracks were constructed near the golf club, which had been given 144 acres by Lea's Belle Meade Company. The first of three surveys placed the proposed rail line at the far end of the property so it did little or no damage; the second practically divided the property; and the third nearly ruined its value as the proposed route of the railroad was almost identical to the then unannounced boundaries of the golf club.

Lea knew if the railroads decided to build a cut-off from the N C & St. L's Memphis line to Radnor Yards on the L & N tracks, they could do so either by eminent domain or laws they could have enacted. Therefore, he watched and waited while engineers surveyed routes through Belle Meade and Lealand, and also through Royal Oaks, the property recently purchased by his father-in-law, Percy Warner, fronting on Harding Road close to Belle Meade.

Finally Lea determined to find out whether the railroad intended building a beltline through Belle Meade or a pipeline through Lealand, lessening the value of those properties, or whether their frequent surveys had been merely attempts at blackmail. He stated the railroad could have at no cost the right-of-way for the pipeline through Lealand on either of two conditions: first, the railroad would exchange the $210,000 of bonds, which it held on the plant of the old *Nashville American*, for property in Belle Meade of equal value; or second, the railroad would grant the owner of Lealand the right to tap six times free of charge the water main crossing the property.

Lea believed that if the railroad planned to construct a tract through Belle Meade, it would choose to pay for the land in securities rather than in cash. If the railroad did not intend to build a track across Belle Meade, it would allow the right to draw on the proposed water main or offer a cash payment.

Lea received a telegram on March 16 that indicated the railroad would accept his proposal of exchanging the *American* bonds for Belle Meade land. Only a few weeks later, however, the railroad announced that plans had been abandoned to run a track through Belle Meade.

After Mrs. Overton Lea filed suit in July 1915 to keep the pipeline from crossing her property the railroad eventually desisted in its efforts, and no pipeline was laid through Lealand.

Two and a half years elapsed between the time Lea introduced S.R. 153 and the beginning of the Interstate Commerce Commission's hearings in Nashville in the spring of 1916.

During the hearings,[18] members of the 1913 Tennessee General Assembly testified under oath that they had received free passes themselves and that they had secured a large number of free passes for their constituents. Records indicated 671 passes were issued to M.H. Taylor of Jackson who served one term and that the mileage traveled on them represented $6,372.71; 423 passes were issued to W.E. Weldon of Paris, and on and on, indicating that the practice was widespread. Witnesses were unable to state from personal knowledge that it was impossible for a person hostile to the railroads to be elected to public office in Tennessee; however, they admitted it was common knowledge that the railroads were actively engaged in the politics of the state.

After three days and nights of testimony in Nashville, the hearings were resumed in Washington. The first witness, L & N president Milton H. Smith, refused to divulge his company's political campaign contributions (*The Nashville Tennessean and the Nashville American* 5 May 1916). He was questioned about his meeting in Kennesaw, Georgia, on October 28, 1894, with Samuel Spenser, president of the Southern Railway. At that meeting, a memorandum concerning which was taken unsolicited to Lea, Smith, referred to as Pizarro, and Spenser, as Cortez, were reputed to have divided the new world between them, deciding which line would control what territory.[19]

Interest in railroad legislation had lessened as more and more public attention had become focused on the European War and the possibility of America's involvement. Therefore, despite charges of monopoly and domination of state politics, the only lasting reform effected by the investigation was the enactment of anti-pass legislation, but that in itself was highly important.

When Lea introduced the resolution to have the L & N Railroad investigated, the fight between Nashville's two morning newspapers was bitter and unrelenting. Not quite a year after he had acquired the *Nashville American*, another newspaper had begun publication in Nashville in September 1911. The reason the *Nashville Democrat* was started, Lea believed, was to attempt to put his newspaper out of business and to destroy him politically and financially. The new paper was financed by the L & N Railroad, which had formerly owned the *Nashville American* for a period of 20 years, and by the united liquor interests under the direction of V.E. Shwab and his son-in-law, Paul M. Davis.[20]

This new paper proved a vigorous competitor to *The Nashville Tennessean and the Nashville American*, every share of whose voting stock was owned by Lea.[21] However, the *Nashville Democrat* ceased publication on October 13, 1913. Lea attributed its demise either to the railroad's assessment of it as a liability, or to the railroad's decision to use as its organ the *Nashville Banner*, whose owner, Major E.B. Stahlman, had formerly been connected with the L & N. At any rate, the *Banner* took up the battle and its attacks against Lea became increasingly vitriolic after the Senate's passage on November 6 of his resolution to investigate the L & N.

It was unusual perhaps that competitors ever enjoyed the close relationship, both personal and political, that Lea and Stahlman once shared. Their commitment to the temperance crusade had made them fast allies, but their differing opinions on an increasing number of matters had developed into bitter animosity.

The senatorship undoubtedly had a part in the rupture between the two publishers. When Lea was elected to the Senate in 1911, Governor Hooper had wanted Major Stahlman to get the post. Stahlman reputedly was concerned whether the Senate would seat him because of its investigation of the government's payment a few years previously of a claim he had lobbied through Congress of the Methodist Publishing House,[22] the proceedings of which investigation were contained in Senate Report 1416.[23]

When a seat in the Senate became vacant for the third time in as many years, the major, apparently having changed his mind, wanted to have the honorary though brief appointment accorded W.R. Webb. Stahlman became bitter toward Lea because he refused to try to have the vote recounted in the major's favor.[24]

The differences of opinion between Lea and Stahlman became so constant and so rancorous that the general public wearied of reading what they said about each other. A.B. Ransom, president, and William R. Manier, secretary of the Commercial Club of Nashville, sent a joint communication to the two publishers requesting that in future political controversies all personalities be omitted.

Lea replied:

...The controversy between *The Tennessean and American* and the *Banner* and E.B. Stahlman and myself is neither of my making nor choosing.... I do not desire to continue the controversy, but will, whenever Stahlman attacks me, make such vigorous defense and complete exposure of him as the circumstances warrant....[25]

Both publishers having strong convictions and nearly always supporting opposing candidates, it was difficult in the heat of a campaign to keep their personal differences from spilling onto the printed page. Consequently the controversy between them would continue to erupt from time to time.

Chapter Five
Politics in Tennessee
and the Bid for Reelection

Despite repeated pronouncements that harmony had been restored to the Democratic party in Tennessee, in-fighting between the Independents and Regulars continued into 1914. Lea believed that the liquor question, which had caused the disruption, had finally been resolved by the Regulars' acceptance of the Nuisance Act, which had gone into effect in March of that year. However, that act was not nearly as effective in stopping the liquor traffic as its supporters had hoped. Crump controlled the police in Memphis, and little effort was made there to enforce prohibition (Isaac, *Prohibition and Politics* 228-29). Also, the die-hard Independents so mistrusted the Regulars that they refused to join the harmony movement and remained a separate faction (Isaac, *Prohibition and Politics* 233) of which the *Banner* was the spokesman.

Lea became convinced that spring that Thomas C. Rye of Paris could not only harmonize the independent and regular factions but could also defeat Hooper for the governorship. The odds against Rye were formidable. He was relatively unknown outside of the thirteenth judicial district where he was attorney general. However, he had an engaging personality, was a staunch prohibitionist, and was known to have political aspirations. Lea did not want to campaign for him openly because he did not want anti-Lea people to be against Rye, so the senator sent his secretary, John D. Erwin,[1] to Nashville until after the primary as his political representative. Their daily correspondence during April reveals that Lea mapped out much of the campaign strategy by suggesting towns in which it would be helpful for Rye to speak, persons in various counties to be contacted, and how money should be raised.

With the backing of the Davidson County delegation, in one of the few times Lea and Mayor Hilary Howse supported the same candidate. Rye won the Democratic nomination for governor on May 27, 1914.

The state Democratic convention adopted the following plank aimed at winning the prohibitionist vote:

The Democratic party has always stood for temperance and good government. All the laws now in force were enacted by votes of the majority of the Democratic members of each branch of the Legislature. We are opposed to the repeal of any of the temperance laws now in force, and we pledge the Democratic party to their maintenance and to such additional legislation as may be necessary to ensure their rigid enforcement. (Isaac, *Prohibition and Politics* 233)

Both the Republicans and the Independents nominated Hooper for a third term. The platform on which he ran, as it related to temperance and law enforcement, differed little from that adopted by the Democrats.[2]

Rye did not name a campaign committee but left management of his campaign to the state Democratic committee, several members of whom had opposed his nomination. The campaign being organized differently from the way Lea had been informed was an indication to him, according to his papers, that his active connection was not desired. Nevertheless, he carried through his agreements and received President Wilson's endorsement of Rye and commitments from several senators and members of the cabinet to go to Tennessee to speak in his behalf.

Lea bore the cost of a special train for William Jennings Bryan's trip through the state, but because Congress continued in session, neither he nor any member of the Tennessee delegation was able to accompany the secretary. Bryan's trip through Middle Tennessee on October 16 was a huge success, and he was met by enthusiastic crowds at every stop. Between 1,000 and 3,000 persons were turned away from the Ryman Auditorium that evening to hear him speak.

Hooper's supporters, who still called themselves Fusionists, did not at first attack Rye, but rather assailed Lea, once the leader and champion of the cause he considered won, but they believed still must be waged. Stahlman labeled Lea a traitor, liar, and all-round skunk (Isaac, *Prohibition and Politics* 236). Hooper devoted a large portion of his opening campaign speech to Lea, but finding that his attacks on the senator were not popular with his audience, the Republican candidate dropped that course and began to attack Rye.[3] The main issue in the gubernatorial campaign came to be whether legislation should be passed giving the governor the power to remove officials holding elective offices, or whether this power should be vested in an especially created commission, or placed in the state courts through the medium of recall.

In the general election on November 3, Tennessee returned to the Democratic fold as Rye defeated Hooper by a sizeable majority. This victory that was generally regarded by many as greater for Lea than for the governor-elect, seemed to insure the senator's reelection in 1916. Prior to the balloting the senator was the center of attack by various factions, but after the votes were counted, Lea was the recognized political leader in Tennessee.[4]

Rye was a great conciliator, but the seeds of disunity were not all harvested by his election. Although the reunited Democrats had control of both houses of the legislature, the party was still fractured and nearly every county had one or more competing factions that did not trust the other.

Despite continued strong opposition in Memphis, Nashville, and Chattanooga, prohibition after 1914 was accepted by all political factions in Tennessee (Isaac, *Prohibition and Politics* 248). Although the fight there for prohibition had more dramatic political consequences than in most states, it was nevertheless part of a general grass-roots reform movement that swept the nation. Temperance leaders were sincere in their belief in the corrupting influences of liquor. The great experiment was tried and failed in Tennessee before it was tried on the national level that proved a failure (Isaac, *Prohibition and Politics* 266), and where enforcement also became enmeshed in politics. Closely linked with the temperance crusade, progressivism in Tennessee advocated also stricter railroad regulation and election reform.

One of the first acts of the General Assembly in January 1915 was passage of the Ouster Law which provided for the removal of officials who did not perform their duties (Isaac, *Prohibition and Politics* 240). Lea opposed this law under which Hilary Howse, mayor of Nashville, would soon be removed from office for failure to enforce the prohibition laws. E.H. Crump resigned as mayor of Memphis before he was ousted, but the state Supreme Court upheld his removal and declared him ousted anyway. Both men, however, would maintain their power-base and regain their political influence.

The Democratic Davidson County delegation that same month nominated Hill McAlister for state election commissioner, a nomination that Luke Lea considered the opening gun in the campaign to defeat his reelection the following year. That campaign, he was informed, was planned when Major Stahlman had recently been in Washington and had secured the active participation of Senator Shields and Tennessee congressmen Hull, Moon, McKellar, and Garrett, whom Lea dubbed "the Allies,"[5] and who differed with him on a variety of political issues.

Attorney K.T. McConnico, a dominating influence in the Nashville machine, but a personal friend of Lea and allied with him against the L & N Railroad, engineered a truce between him and Mayor Howse.[6] The support of that machine would be helpful to Lea in the forthcoming senatorial contest. But during that truce, which turned out to be quite temporary, a scandal over appropriations erupted in the city administration.

The *Banner,* quick to take advantage of the situation, tried to lay the blame on Lea for an alleged misuse of public funds. It was at this point that anti-Lea men gained control of the state election commission.

Congressman Cordell Hull of Carthage conceived the plan of a primary called a year earlier than it ordinarily would be scheduled, because he believed that by so doing Lea would not have time to gain control of the election machinery (Hull, *Memoirs* 77-79). The

Democratic executive committees of Henry, Robertson, and Rutherford counties, controlled by anti-Lea men, pressured the state Democratic executive committee into holding a special session on August 4, to consider resolutions that Lea run for reelection in an off-year, instead of in 1916 at the same time as the president of the United States, the governor, and ten congressmen from Tennessee.

After sharp debate, the committee set the senatorial primary for November 20, 1915, with a run-off scheduled for December 15. A primary when 16 months of the incumbent's term remained and a year before the nominee would run in the general election was without precedent in any state of the union.[7]

After Lea went on record opposing the early primary, he announced his candidacy and stated that his newspaper would support the nominee. He exuded confidence, but he realized that he would have an uphill fight against formidable odds.

Never having run for office, he did not have a statewide organization. Consequently he would have to rely on key men in the various counties.[8] He would be severely hampered by lack of funds in getting his record before the people, but perhaps the greatest obstacle he had to face was the opposition of the L & N Railroad, the enmity of which he had incurred by his determination to have its operations investigated.

Congressman Kenneth D. McKellar made the long expected announcement on August 16 that he was a candidate for the Senate seat, and following much speculation former Governor Malcolm Patterson threw his hat into the ring on September 2.

John L. Parham, a member of Crump's organization, wrote Lea almost daily in mid-August assuring him that at the proper time Crump would throw the support of the Memphis machine behind the senator. Lea tendered a top spot in his Shelby County campaign committee to Parham on September 12. After consulting with Crump, Parham replied that Crump had decided it best for "all the boys to be together and to be for McKellar."[9] Having carried through all the Fusionists' agreements with Crump, Lea naturally had hoped to have the support of Shelby County, and the loss of that large block of votes was a severe blow.

From the outset, the race created wide interest. It was perceived as a contest between arch foes: Lea, who had led the purge of the Democratic party of its domination by the liquor interests, fused the Independents with the Republicans to enact election law reforms and prohibition, then striven to reunite the Democratic party; and Patterson, who as governor had opposed prohibition and election law reform, but who had repudiated his former stand.

Lea opened his campaign September 11 in the historic old courthouse of Weakley County by outlining his position on important issues before the Senate. Running on his record, he made the alleged corrupt practices of the L & N Railroad one of the main issues of his campaign. He reiterated his belief that the greatest guarantee of peace was preparedness. Strongly in favor of the construction of good roads, he thought the federal government should bear its share of their cost.[10] It was his hope that his opponents would permit the campaign to be a discussion of issues and the position of the candidates thereon, rather than degenerate into a contest of personalities.[11] In his first 32 speeches, Lea did not refer in derogatory terms to either of his opponents. He did not even mention them or their records except as it was necessary to present his own position.[12] As the campaign progressed, however, the high road was not maintained.

To Patterson's charge that Lea had betrayed him, the senator replied he had never betrayed any man. Sometimes he had supported men for office who had betrayed, as Patterson had, the principles they advocated as candidates, and that therefore he had refused to support them further.[13] Attacks once launched, Lea and Patterson throughout the remainder of the campaign lambasted each other.

In answer to McKellar's charges against Lea in October, the senator stated that he would not only quit the race but would resign his seat if McKellar could produce a single man to whom Lea had promised a judgeship or his support for governor in exchange for his support of Lea in his bid for reelection.[14] The charges were not substantiated.

His opponents bore down heavily on Lea's absenteeism from the Senate. Despite being at his wife's bedside several times when she was gravely ill, he was, according to the *Congressional Record*, absent during the 63rd Congress only three times more than Tennessee's junior senator, John K. Shields. A large number of Lea's constituents, however, did not understand his frequent absences, although he made certain that his vote was protected by a pair, as was customary.

In keeping with Tennessee's tradition of great debates by opposing candidates, Patterson challenged Lea to meet him on the stump. Their several joint speakings attracted large crowds as both candidates were gifted orators with attractive personalities and caustic tongues. In the beginning they almost completely ignored McKellar, who was not considered a factor. Lacking ability as a debater, McKellar, a square-faced man of medium height, quietly covered the state talking with the voters and shaking hands.[15] As the campaign progressed it became evident that both Senator Shields and Congressman Hull were working diligently for him.[16]

In his avowed intention of going into all of the 95 counties in the state, Lea's hearty constitution and excellent voice stood him in good stead. Up early every morning he traveled many miles each day, making two or more speeches, which number would increase as the election neared, and he was temperamentally suited to take the unexpected with equanimity. In order to make his scheduled speeches in Hohenwald and Centerville on November 4, it was necessary to go by automobile. Enroute the car swerved and hung uncertainly over a chasm nearly 100 feet deep. The passengers managed to climb out, the car was gotten back on the road, and the journey continued.

The next day the car stalled crossing a creek, and the occupants had to take off their shoes and wade to the other bank. The rest of the trip was made on a badly battered rim minus its rubber tire, but Lea was in fine fettle when they got to Centerville, and the warm welcome he received made the harrowing trip worthwhile (*The Nashville Tennessean and the Nashville*

American 5 November 1915). By the middle of November Lea had visited more than 80 counties and made over 130 speeches, a record unmatched at that time by any other candidate in Tennessee's history.[17]

Lea's strength was in rural areas, and he had to get enough votes there to overcome the big city districts where he was expected to run poorly. His campaign was boosted by George L. Berry, president of Pressmen's Union, and later a United States senator, who, contrary to custom, endorsed the senator's candidacy. Berry wrote labor officials across the state that Lea had uniformly supported measures advocated by organized labor, such as the eight-hour law and workman's compensation; that his newspaper had always backed measures benefiting labor both on the state and national levels; and that the papers had been operated under union conditions.[18]

During the closing days of the campaign, the *Banner's* charges reached a shrill crescendo. Squibs stated that Wilson had not said anything for Lea yet; the only part Shields had taken in the campaign was to make certain that he would be the senior senator; if Rye had done anything to help Lea, he had been very quiet about it. The day before the primary a *Banner* editorial proclaimed that:

> It is opposed to Luke Lea because neither his character nor his intellect qualify him for the post of United States Senator.
> In the brief time Lea has been in Tennessee politics he has been on all sides of all questions, and has betrayed every person and every cause with whom or with which he has been associated. He cannot be trusted in anything.
> His record in the Senate, in so far as national policy is concerned, has been a blank.... Nor did Lea give any attention to matters affecting directly the interest of the state.... (*Nashville Banner* 19 November 1915)

A *Tennessean* election day editorial charged the L & N had poured money into the campaign in an effort to stave off the investigation into its practices until Lea's term was over so it could continue its illegal ownership of the N C & St. L.

As returns began to come in, votes for the three candidates

were almost equal. Then Patterson gained the lead, which he maintained until Shelby County reported its heavy majority for McKellar. At that point McKellar took the lead and kept it, and the result soon became clear.

Mrs. Lea was at her husband's side throughout the evening.[19] At ten o'clock the senator conceded and made the following statement:

> Political postmortems are never interesting. The result is accepted cheerfully on my part and there are no sores or wounds to be healed. I shall cordially support whoever is nominee of the run-off and will always remember with deep gratitude the unselfish loyalty of the friends who fought with me in this campaign. (*The Nashville Tennessean and the Nashville American* 21 November 1915)

The next morning the following unofficial figures were reported in *The Tennessean*:

	McKellar	Patterson	Lea
East Tennessee	10,803	4,850	9,202
Middle Tennessee	14,216	22,961	15,909
West Tennessee	16,216	11,273	7,536
Total	41,235	39,084	32,647

In analyzing the returns, *The Tennessean* stated the next day that the voting contained many surprises. Patterson supporters had predicted he would poll almost 20,000 more votes than he did, while McKellar's most optimistic backers did not foresee that he would get so large a vote. However, few counties gave either of the three candidates a clear majority over the other two combined. In most counties, the race was close between the three. In Madison there was less than 100 votes difference between the candidates. Shelby County, as always, was influential in the outcome, and Lea polled only 173 votes in that county (*The Nashville Tennessean and the Nashville American,* 21 November 1915).

Many factors contributed to Lea's defeat. He was undoubtedly hurt by his continued involvement in state politics from which he found it difficult to remain aloof. Continually he was beseeched by one faction or another to exert his influence to maintain election law reforms and temperance legislation. Those two goals, for which he had consistently fought, had been gained, but for his political fortunes it was a Pyrrhic victory. Caught in the crosscurrents of the often conflicting opinions of the Democratic voters, his actions were misunderstood by many. The temperance forces thought he had not gone far enough in advancing the prohibition cause. Many independent Democrats had become disenchanted with him because he was willing, once the liquor question had been settled, to work with Regulars to try to reunite the Democratic party in Tennessee. Some regular Democrats mistrusted him still because he had allied himself with Republicans to bring about election law reforms and prohibition.

He was also hurt by Governor Rye's not coming out strongly for him. Had he done so, some thought the governor could have gotten Lea renominated without opposition.[20] However, not wanting to jeopardize his position, Rye was cautious about becoming embroiled in the senatorial primary.[21]

The Banner was vitriolic in its attacks on him and aligned against Lea were the whiskey interests and the big city machines. During his temporary truce with Mayor Howse of Nashville, Lea received some of the blame, although he was in no way responsible, for the financial scandal that erupted in city hall.

The greatest single factor, perhaps, in Lea's defeat was the L & N Railroad. It was reported by his Knox County campaign manager, A.M. Gains, that the L & N poured money into McKellar's coffers there,[22] and the railroad attorneys throughout West Tennessee counties organized their counties against him. Lea had little money with which to combat the unlimited funds the railroad apparently was willing to spend to insure his defeat.[23]

For a time Lea had managed to hold together a working coalition of the various factions without which Tennessee would likely have sunk back into the quagmire from with it had recently extricated itself. Possibly no person who had been a leader in those battles and antagonized the inevitable numbers of people necessary to bring about those reforms could have mustered enough votes to be reelected. However, progressive reformers of that era, among whom Lea was numbered, succeeded in making state government more honest, more representative of the people, and more responsive to their needs in a period of rapid and confusing change. In so doing, they charted the future development of Tennessee (Shahan, "Reform and Politics in Tennessee" 382, 384).

In the December 15 senatorial run-off, bad weather and lack of interest held the vote to approximately 25,000 less than in the November primary. McKellar won by 20,000, and again stunned prognosticators by his margin of victory (*Nashville Banner* 16 December 1915).

It had been a foregone conclusion that former Governor Ben Hooper would be the Republican nominee for the Senate. In the general election the following autumn, McKellar, who would become part and parcel of the Crump machine, would defeat Hooper and in 1917 begin his record-breaking tenure of 36 continuous years in the United States Senate.

Lea returned to Washington on December 6, 1915, for the opening of the first session of the 64th Congress. With an entire session ahead of him and 16 months of his term yet to be served, he was already a lame duck. Not given to bitterness, he did not brood upon his defeat, but rather he looked to the future.

In that congress, Lea continued to serve on the Military Affairs, Appropriations, Rules, Post Office and Post Roads, and Privileges and Elections committees and was chairman of the Committee to Audit and Control the Contingent Expenses of the Senate. He introduced bills to codify and revise laws governing the judiciary; to regulate the Civil Service Act; and to establish additional national parks and construct more post roads (Congressional Record 1916; 9032, 12825, 13873).

He voted to confirm the president's nomination to the United States Supreme Court of the controversial Louis D. Brandeis; supported the Shipping Act of 1916, which created the modern merchant marine; and voted in favor of the progressive Revenue Act of 1916, which increased taxes on large properties and eased the burden on lower and middle incomes (Link, *Woodrow Wilson and the Progressive Era* 192, 196). Although he did not approve of compulsory arbitration in labor disputes[24] he voted to prevent an impending railroad strike thereby giving Congress time to consider the issues involved.[25] Not surprisingly he had earlier introduced a bill to outlaw intrastate railroad passes. Due in no small measure to his untiring efforts, as well as in response to public opinion, the Tennessee legislature would later enact a law forbidding free railroad transportation after December 31, 1917.[26]

Lea consistently supported immigration legislation[27] and he favored the Muscle Shoals Falls in the Tennessee River as the site for the government nitrate plant recently authorized by Congress.[28] He also advocated a constitutional amendment providing for the direct election of presidents of the United States.

Lea fulfilled his senatorial duties and continued to look after the concerns of his constituents, but his influence was lessened by his defeat for reelection. His interest, not in the great issues with which the Congress had to wrestle, but in the routine mechanics of government, also was probably diminished.

Mrs. Lea's health had not improved as much as had been expected, and because of her illness the senator had become interested in the von Ruck treatment for tuberculosis. Doctor Karl von Ruck had a sanitarium in Asheville, North Carolina, and had worked for more than 20 years on trying to prevent tuberculosis. He had devised a vaccine made from a culture from the blood of persons infected with the disease.[29] Although the von Ruck method was controversial, thousands of persons had submitted to his treatment, and hundreds claimed to have benefited. Moreover, there was no evidence that any patient had been injured by the treatment, which also included a strict diet, exercise, and fresh air.

Senator and Mrs. Lea decided there was nothing to lose by her becoming a patient of von Ruck (*New York Times* 29 May 1913). Asheville's closer proximity than Denver to Nashville and to Washington probably weighed in their decision. When Congress was not in session, Lea was needed in Nashville both because of his business interests and the state political situation in which all that he had fought for was continually being challenged.

Lea had been instrumental in the Senate's passing a resolution on May 13, 1913, to try to establish the merits of the von Ruck treatment, but the results were inconclusive. Nevertheless, it seemed to be beneficial to Mary Louise, and she was quite comfortable at Rosebank Cottage, a house they rented on the grounds of Grove Park Inn.

However, she continued to suffer set-backs from time to time. In the late winter of 1915 she was stricken with severe hemorrhaging. Luke rushed to Asheville where he spent ten days until she was considered out of danger.[30] She contacted pneumonia the middle of September 1916 and was desperately ill. After a week of fighting the disease, she suffered three severe heart attacks, but each time rallied when strong stimulants were administered hypodermically. Luke was in her room day and night until slowly she began to improve.[31]

As high altitude was considered beneficial for people with tuberculosis, Lea decided to build atop the highest hill in Lealand a small clapboard cottage so Mary Louise could spend some time in Nashville. The site was selected, plans drawn, and the house completed in time for the family to celebrate the following Christmas there. That, however, was to be the only occasion it was ever occupied.

Lea's belief that Belle Meade was the direction toward which Nashville must inevitably grow was being proven correct, and by 1916 it was becoming the city's most prestigious residential area. Many lots, priced at $1,000 to $6,000 had been sold, and quite a few handsome homes and the Belle Meade Apartments had been built or were under construction. The Nashville Golf Club, having accepted the Belle Meade Company's offer of land to relocate in Belle Meade, had moved into its beautiful new clubhouse. Forty lots in the new subdivision were offered at auction on June 26, 1917 (Tidwell, *Belle Meade Park* 31). To increase the water supply, Lea that year authorized the building of a reservoir on one of the highest hills in what is now Percy Warner Park and the digging of a well and construction of a stone pump house from which a water main was laid so water could be pumped to the reservoir (Tidwell, *Belle Meade Park* 18).

The Tennessean and American had moved in the spring of 1916 to Fourth Avenue into the remodeled building previously occupied by the Southern Turf, a renowned saloon. The paper's new home was considered to be one of the finest buildings in the South devoted entirely to publishing a newspaper and the mechanical equipment was of the latest design (*The Linotype South* May 1916).

J.H. Allison had been placed in charge of the daily management of the newspaper when Herman Suter had resigned in the autumn of 1912 to become general manager of *The Philadelphia Times*. Lea hated to lose the expertise of Suter, who more than anyone had helped organize *The Tennessean*, and had also handled much of the senator's personal and political business, but he never stood in the way of anyone advancing himself.

The Tennessean and American supported the planks of the state Democratic platform in 1916 calling for the abolition of free railroad passes, the outlawing of legislative lobbies, the strengthening of election laws, and a compulsory primary for the nomination of party candidates.[32] Lea directed that the paper lead the fight to change the charter of the city of Nashville and to spearhead the drive to lower the tax rate to not more than $2.25.[33]

By the summer of 1915 while the primary in which Lea was defeated was being agitated, there was nationwide concern over the continued refusal of the warring factions in Mexico to end hostilities (*The Nashville Tennessean and the Nashville American* 11 July 1915). Despite the gravity of that situation, however, the European War dominated the news. Germany had declared in February, as its submarines tightened its blockade of Great Britain, that the waters around that island, including the English Channel, were in the war zone. Merchant ships, even those of neutral nations, found in that zone would be sunk. The British passenger liner, the *Lusitania,* was torpedoed and sunk May 7, off Kinsale

Head, Ireland. Among the nearly 1,200 persons drowned, 124 were Americans.

The sinking of the *Lusitania* coupled with Germany's refusal to meet President Wilson's demands concerning the matter made Lea wonder how much longer the United States could remain neutral. The issue of war or peace weighed heavily on him. Before a large audience at the dedication on June 8, 1915, of the Confederate monument at Dresden, Tennessee, he said:

> Today we are confronted by the greatest crisis in history.... Today, as yesterday and tomorrow, Death disguised as Mars, is drawing nation after nation into its ever widening whirlpool of blood, until half of the world is running red.... the question upon the lips of every patriotic and country-loving American is, "Are the waters of the Atlantic deep and broad enough to quench the fire of hate and death kindled last June by an assassin's bullet, or must America, too, pay its toll of death without having incurred the debt of war?"...War has no place in a civilization whose foundation stone is the life of Christ....[34]

His desire for peace was evident in the commencement address he delivered at the University of the South on Tuesday, June 15, when he was awarded the honorary degree of Doctor of Civil Law. In discussing the responsibilities of citizenship he stated that a person's foremost duty at that time was to try to prevent the war from annihilating all civilization. If there were no provocation however great, save self-defense, that justified a man to kill another man, neither could there be any provocation, save actual self-defense, that would justify a group of men designated as nations, by arbitrary or artificial boundaries, to kill another group of men. To meet the responsibility of worldwide citizenship the United States must lead the way in establishing an international court of arbitration, empowered to enforce its decrees through the deployment of the armies and navies of peace-abiding nations to quell any country daring disregard of its mandates. In his repudiation of war and advocacy of compulsory arbitration of international disputes, Lea was in the mainstream of progressivism (Link, *Woodrow, Wilson and the Progressive Era* 180).

The events of 1916 transpired against the tapestry of worsening relations between the United States and Germany. In May, after nearly a year of diplomatic correspondence over the submarine issue, the German note, stating that in the future German subs would warn ships before torpedoing them and would also assist in rescuing passengers on those ships, was accepted by President Wilson as fulfilling his demands (*The Nashville Tennessean and the Nashville American* 6 May 1916). A diplomatic break was thereby averted, but the crisis remained unresolved, and as it deepened, public opinion shifted from a stance of strict neutrality to sympathy with the Allies.

Woodrow Wilson was elected in November 1916 to a second term in a race so close that his Republican opponent, Charles Evans Hughes, went to bed election night believing that he was the president-elect. Lea was afraid that the kaiser and his advisors, not fully comprehending the American political system, might think the closeness of the race indicated that the United States was divided on foreign policy.

His fear was shared by the German ambassador to the United States. Count Johann Heinich von Bernstorff was reported to have stated that he could not convince his government that the American people, almost evenly divided in their preference of two candidates who had opposing views in regard to foreign policy, could ever unite sufficiently to enter the war to help the Allies. He feared Germany's misunderstanding of the American election would result in unrestricted submarine warfare, which in turn would quickly bring about war between the United States and his country.[35]

Strongly opposed to the United States becoming involved in the war, Lea believed that Wilson would call for a declaration only as a last resort.[36] However, he considered that it was his duty to support the president in whatever course of action he deemed necessary.

During that fateful second session of the 64th Congress, December 4, 1916 to March 4, 1917, Lea voted yea on February 20, and the Senate passed a bill to punish espionage acts.

One of Lea's last votes cast late the evening of February 28 was in favor of a bill to arm merchant ships, the passage of which enabled them if attacked, to fire on submarines.

Wilson's peace overtures to the belligerents on December 18, 1916, had little effect, and on January 31, 1917, Germany, as Count von Bernstorff had predicted, announced her intention of sinking all vessels in the war zone around the British Isles. The United States responded by severing diplomatic relations with Germany.

The United States made public on February 28 a communication from Germany to Mexico proposing an alliance and offering as an inducement the return of the territory of Texas, New Mexico, and Arizona, formerly under the control of Mexico. American ships were torpedoed on March 18 and 21 and again on April 1 and 5. President Wilson announced on April 2 that because of Germany's acts, war had already begun; and that America's aim in becoming a combatant was "to make the world safe for democracy." Four days later, April 6, Congress declared war, and the world would never be the same.

Chapter Six
Colonel of the 114th Field Artillery

Luke Lea was opposed to war and had earnestly hoped that the United States could remain neutral.[1] He was over the draft age and had an invalid wife and two young sons. No one would expect him to enlist. He was of the opinion that soldiers who fought in this war 4,000 miles from home would not gain the glamour and glory that had surrounded soldiers of former wars. He recognized that promises made to enlistees probably would not be carried out to ex-servicemen once peace came and they returned home. Yet because he believed that preparedness was the surest avenue to peace he had voted in the Senate for every measure that had aided America in getting ready for the conflict into which she had been drawn. Therefore, he believed he was compelled to volunteer for active service. Daily his newspaper advocated enlisting, and he could not urge what he himself did not do.

He had decided several months previously that should the United States go to war, he would raise a volunteer regiment and tender it to the federal government for active service in France. He discussed this plan early in 1917 with several top War Department officials, whom he knew from his work on the Senate Military Affairs committee and was assured that such a regiment would be accepted and fully equipped.[2]

Lea began the end of May 1917 to recruit. "Join the artillery and ride," "Tennessee's only mounted regiment," and "Go with those you know" were favorite slogans. Later at the front, when scarcely enough horses were left to pull the guns and the men had been marching on foot for days and nights, some soldier would frequently yell out, "Join the artillery and ride," which always evoked loud hoots.

Regimental headquarters was established in Nashville. The four larger cities—Memphis, Nashville, Knoxville, and Chattanooga—each furnished a battery. Many more men applied for enlistment than could be accepted, so the examining surgeon adhered to rigorous standards, both physical and mental. The percentage of illiteracy was quite low. A large number of the enlistees had some high school education, and many were either college graduates or students.

The regiment went into state service on July 25 as the First Tennessee Field Artillery. The previous evening Governor Tom Rye commissioned Lea lieutenant colonel, but in the absence of a full colonel, Lea continued in command. All national guard units were drafted into federal service August 5, and Lea was notified at the end of the month that the regiment would be trained at Camp Sevier in Greenville, South Carolina.

The men of batteries A, D, and F were assembled at Union Station on September 9 by 2:00 P.M., as the sun broke through the clouds. Led by Lea and his staff mounted on splendid horses, the regiment paraded through the business district. Instead of the few thousand relatives and friends expected to tell the men goodbye, the streets were lined that Sunday with a crowd estimated at 50,000.[3]

The first section of the train reached Paris, South Carolina, before daylight September 11, and the regiment immediately began marching to Camp Sevier, named for the Revolutionary War hero of King's Mountain. To their dismay, they discovered the camp consisted only of a few mess halls amid a dense forest of pine. Picks and axes were distributed, and before nightfall enough land had been cleared for tents. Blankets were in short supply and it was quite cold, but luckily wood was plentiful, so fires roared through the night.

While the site was being cleared, the division was organized. Lea's regiment became the 114th Field Artillery; the First Tennessee Infantry, commanded by Colonel Harry S. Berry, a West Point graduate from Nashville, became the 115th Field Artillery; the First North Carolina Artillery, under the command of Colonel

Albert L. Cox, became the 113th Field Artillery; and Troop D. Tennessee Cavalry of Knoxville, captained by Ambrose Gaines, became the 105th Trench Mortar Battery. These four units made up the 55th Artillery Brigade of the 30th Division.

Brigadier General George G. Gatley, a West Pointer, was charged with the tremendous task of transforming civilians into soldiers. When he was informed that one of the regiments to be under his command was led by a former United States senator, he had dark forebodings and envisioned an elderly and portly gentleman, more familiar with an easy chair than a saddle and more inclined to give orders than to carry them out. However, as he came to realize that both the officers and men of the 114th knew they were utterly lacking in military knowledge but were eager to learn, he grasped the regiment's potential and set out to develop it.

Lea was promoted on October 20 to full colonel, and General Gatley pinned the eagles he had worn for 20 years as a colonel on the shoulders of the Tennessean.[4] From the outset Lea had his men's respect and admiration, which during their service together grew steadily. The colonel did not give his men a stiff, cold salute. He spoke to them, calling most by name.[5] He maintained strict discipline but was eminently fair, and his energy and enthusiasm set an example for the entire regiment.

Lea was ordered the first of December to the school at Fort Sill, Oklahoma, considered by the officers the most tortuous they had to attend. Next he was sent to Fort Sam Houston, "the canning factory for national guard colonels," as it came to be called.[6] He was one of 13 out of the 42 to pass the course.[7] He then received orders to return to Fort Sill, where he completed his training on March 22 and rejoined his regiment.

Colonel Hammond arrived on April 29 from Washington to inspect the troops. The day before the inspection Lea found the guns were dirty, an artilleryman's cardinal sin, and took drastic disciplinary action. At the inspection everything went wrong. The guns had been improperly cleaned, and the entire regiment was placed under arrest. Nervous because they were being inspected, the batteries made basic mistakes. One was not called to attention; another appeared without blankets for mounted drill; one failed to lay a gun properly, and on and on. They failed on every phase of the inspection. During the break for dinner, Lea met with the officers and instructed them in no uncertain terms to make sure their men shaped up, but the batteries were slow in working the reconnaissance problems that afternoon.

The inspector's attitude, in Lea's opinion, had been hostile throughout the day. He later heard rumors that his political enemies in Tennessee had pulled strings to have him "found" at the inspection so that he would be relieved of his command and the regiment he had raised would go abroad without him.

Lea issued orders that night correcting the regiment's mistakes. The next day the performance of the 114th merited only commendation, and Lea was not "found."

After another inspection the following week, the colonels of the three artillery regiments were informed their units were ready for active service. Lea went into town to break the news to Mary Louise that the 114th would probably be shipped out in about ten days.

Each was determined to be cheerful, and so much had to be done before they left Camp Sevier, there was little time to dwell upon the coming separation. A special celebration of Holy Communion for the colonel and Mary Louise was held at Christ Church on Monday, May 20. The regiment left Greenville that night by train and arrived early on May 23 in New York.

The following day Lea received orders to embark Sunday, May 26, by 8:00 A.M., and for him, Adjutant Thomas W. Pointer, and Major Larkin Smith to go on board Saturday, reporting before 9:00 A.M. to Pier 1, Hoboken, New York. His heart sank at the thought of leaving Mary Louise and the boys so soon, but he determined not to let her know in advance the date of his departure, which was the first time he had ever kept anything of importance from her. He was able to spend the night with his family at New York's Hotel Martinique and the next morning had a business conference with Percy Warner, William Nelson, and Jim Allison.

On reporting to Pier 1, he received orders for embarkation on the *SS Karoa*, Pier 54, N. River, New York City, and was given an hour and a half to get his baggage. Mary Louise helped him pack. At Pier 54 he presented his orders, inspected the *Karoa*, a small British vessel, formerly in the Indian trade, and spent the afternoon going over orders.

He was able to go back into town where he spent a delightful evening with Mary Louise and the boys. Throughout his training period, his family had been near him—in Greenville and San Antonio and in Lawton, Oklahoma. He would always remember his last glimpse of them—the boys asleep and Mary Louise's eyes glowing as she kissed him goodbye and after she thought he had glanced back for the last time, a tear rolling down her cheek.

The troops arrived by ferry a few minutes before eight the following morning and were loaded by 9:30, the regiment being commended by the commanding general on the speed with which it had boarded. Boat drills were held, and the men were instructed about lowering the life boats.

The fog was so heavy that the 14 ships in the convoy—eleven troop ships, a British cruiser, one freighter carrying ammunition, and one old camouflaged cruiser—did not get under way until nine o'clock the following morning. Because of the submarine menace, boat drills were held daily, and on Wednesday Lea commenced schools similar to those he had instituted at Camp Sevier. The officers of the regiment were divided into two sections, with Lea taking one and Lieutenant Colonel James A. Gleason the other. Physical drills were started, and daily baths ordered.

The convoy, Lea thought, was a farce. Should a ship be torpedoed, the others were to steam away quickly with the exception of the cruiser, which, if possible, would help. When the most dangerous submarine zone was reached, the men and officers were ordered to wear life preservers at all times except when eating and sleeping and then to have them close at hand. Late the night of June 4 the captain sent word to Lea that the ship to their port side had been fired upon. Lea immediately dressed as warmly as possible and went to the bridge. The fog was quite thick, and the entire convoy deviated from course and steamed due north. Although much alarmed, the captain stated it was not advisable for the men to be brought on deck. Since there was nothing Lea could do, he went back to bed.

The next day the captain continued to be so worried that he did not take any meals with the officers, and the weather was so bad, boat drills were cancelled. By then each man knew his assigned place on deck in case of attack and could get there within a minute or so after the gong was sounded. Because of the deviation the previous evening, they were 60 miles north of their rendezvous with the torpedo destroyers, and the convoy's cruiser had returned to the United States at the time it was most needed.

However, eight destroyers capable of great speed joined them early the next morning, June 6, and their arrival greatly allayed the men's fears. It was terribly rough that night, but the officers' schools had the scheduled exams. A lighthouse sighted about 9:00 P.M. was a most reassuring sight. Land—Scotland—was visible the following morning. Destroyers and small armed craft of all kinds darted about, and two dirigibles hovered overhead as the convoy sailed between the shores of Scotland and Ireland. The *Karoa* was docked by 10:30 that evening.

The regiment, with the exception of those who remained on board to police the ship, disembarked at 10:30 the next morning. With standards uncased and band playing, they marched five miles to West Camp at Knotty Ash, on the edge of Liverpool, England. Their route was crowded with women and children and a sprinkling of old, crippled men, who welcomed them with enthusiastic cheers. Early the next morning the regiment again marched through the streets with the band playing and entrained for Winchester.

After being reviewed by the Duke of Connaught, the regiment departed for Southampton where it boarded *La Marguerite*, an old sidewheeler, to cross the English Channel. The ship had no quarters for the approximately 1,000 troops that were crowded into a space that would poorly accommodate 200. Had the boat been torpedoed, the fatalities would have been terrible. Lea sat on deck until nearly midnight, then laid down in his clothes and slept soundly. By 4:00 A.M. the ship reached Le Harve.

The regiment spent that day and the next at another poorly provisioned rest camp. Twelve or 13 men were assigned to a tent only large enough for two. The officers were quartered in huts but had to sleep on the floor. The roar of guns on the front was distinctly audible. The second evening there Lea took the wrong streetcar from town and found himself at a German prisoner of war camp. He was delightfully surprised to see the prisoners were ignorant-looking and either very young or quite old.

The regiment left at midnight for their new station and arrived Sunday, June 16, at Camp Coetquidan in Brittany some 20 miles south of Rennes, where they were to receive their final training before going to the front. The camp was one of several artillery training centers for the American Expeditionary Forces rented from France by the American government. Coetquidan, used by Napoleon for training his artillery, was laid out on extensive lines and could accommodate two brigades. Lea allowed the men and officers to rest the following day, and then work began in earnest.

The course at Coetquidan was expected to last six to eight weeks, and the training on the French 75mm guns would be similar to that at Fort Sill on the three-inch American guns. About six hours daily would be spent in classes of general instruction and the remaining time would be devoted to firing under field conditions. For the first time horses and equipment were plentiful, and with his tremendous energy Colonel Lea set an incredible pace for his officers and men.

As the training progressed, the men began to see a purpose for the seemingly endless drudgery they had endured in the States. Their esprit de corps steadily increased as they set about acquiring as much military knowledge as quickly as possible. Colonel Lea made competitive Saturday afternoon inspections, which included men, guns, stables, barracks, and kitchens. A spirited rivalry developed between the various units for the honor of winning these contests, results of which were published in regimental orders.

To celebrate the Fourth of July the three artillery regiments were reviewed by General Gatley, General Hugay, the French commanding general, and French Senator Humbiert. The brigade never looked better, and General Gatley beamed with satisfaction.[8] On behalf of the brigade, Lea made a brief speech to the assembled soldiers.

In addition to the interminable paperwork, which frequently was quite burdensome for a regimental commander, Lea also tried to answer all his correspondence. He wrote his friend Thad Cox on June 11 that the mountains and fertile valleys of France dotted with small farms reminded him of Middle Tennessee, the height of compliments, and that he was impressed with the warmth of the people. His pride in his men often shone through his letters as when he wrote Mann Wills in Brownsville, Tennessee, on June 28 that he was confident they would give a splendid account of themselves.

Lea wrote as much as censorship allowed about the activities of the regiment to Percy Warner, who kept his son-in-law advised on political developments and went almost daily to *The Tennessean* office to go over policy and finances with general manager J.H. Allison. Lea allowed nothing to interfere with at least a brief note dashed off daily to Mary Louise, and according to long established custom she wrote him every day.

News was received on July 15 of new German offensives, followed three days later by a communique that the Allies had counter-attacked. From aerial photographs that Lea viewed at the nearby aviation school, he deduced the Germans had control of the air.

A complicated barrage of heavy artillery fire worked out by the staffs of the regiment and fired by the batteries the middle of August completed the training at Coetquidan. Departure for the front was imminent.

When orders came for the regiment to entrain for Toul, Abe Frank, a private desperately ill with highly infectious spinal meningitis, had to be left behind. Lea put aside for half an hour the many matters demanding his attention and disregarding the strict quarantine went to the hospital to say goodbye to the soldier. His visit was not known until the regiment returned to the States and was rejoined by Frank, who in later years would grow eloquent in recalling how his colonel had saved his life by rekindling his hope and courage to fight to get well.[9]

Half of the regiment left Coetquidan the morning of August 20, three months to the day after their departure from Camp Sevier, and the remaining half followed the next day. A special train of 51 passenger and flat cars transported the men, horses, and guns over a track that had been cleared, reaching Toul in a little over 40 hours.

Lea and three other officers made the trip by motor and arrived in Toul as the regiment was detraining. Lea reported to camp headquarters, met General Lassiter, and proceeded to the little village of Troussey, where he and his men were to be billeted. Lea was assigned a Dodge automobile, and accompanied by an officer of the 113th and one from the 115th, he made a reconnaissance of their bivouac position near the Etang (Lake) Rovie, about ten kilometers from Troussey. It was easy to tell that they were at the front. No lights burned at night, and airplanes, friendly and hostile, continually flew and fought over them.

Orders for the 55th Artillery Brigade to proceed to the Toul sector had come as a surprise because it had been expected that it would rejoin the 30th Division stationed in Belgium or northern France. However, after the Allies were victorious at the Second Battle of the Marne in July, General Pershing decided to form the American First Army and attempt to wipe out the St. Mihiel salient, a deep wedge driven into the French lines in the first German offensive in the fall of 1914.

The German objective had been to capture Verdun, the most powerful of the French fortresses, and cut the two-track railway line from there to Paris, thereby severing eastern France from the rest of the country. The Germans were entrenched on three sides of Verdun, and the railroad was pierced for about two kilometers south of St. Mihiel. If the Americans could eliminate this salient, the length of the front would be shortened from approximately 65 to 40 kilometers and the immense coal deposits of the area would be easily accessible for future American drives.

General Pershing's strategy for eliminating the salient was a beautifully simple pincer movement. Les Eparges and Pont-a-Mousson he envisioned as the hinges of two great doors that opened southward toward St. Mihiel. These doors would swing together, closing just north of Vigneulles. The French, stationed at the bottom of the pocket, were to engage the German troops opposite them and take them captive after the doors had closed and their retreat had been cut off.

Nine American divisions, totaling 215,000 men, were moved into the line for this attack, and another 190,000 were held in reserve, while 50,000 troops were supplied by France. After two days rest at Troussey, the 114th Field Artillery advanced the night of August 24 to the Sanzey Woods, where its camp of pup tents and horse lines were concealed by dense trees from German planes. Two nights later orders were received for batteries B, C, D, and E to occupy their positions. Lea traveled nearly 140 miles in his car overseeing the move which took hard work all night, but by 6:00 A.M. it had been accomplished.

The complicated planning for the forthcoming offensive was shrouded in secrecy, but as troops converged by road and train in the darkness, indications pointed to a great push. Lea did not go to bed four of the first eight nights they were in the St. Mihiel sector, only lying down for a short time early in the morning before beginning his administrative duties.[10] Lea and two other officers walked 15 miles on September 2 to pick defensive positions for the forward batteries and four defensive positions for the remainder of the regiment. That evening Lea conferred with all battery commanders about alternative defensive positions in the event the offensive should fail or be preceded by an enemy attack. He had the routes marked, the data calculated, and each gun position selected to enable the batteries to move rapidly.

After the troops had dug trail pits and shelter trenches and built and camouflaged ammunition racks, they began hauling ammunition to the front. Each battery was allotted over 4,000 rounds, which proved to be greatly in excess of what was actually used. At dusk the horses were hitched up, and all night long for over a week they pulled the heavy caissons, floundering through the rain and mud over incredibly slick roads. Part of the route could have been visible to the Germans had the nights not been so dark and rainy. The roads were often jammed with traffic forcing the horses to stand in traces for hours. The strain of moving that much ammunition coupled with two more weeks of severe work rendered most of them almost useless.

Lea usually supervised his soldiers' hauling of ammunition. One night the regiment became stalled in a traffic snarl that he saw could be unraveled only from the head of the column. He rushed forward in his motorcycle sidecar because he knew that highway was frequently shelled by the Germans in the early morning. A small French train dummy engine had stalled as it crossed the highway unable to pull across or to back up the heavily loaded railway cars. Lea ordered sufficient soldiers to get off the stalled trucks to move the engine from the road. When word went down the line that Colonel Lea was at the head of the column directing traffic, Private William A. Farmer of the 114th began to boast, "Thank God! We are safe now. My Colonel will get us by."[11]

Before going to the front, Lea had met privately with each soldier in his regiment confined to the guard house. Each was assured that his military record would be determined by his future conduct and then was released. Private Farmer had stated that the main reason he wanted to be freed was so he could kill Colonel Lea, whom he would rather kill than 1,000 Germans. After that night, however, Farmer was both an excellent soldier and loyal to his colonel.

Finally all was ready for the launching of the attack. Lea and his regimental majors reported to artillery headquarters early on September 11 for instructions. Lea then conferred with his battery commanders, gave them maps, and carefully checked their plans of fire. All batteries of the regiment were in place. The 114th was to assist in the support of the 89th Division, commanded by Major General W.M. Wright, which was positioned along a two-and-a-half kilometer front extending from Flirey eastward to Limey. Had they been placed in a straight line, there would have been one gun about every 17 yards on a front extending a mile and a half. After many frustrating delays, the orders finally arrived at 12:40 A.M. The 114th was to begin firing at 1:10.

The battle was on. The very earth seemed to shake from the bombardment as the guns roared in unison and the darkness of the rainy night was lighted by bright flashes of flame from exploding shells. Two thousand guns fired as quickly as they could be reloaded for four hours. Precisely at 5:00 A.M. they ceased, and the ear-splitting noise gave way to deathly stillness. Twenty minutes later the guns roared again as they laid down a rolling barrage in front of the infantry. The infantry jumped out of the trenches and advanced across no-man's land under cover of the barrage, which lasted five hours and 45 minutes. The Allies made a general advance of about eight miles.

The tremendous artillery fire simply blew the Germans out of their trenches and approximately 2,500 prisoners were taken.

Lea moved his headquarters to Flirey at ten o'clock that morning and at 3:00 P.M. reported to division headquarters. He was asked if he could get his artillery over the trenches and to an advanced position. He replied that he would. It took six hours of pushing and pulling, but somehow the guns were dragged across the recently excavated German trenches. Of the 20 artillery regiments in that sector, only one, the 114th, was forward that night to support the infantry.

Early the next morning Lea supervised getting the combat train with ammunition and supplies past Flirey and then rode toward the front. Later he moved his headquarters to the abandoned headquarters of a German brigade commander just south of Bouillonville. He discovered the next morning that in their hasty retreat, the Germans had left behind important documents and maps, which he dispatched to brigade headquarters.

General Pershing and the Allied commanders hoped that victory could be won before the coming of winter if the heavy assaults all across the front, begun more than a month previously, could be continued. Therefore, the 114th received unexpected orders late the afternoon of September 14 to evacuate the St. Mihiel sector.

The regiment was far from fit as it began its long march to participate in a much larger battle than St. Mihiel, which, however, had won a distinguished place in American military history, and in which the 114th Field Artillery had made a glowing record. Only three men of the regiment had been killed in the attack, but both officers and men were near exhaustion from loss of sleep and the heavy work of hauling ammunition before the battle. The horses were in even worse condition.

The ten nights march from Bouillonville to Brocourt Wood, from the St. Mihiel sector to the Meuse-Argonne, was one of the worst ordeals of the regiment during its 11 weeks of continual service at the front. They marched by night to avoid detection by German planes. All must be camouflaged before daylight, so during the day the men and horses got what rest they could in the woods or little towns along the route. At dusk they began again their march along roads jammed with other troops, usually arriving at their destination about three or four o'clock in the morning.

The 114th was ordered to clear the town of Essey by midnight on the first evening's march. No sooner had they passed through than the Germans began to shell the town with long-range guns. The regiment reached Rambucourt at 5:00 A.M. and took cover there for the day.

To protect his men, Colonel Lea violated both corps and brigade orders by halting the regiment at Rambucourt instead of in a prescribed woods, which in reality was practically a swamp. He went immediately to brigade headquarters and reported the regiment's location and the reason it had been changed to General James A. Shipton, who had replaced General Gatley. That evening the regiment marched for 12 hours to the village of Pont-sur-Meuse, which strangely had not been shelled.

The men were so fatigued by the long, hard marches they were given a night of rest, but the next evening they marched to Pierrepit, and the following night to Beauzee. The next evening, because of congested traffic, the regiment was not able to reach its destination. Lea concealed the regiment at daybreak in what remained of a French village, then immediately proceeded to the temporary brigade headquarters to report to the brigade commander the location of the regiment.

So the regiment would have no excuse for not reaching its destination that night, General Shipton ordered Lea to resume marching that afternoon at three o'clock despite the general order prohibiting troops in the war zone from marching in daylight.

A brigadier general, coming upon the regiment in marching formation, demanded to see the commanding officer. Lea came forward and saluted. When asked what he meant by preparing to march in daylight in the war zone, Lea repeated his order from brigade. Finally convinced of its accuracy, the brigadier general ordered Lea to halt the regiment if a German plane should fly over so the aerial photographs would not show troops in motion. In that way the danger of giving away troop movement would be minimized.

They had been marching less than an hour when an observation plane flew from the American lines very low over them. As it was a friendly plane, Lea did not halt the regiment.

Early the next morning General Shipton arrived at regimental headquarters and fairly yelled at Colonel Lea: "Why in the hell did you take it upon yourself to violate general orders and march in daylight?" In a steady voice Lea replied, "Because, over my protest, General, you ordered me to march in daylight as you know full well."[12]

General Shipton turned abruptly and left. About dusk that clear September afternoon Lea was ordered to report to brigade headquarters. Coming quickly to the point, General Shipton said:

> I have all the advantage of you, Colonel....
> If you are relieved of the command of your regiment, as you will certainly be unless you do what I tell you to do, you will be destroyed....
> I have a way out for both of us. Your adjutant is a very young man....
> Your marching in daylight was due to your young and inexperienced

adjutant misunderstanding my orders. Neither of us need suffer. What do you say, Colonel?

Lea replied, "General, you have no authority to order me to commit perjury. Have you any proper orders to give?"[13]

In the silence that followed, the general's face flushed a dark crimson; his mouth moved but no words came. After a moment's silence Lea saluted, did an about face, and left. Shortly thereafter Shipton was relieved of his command of the 55th Brigade.

The regiment continued to march at night through the mud that came to symbolize all that was disagreeable and that impeded their forward progress. Cold and tired they arrived about daybreak the morning of September 23 at the Bois de Brocourt. In the Argonne sector, a tangled jungle of trees and underbrush, they supported the center unit of the nine American divisions selected by General Pershing to open the drive. Montfaucon, the highest point in the whole region, was directly ahead and several kilometers behind the German lines.

The front for this, the greatest offensive in which American troops had ever participated up to that time, extended from the edge of the Argonne Forest at Vienne-le-Chateau on the west to the Meuse River, a distance of about 30 kilometers. Ahead, behind a natural barrier of hills, stretched the intricately fortified Hindenburg line, which protected the hub of the German transportation system. General Pershing proposed to drive a wedge through to Sedan and cut the four-track railroad that was the main link between Germany and her armies in France.

Lea was awakened about three o'clock on September 25 by a terrific bombardment, which lasted nearly three hours. At first he thought the battle had started and that orders for the regiment had miscarried, but he soon discovered the shelling was by the Germans who evidently feared an attack. Lea reported to headquarters and after two conferences made an inspection of all his batteries.

The regiment's orders for the attack did not come until after 11 o'clock that night, a half hour before the great bombardment by the heavy artillery in that sector began. At precisely 2:30 A.M., September 26, as ordered, the regiment began shelling. To tour his batteries, Lea had to cross a road being shelled by the Germans on which ten men had just been killed. Having been given road right-of-way for the middle of the following day, he led the second battalion forward to its new position in the woods north of Avoncourt, then went back and led batteries C and A forward and sent a guide to escort battery B to its new position.

After a hasty reconnaissance the following morning, September 27, batteries A and C again moved forward, and battery B advanced to quarters recently evacuated by the Germans on the edge of the Bois de Chehemin. Those batteries fired effectively throughout that day and batteries D, E, and F advanced the following day to positions close to battery B. Lea spent the afternoon at division headquarters, quite near the front, arranging the artillery fire of his regiment together with some French batteries temporarily under his command. On inspecting batteries A and C he was delighted to find two German guns and a large supply of ammunition had been left behind. His men had wheeled the guns around and were firing at the enemy with their own guns and their abandoned ammunition.

The front line wavered, broke, and regrouped constantly. The 114th was only 2,000 meters behind the front lines. The regiment had gained confidence in the St. Mihiel drive, and its morale was high. The troops were determined to stop the Germans, should the infantry fail. Their guns were in a commanding position, and firm platforms had been built to prevent the wheels sinking into the mud. The gun squads functioned most efficiently and kept the guns firing at top speed. The demands on ammunition were terrific, but the 114th, fortunately, despite the condition of the roads, had managed to haul explosives every night and had more on hand than the other regiments.

The night of September 29 and all the next day, the 114th kept up a heavy, harassing fire on sensitive enemy points. It proved particularly effective upon several machine gun nests and upon a column of German artillery being rushed forward on the Graves and Romaque highway. All day until his voice was entirely gone, Colonel Lea gave orders to the artillery he had assembled under his command. Seldom would he stay back at the command post. Leaving Lieutenant Colonel Gleason in charge there, he would go to the front with his men.[14]

Finally relief came. The 32nd Division arrived September 30 to relieve the depleted 37th that evening. The assignment of the 114th was to deliver a sham of irregular fire to protect the infantry as one unit went forward and the other unit went to the rear.

The German front had been penetrated to a considerable depth during the first two days of the offensive, but the artillery as well as the infantry had suffered terrible losses. The momentum slowed as the enemy contested foot by foot the advance of the Americans through the Argonne (*The Nashville Tennessean*, 15 June 1930).

A French artillery officer served as liaison with each artillery regiment, and Lieutenant Louzier was attached to the 114th. One day during the Meuse-Argonne offensive, he and Lea started for the new positions gained by the infantry the 114th was supporting. At a road being heavily shelled, Louizer begged Lea not to cross. Lea insisted upon going on as he believed it was his duty to confer with the infantry commander. Shortly thereafter, to avoid being blown to bits, the two men had to dive into a shell hole. When the German barrage lifted, Lea proceeded on to the front line and arranged for one of his batteries to move forward that night. The move was accomplished without casualties, which likely would have been heavy had he not conferred with the infantry commander.

All along the line, an attack was mounted the morning of October 4. Infantry General McCoy had Lea with him during the beginning of the battle. Despite the delay in receiving final orders for the rolling barrage, the regiment opened fire on time. The attack did not go as well as anticipated. Several machine gun nests and the town of Cierges were captured, but heavy casualties were sustained. Another attack was scheduled for the following morning.

General McCoy sent for Lea at 2:00 A.M. on October 5 and

asked him to plan the attack for the artillery brigade. Lea went over the infantry orders, determined the artillery support needed, and arranged the barrages to be fired by the 113th and the 115th as well as the 114th. He also directed those three regiments to smother with fire certain spots where he thought enemy batteries and machine guns were located.

The attack began on time, and the artillery gave superior support. The infantry to the left of the 114th captured the Bois Mariner, but the infantry to the right was not able to gain its objective as the Germans seemed determined to hold that key position at all costs.

The 55th Brigade, relieved of duty in that sector, began its withdrawal the next evening after dark. Placed under the command of Brigadier General John W. Kilbreth, Jr., the brigade was to proceed to Troyan in the Woevre sector where it would go into the line again in what was regarded as a quiet sector to rest and re-equip. The line there had stayed practically the same since 1915 until the Americans, in their great drive that had begun the middle of September, had captured the German positions on the south end, thereby forcing the enemy to abandon the ridges and high ground and retreat into the Woevre Plains. Those heights were quickly occupied by Allied artillery, and such a complete plan of defensive fire had been worked out as to make recapture almost impossible.

After the arrival of the new American units in that desolate area pitted with shell holes, the German artillery became quite active, peppering the Allies with both gas and high explosives. The gun squads of battery B of the 114th, which went forward the night of October 9, received a heavy dose of gas, and nearly all of the men had to be hospitalized. Due to the continual and accurate German shelling, battery positions had to be shifted often. The hardships the 114th endured during the ensuing weeks and the casualties it sustained in this supposedly quiet sector were greater than at any other time during its service at the front (*The Nashville Tennessean*, 15 June 1930).

Lea was able to buy newspapers Sunday, October 13, in a

small French village and hungrily read Germany's reply to Wilson's latest note. He believed that Germany would like to be allowed to pull out of France and Belgium and not be pursued. An armistice would be a great victory for the Germans, and he devoutly hoped Wilson would remain firm. On October 28 the Americans at the front learned that Austria had capitulated. Lea believed that peace finally was near.

General Kilbreth notified Lea on November 1 to be ready for an advance, which he interpreted to mean that with the elimination of the Austrian troops in front of them, the enemy would be forced to retreat if an attack were made. Lea had less than a third of the number of horses to which he was entitled, but he told the general the regiment could make the advance. Instead of an advance, however, reconnaissance work on the plains was ordered for the purpose of trying to determine Germany's plans; whether its soldiers would stand their ground or retreat before the great offensive planned by the American Second Army, which had as its objective the outflanking and capture of Metz. Several raids during the early days of November were made by the infantry in order to capture prisoners and obtain that information. Five regiments were placed under Lea's command, and that combined artillery supported the November 7 raid against the Chateau D'Aulnois, which was highly successful.

That morning the division to which the 114th was attached intercepted radio messages from the German high command requesting a meeting to discuss an armistice. Lea knew then the war was over. Yet that night battery F was heavily shelled. All four guns were hit, but miraculously there were no casualties.

While Lea was inspecting the battery positions next day, word came that Germany had requested 72 hours to consider the terms of the armistice. That time, which would expire at 11:00 A.M. the following Monday, had been granted.

The largest of the November raids made by the infantry was on the morning of the tenth against Marcheville, a strongly fortified village and the key to German positions in the sector. Lea arranged the artillery fire, consisting of a box barrage, a rolling barrage, and neutralization fire by the corps artillery. Due in large measure to the precision of the artillery fire, the raid was a success. Five officers and 77 men were captured, and a good many more were killed and wounded, but the Americans also sustained quite a few casualties.

After the raid Lea was summoned by General King and informed that the infantry attack originally planned for the first of the month was scheduled for early the following morning. The advance guard was to be the 65th Infantry, and Lea would be in command of the first battalion of the 116th as well as his own regiment, which together would constitute the artillery of the advance guard. Lea was also told that the kaiser had abdicated, the crown prince had renounced his rights to the throne, and the Reichstag had proclaimed a republic. Lea spent the afternoon making plans for the attack even though he thought peace would be declared the following day.

Lieutenant General R.L. Bullard ordered the American Second Army to attack the morning of November 11 on a front of several kilometers. The attack was to occur simultaneously with the new drive mounted by the American First Army east of the Meuse River. The capture of the coal and iron belt around Longwy, Briey, and Conflans was the objective of the combined attacks, which if successful would have a disastrous effect on Germany, should the armistice not be agreed upon.

Marshall Foch's order that all fighting would cease at eleven o'clock was known at 5:00 A.M. Yet the infantry attack was not called off in spite of the protests of brigade and division commanders and their efforts to have the order countermanded. About eighty men would be killed and many more wounded with peace only a few hours away.

The American advance started at five o'clock. All the batteries under Lea's command were on the Woevre Plains. The advance was slow, but by eight the troops had taken Riaville and the suburbs of Pitchville and Marcheville. At 8:21 orders were received to cease firing. The armistice had been signed.

The Germans continued to fire until exactly 11 o'clock when

the armistice became effective. Perhaps they were angered that the infantry attacked that morning. Whatever the reason, Lea found it extremely difficult not to return fire while his regiment was under heavy shelling for over two hours after the Germans knew the armistice had been signed and the Americans, in accordance with it, had ceased firing.

Precisely at 11 A.M. all firing ceased. After having become accustomed to the roaring of guns and the screaming of shells, Lea found the silence eerie. There was no cheering or shouting, even though everyone thought the armistice meant peace had come. The officers and men continued quietly with the tasks at hand. As the realization sank in that it was safe to move around in daylight in plain sight of the Germans, the men started to collect souvenirs and war trophies.

The next morning Lea made a reconnaissance of the plains to determine the best way to withdraw the batteries. Accompanied by some of his officers, he went that afternoon into Baile Duc to cable home. They were embraced by the villagers with undiluted joy at the war having been won.

It was reported that the 114th was to be one of the artillery units to go into the front lines on its side of the Rhine. Lea worked out a line of march, made a careful inspection of all wheeled material, and cancelled all requested leaves. Then it was reported they were not to be a part of the Army of Occupation. Lea, however, still hoped they would march into Germany at an early date, and his hope was strengthened after the 114th received horses and mules from other brigades.

The marking of time in the mud where the regiment had been when the armistice came was tedious and trying on all the men. Inspections continued to be held routinely. Drills were impossible, but an area of about six kilometers square was cleared of all salvageable material, which was hauled to the railroad. Next work was begun to improve the 114th's makeshift quarters.

Lea received orders the night of December 5 that the 55th Brigade was to accompany the 33rd Division to take command of part of the bridgehead on the Rhine. Preparations got under way at once: guns and caissons were quickly painted, harnesses washed and oiled, and horses readied.

The regiment, with flags flying, began its march for Germany the morning of December 7. To ensure complete uniformity throughout the regiment, Lea had issued detailed orders concerning equipment, horses, and uniforms, including even to which side the buckles of helmets should be worn, the number of cannoneers who should walk behind each carriage, and the exact order in which the carriages of the combat train should march. Stretching two miles or more, the regiment made an impressive sight as it marched over the last ridge of the Woevre Plains across shell-pitted roads to Boncourt.

The point to which the Germans planned to expand their territory was clearly discernible by the lack of devastation on what was to have been the German side and the complete destruction of what was to be left to France. In the sections the Germans expected to make a part of Germany, the roads had been improved and the fields had been cultivated.

The 114th crossed the border on December 12 into Luxembourg where the people, the land, and the towns all seemed cleaner and less ravaged. The troops marched through the beautiful country, the hillsides on which were terraced vineyards, to Ehnen, a village on the Moselle River, across from which stretched Germany. On arrival at the German border, Lea received the news that because the French had taken over part of the Zone of Occupation, the American bridgehead on the Rhine had been reduced, and therefore no more divisions were needed. The men of the 114th were disappointed not to continue the march to Coblenz and be a part of the Army of Occupation, but Lea thought the change of orders probably meant an early return to the States.

The regiment was assigned the occupation of the area around Mersch in the Duchy of Luxembourg. The German army had retreated through Luxembourg less than a month previously, but on the three-day march to Mersch, Lea saw no evidence of the disorganization about which he had heard. No discarded property was seen along the roadside or in the villages, nor was there any sign of lack of system or policing.

The wind was high, and a cold rain turned to sleet and snow the third day of the march. The men were half frozen when they reached their destination, which could not provide sufficient accommodations. A couple of days later the regiment was ordered to move 10 or 12 kilometers to the village of Brouch and the larger towns of Saeul and Tuntingen, in which regimental headquarters was established. Their new quarters were more comfortable than the men had had in many months. It was reported they were to be there a month and a half, but no one knew whether this was true. Even in the depth of winter, Luxembourg, with its quaint villages, marvelous old castles, excellent roads, and carefully cultivated fields, had a charm and beauty that beguiled its visitors.

It was reported on December 30 that the 55th Brigade would leave January 6 to join the 28th Division in the Minorville area and would then join the 13th Division, which was on a priority sailing list. Lea could hardly wait to see Mary Louise and the boys. The high point of the day were her letters, and the regular delivery of mail, even at the front, had been a great boost to morale. In her December 11 letter she asked the question uppermost in the minds of all wives whose husbands were overseas:

When do you think you will get back?

Have another picture of you on my sewing table so I can see you all the time—it makes the eighth picture in my room. This picture is very good of your body, arms and hands—as if I could take hold of your hands, which I am crazy to do and be in your arms again.

We will have so much to talk about, it will take months, and then it will only be a start. I won't let you stop long enough to sleep. How happy we will be.

Lea was extremely proud of the outstanding record made by his regiment. General Kilbreth, who prior to becoming brigade commander was chairman of the rating committee of the artillery units in France, stated that the 55th Brigade received the highest rating of any artillery trained in France. Their excellent rating, Lea thought, explained why that brigade was the only one that went directly from the training area into a great offensive and why after a few days in the line it was made "shock" artillery at St. Mihiel, the Argonne, and the Woevre Plains. The 55th Brigade was on an active front continuously from August 26 to November 11, 1918.

After it went to the front the 114th distinguished itself in all the intense fighting thereafter until the armistice. It was the first artillery across no-man's land in the St. Mihiel drive and again in the Meuse-Argonne offensive. His service with the regiment would be a life long satisfaction to Colonel Lea, who many years later would write:

In a varied life that has run the gamut of all human emotions from the sublimest of joys to the most tragic of sorrows, from the heights of fame and fortune to the depths of defeat and degradation, the greatest honor of my life has been that of commanding and leading the 114th Field Artillery in battle for flag and country.

Success was not able to add to nor failure to subtract from the satisfaction that service with the regiment at the front gave. That is wholly mine. No court can declare it the property of another. No decree of any judge can place it in receivership. No judicial fiat can enjoin it. No stripes can mar its beauty. No bars can imprison it. Not even death can erase its glorious memory.[15]

Chapter Seven
Attempt to Capture the Kaiser

For audacity of purpose and daring, Luke Lea's brief trip into Holland in January 1919[1] was one of the most colorful exploits during World War I. Had it succeeded, and it came within a hair's breath of so doing, the history of the world might have been different.

Lea had conceived the idea over teacups in England six months before on June 11, 1918. On that day the 114th Field Artillery paraded before the Duke of Connaught. Afterwards the field officers were guests of His Highness for tea.

The duke, in the course of conversation, remarked, "I rather fancy you American chaps do not know it, but I am the same relation—the uncle—to his Imperial Majesty, the Emperor of Germany that I am to his August Majesty, the Emperor of Great Britain and India."[2]

The high idealism that brought the United States into World War I must be remembered to comprehend the effect of that statement on Lea. He was filled with disgust for that tinseled soldier whose tone of voice betrayed no difference in affection for his two nephews, although the kaiser was generally regarded in Britain as the cause of her desperate plight. The Americans had crossed the Atlantic to fight and perhaps die to preserve for all men the liberties won by their forebears. The duke's boast indicated to Lea that no matter how the war ended, there would be no establishment of war guilt, even though the battle cry of England at that time was "Punish those responsible for the war."

Then and there, during tea at Windle Downs, Luke Lea determined that if the Allies gained victory, he would try to

105

gather the data that would demand that Germany's "All Highest" be punished. Since America's entry, the war had been directed against the Imperial German government, typified by the kaiser, not against the German people. Lea's conviction that the kaiser should be held accountable for the death and destruction he had caused grew during three months of hard fighting at the front.

When Germany capitulated, the kaiser first fled to the British army. Next, he sought asylum in neutral Holland, whose monarch reportedly was sympathetic with both the German and the British crown heads. Lea knew that small, peace-loving Holland, after maintaining her neutrality when Germany appeared on the verge of victory, would not on Germany's defeat have offered asylum to Kaiser Wilhelm Hohenzollern without at least an informal sanction of the Allies.

The primary aim of Lea's trip into Holland was to seize the kaiser, take him to Paris, and present him to President Wilson. Had the kaiser been taken to Paris, he undoubtedly would have been tried and convicted of war crimes. His punishment would in all probability have prevented many of the heavy reparations imposed by the Versailles Treaty. Lea believed that those harsh terms, levied not against the kaiser but against the German people, would tragically sow the seeds for yet another world war.

Lea's plan in no way violated the neutrality of Holland. He hoped by a surprise visit to be able to get the kaiser into his automobile and drive him to Paris. His alternate plan was to secure and give to the American delegates to the Peace Conference information concerning the kaiser's living conditions: whether he was directing the reorganization of Germany, if he were able to keep in close touch with various governments through radio, and the state of his health.

Lea presented to General Oliver L. Spaulding, commander of the 55th F.A. Brigade since the armistice, the following order for his approval on January 1, 1919:

In accordance with authority contained in General Orders No. 6, General Headquarters, American Expeditionary Forces, January 8th, 1918—

> Colonel Luke Lea
> Captain Leland S. MacPhail
> Captain T.P. Henderson
> 1st Lieut. Elsworth Brown

of the 114th Field Artillery, are granted leave from this date to and including Sunday, January 5th, 1919, with permission to visit any place not prohibited by orders from General Headquarters, American Expeditionary Forces.[3]

General Spaulding read the order twice. Then he turned it sideways and read it again. Finally he asked Colonel Lea where he intended to go.

Lea answered, "Nowhere forbidden by orders of G.H.Q. I don't want to tell you where. I do not wish you to be responsible for the trip."

The general read the order again and exploded, "It's the damnest order of leave I have ever read. But it violates no general or special order so I'll sign it."[4]

Lea had carefully selected the men to accompany him. Captain Thomas P. Henderson, commander of battery F, was a life-long friend; Captain Leland S. MacPhail, commander of battery B, was resourceful and an accomplished linguist; Lieutenant Elsworth Brown was a radio expert; Marmaduke Clokey, the colonel's motorcycle orderly throughout the 114th's service at the front, was absolutely fearless under fire; Sergeant Dan Reilly was an expert radio, telephone, and auto mechanic; and Sergeant Owen Johnston was a jack-of-all-trades and good at all.

On a two-day pass over Christmas Lea, accompanied by those men and Sergeants Robert Dale and John Tolliver, had driven to Leige and secured road maps of Germany, Holland, and Belgium. In Cleve Lea had met by chance a Holland merchant who gave him much information about Amerongen, armed with which Lea determined to return the following week.[5]

He told no one his purpose or destination. He merely asked if the men wished to accompany him on a five-day leave. The journey would be exciting; it might be dangerous. All wished to go.

The trip got underway a cold January afternoon. From Luxembourg, where the regiment was stationed, Lea planned to return to Liege, Belgium, where he expected to procure passports to neutral Holland and then to drive directly to Amerongen, the castle of Count Bentinck in which the kaiser had taken up residence.

The seven men, ladened with blanket rolls and an extra supply of gasoline, piled into the regimental car, a seven-passenger Winton, the Archillean heel of the regiment throughout its service at the front. Always needing repairs, the car had 16 tire punctures in one night on the 114th's march around Verdun to its position in the Meuse Argonne. True to form, the Winton had not gone 30 kilometers before it erupted near Arlon, Belgium.

An American corps truck fortunately came by in a short time, and Clokey was put on it with instructions to return posthaste with the regimental car of the 115th, which regiment was stationed adjacent to the 114th. About midnight Clokey returned with not only the car, an eight-cylinder Cadillac, but also Egbert Hail, the 115th regimental chauffeur and a fearless soldier. Reilly and Johnston by then had repaired the Winton, and the trip was resumed. Many long, cold hours later, the half frozen soldiers arrived at Liege.

Unable to cut through the red tape for processing passports, they set out on another long, cold drive to Brussels to see Minister Brand Whitlock, whom Lea had known in Washington. There Lea ascertained that passports could be obtained but not until the next day. On his application he stated that the purpose of the visit was journalistic investigation. The other officers stated accompanying Colonel Lea as the object of their trip. Lea made it absolutely clear to Minister Whitlock and to the clerk who prepared the passports that he was on leave, the trip was not official business, and that he represented no one. However, his passport was issued in the name of Senator Luke Lea. At the Dutch legation he requested a letter stating the party had obtained permission to travel in uniform and by car, and was given a laissez-passer.

Soon Lea and his companions were retracing their route from Brussels back to Liege. A heavy snow made travel slow, and they were again plagued by car trouble. When they reached Liege, it was already dark, and they learned while having dinner that all roads into Holland were closed for the night on account of a storm.

The next morning they made an early start. At the border of Holland they were halted. The border guard ordered them to go back, stating no American officers were wanted or permitted in Holland. When Lea presented Her Majesty the Queen of Holland's laissez-passer obtained from the Dutch legation in Belgium, the guard snapped to attention and saluted. He informed them that the road into Holland had been reopened and waved them forward.

The minutes and the miles flew past. When the men stopped for an early dinner in Nijmegen, a small boy, not over 15, dashed up talking in broken English, "Interpreter, you want one? Me speak English. Speak very proficient—See here."[6] He waved a high school report card, listing many subjects, including English, below which was the word, proficient. After some discussion, he was hired.

At dusk they ran into a major obstacle—the bridge had washed away over a branch of the Rhine. The river could only be crossed by ferry. The laissez-passer secured their passage on the ferry, but even it could not persuade the operator to wait on the other side of the river until they returned.

Not being able to cross the river immediately upon their return, Lea knew it would be impossible to take the kaiser out of Holland without his consent, as they would be apprehended on the Amerongen side while waiting for the ferry. Lea determined, nevertheless, to continue. He hoped to persuade the kaiser to go with the Americans peaceably by convincing him that his place in history would be greater if he went to Paris and stated that it was he, not the German people, who had instigated the war.

A few kilometers from the village of Arnhem, Lea disclosed to the group the purpose of the trip. He assumed complete responsibility for the undertaking and said each man was free to return to the regiment or wait at the border. He needed only one car, which he could drive himself, to carry out his plan. They all wanted to continue even though they were skeptical that they would gain admission into the castle. Lea stated that he had a plan for entering the building.

They reached Arnhem a little before eight on Sunday night, January 5, 1919. Within minutes they were at the gates of the castle. The colonel could tell from the shadowy outlines of his flashlight that the sentry clad in a Dutch uniform on guard duty at the entrance was unmistakably a German soldier. Lea strode up to him. He reversed the beam of his flashlight and threw it on himself so the sentry could see Lea's Sam Brown belt, the insignia of an officer in all armies. In his gruffest German, the colonel called the sentry to attention. As the guard clicked his heels, saluted, and stood stiff and immobile, Lea ordered him to take them without delay into the castle. The guard responded automatically and immediately escorted Lea and his party through the gates and into the castle, where they were ushered into the library.

In a few moments Count Godard Bentinck, the son of the owner of the castle, came in and greeted the Americans. The young count, affecting many of the mannerisms of the kaiser, had a military bearing and a luxuriant upturned mustache. He wore no military decorations, but was dressed in regulation evening coat, and Lea later recounted that:

The Count's manner, appearance, voice, formed a huge question—Who are you? Why are you here? What do you want? Finally he spoke. Quite formally he asked the object of our visit. I gave him an indirect answer by asking to see the Kaiser and introduced myself and the other officers. The Count repeated his question. I countered by stating that I would reveal the object of our visit only to the Kaiser. The Count seemed much disturbed and no little excited. He then excused himself and left the room. We could hear him talking in the adjoining room, speaking in German. He addressed the one to whom he was talking as "Your Majesty." He also talked over the telephone.[7]

A few moments later, the count returned, and according to Lea's recollection informed them that:

His "August Majesty" had considered our request for an audience and could not grant it unless we stated the object of our interview. While we were sparring over the purpose of the visit, there was an interruption. The door to the library opened and a comparatively young man, also in full evening dress, entered. He appeared completely satisfied with himself and ready to debate at length with anyone who denied he was a person of importance. He was introduced to me by the Count as the Burgomaster of Amerongen. I then introduced to him the other members of our party.

The Burgomaster immediately renewed the questions repeatedly asked by the Count. Why were we there? What was the object of our visit?[8]

In German, Lea began the same replies he had previously addressed to the count. The burgomaster interrupted:

...in beautiful, fluent, Bostonian English...without even a trace of a Dutch accent, "Ah Colonel Lea," he said patronizingly, "I am sure we will progress more rapidly speaking in English. I am a graduate of Harvard University...."

The Count, the Burgomaster, and I then fenced in English for several minutes....[9]

Then with elaborate apologies the count and the burgomaster excused themselves and withdrew. From bits of conversation that filtered through the walls, it was evident there was much commotion in the adjoining apartment. Someone was telephoned—the governor-general at Utrecht it was surmised from the few words that were understood. The word "American" was used over and over as was a Dutch word none of them recognized, but which their interpreter later translated as "soldiers" or "troops."

When the count and the burgomaster returned, the latter stated that his Imperial Majesty refused to receive the Americans unless they disclosed the purpose of their visit and it was of interest to His Majesty. Lea recalled later that he

...then fell back on the laissez-passer.... It made an impression even upon the blasé Bentinck and the Harvardized Burgomaster. They evidently wondered how we had obtained it. It immediately gave an official color to our presence. I added, as I had stated in my application for the passport, that the object of my visit was journalistic investigations.

Both asked, in one voice, what that term—journalistic investigations—meant....

My reply was that the phrase spoke for itself. I was then asked to elaborate my answer. I declined to do so. The situation grew quite tense.... The Count and the Burgomaster again retired—this time without apologies. Again we could hear the hum of conversation interspersed with loud and angry tones.[10]

As their hosts were gone for quite a few minutes, the Americans had time to make a careful check of the luxuriously furnished room lined with bookshelves. The draperies and rugs were handsome and thick; the dark furniture, probably black walnut, ornately carved. Throughout were comfortable chairs, and in one corner stood a large library table on which was stationery with the kaiser's crest. On several tables were bronze ashtrays embossed with "W I" and the kaiser's coat of arms.

Upon their hosts' return there was absolute silence. Finally the burgomaster spoke:

His Imperial Majesty did not appreciate ordinary soldiers, not even one of the rank of Colonel, seeking an audience with him save in response to an invitation. Such an act was never countenanced in court circles. It was simply incomprehensible....

Addressing Lea the burgomaster continued:

His Majesty has been unwilling to refuse to meet you and your officers lest you be here officially. His Majesty has done me the honor to instruct me to say that if you, Colonel Lea, will make the statement on your word of honor as an American officer that you are here as the representative of President Wilson, or of General Pershing, or "even" of Colonel House [a delegate to the Peace Conference who often acted as a personal representative of President Wilson], he will grant you a brief audience. Otherwise His Majesty will decline to grant any audience to any uninvited persons no matter in what form they seek it....[11]

Lea was prepared to take any risk to gain entrance to the kaiser and try to accomplish the purpose of his trip, but he would not make a false statement. He said that he

...was not in the castle as a representative of the President, General Pershing, or "even" Colonel House.

I then urgently renewed my request for an audience with the Kaiser and stressed the importance of his seeing us from his viewpoint.[12]

They fenced verbally for some time: the count and the burgomaster trying to make Lea state the purpose of the visit, and Lea attempting to get the kaiser to see them without divulging why they were his "uninvited guests," as they were continually called. Occasionally one of their hosts would digress to the proposed League of Nations or the amazingly quick and effective organization of the American army. It soon became apparent that their purpose was not to allow them to see the kaiser but to prolong their visit.

Lea guessed their reason for seeking to continue the conversation, but he was willing to accept the unspoken challenge because he wanted additional time for radio officer Brown to inspect the premises and try to locate the radio station that they had heard had been established at Amerongen after the kaiser had fled there.

After the Americans had gained all the information that they believed could be obtained, Lea made the move to leave. He did not know whether they would be speeded on their way or detained. Lea recounted later:

No effort, however, was made to detain us. Cigars and water were again served by the butler. We bowed to our hosts, and left the castle.

As we approached our cars we found they were completely surrounded by soldiers.

Upon drawing nearer we found ourselves actors in a strange drama. Hundreds of civilians formed a background for what was apparently two companies of Dutch Infantry, armed with regulation rifles and side arms.

We had not the slightest idea the kind of reception we would receive from the Kaiser's heavily armed guard or the Dutch civilians. We knew vacillation or hesitation on our part might provoke either attack or detention....

We did not request the soldiers to move but as the cars glided forward, they fell back on either side and formed an armed passageway for us.

We sped through it.... In a few minutes we had cleared the village of Arnhem.[13]

MacPhail then put his hand in his pocket saying he had a souvenir for them. Before he could exhibit his trophy, the colonel interrupted, stating that he did not want to know anything about what he thought MacPhail had done. Conversation then turned to their reception and what they had seen at the castle. When they reached the washed-out bridge they signaled the ferry which at length arrived to take them across.

Lea decided it was advisable for the party to separate. He had arranged for passage across the border when he hoped the kaiser would be with them so he knew one car could return through Germany to Luxembourg. The other car must return through Holland to leave the young Dutch interpreter at Maastricht. Tension mounted as they approached the border. Had the count or the burgomaster telephoned and ordered them detained? Their apprehension melted, however, as the captain of the guard recognized them and waved them across the border.

In Maastricht they got their young interpreter to promise not to discuss the trip with anyone for one year. That period of silence was stipulated because Lea was convinced that the kaiser would prefer charges against them and their trip would be investigated, but that within a year they would be home. In jest, Lea added in parting that he would come back and "hant" him if the interpreter broke his silence.

They made good time to Tuntingen, arriving five minutes before noon. Major Horace Frierson, Jr., senior officer in command during Lea's absence, had the regiment formed, and the colonel's horse saddled at the head of the column to begin the regiment's scheduled march back to France. After a brief conference with Frierson, Lea mounted and gave the command "Forward." All that bitterly cold afternoon, he rode fighting to keep awake. At six they camped at Kehlen for the night. Lea gave the necessary orders, had a light supper, and before seven was in bed and slept for 13 hours.

After a march of several days, the regiment reached Boucq, a village just north of Toul, from which they had begun their drive against the Germans on a hot, rainy night the preceding August. On the march from Kehlen, Lea and the men who had accompanied him to Amerongen had time to analyze what they had seen there, but their first opportunity for a conference was at Boucq.

Lieutenant Brown reported he had spent the two hours outside the castle investigating the radio situation. Through a window in the castle he had heard a receiving set and had discovered an excellent broadcasting station. He concluded that the kaiser could be in continual communication with Germany, and, by code, he could communicate with his agents through broadcasts of commonplace events. From the conversation in the castle, it was apparent that the kaiser was then surrounded by military personnel, and evidence was that he still planned to return to Germany.

After their conference Lea wrote to Colonel House and offered to furnish him with information gained during the trip.[14]

Lea still had several days of leave, and having regimental business in Paris, he obtained permission to go there. On his arrival he learned that Colonel House was ill and could see no one, so Lea communicated the information he had gleaned on his trip to a Mr. Rogers on the committee of public information.[15]

In Paris, Lea hoped to be admitted to the plenary peace conference in the Palace of Mirrors. As his hopes began to wane, James Stuart Bryan, publisher of the Richmond *News-Leader*, and president of William and Mary College, arrived. He recognized Lea and, learning that he did not have an admission card, said he would remedy the situation. Shortly a French major in an elaborate uniform, greatly excited and most apologetic, approached and asked Lea to follow him. Lea learned later that Bryan had gone to the head of the press section and stated that a deplorable breach of etiquette, a major crime in France, had been committed. A colonel in the army, a member of the Associated Press, and a former United States Senator was being kept waiting to enter, and he requested the official to apologize immediately to Lea for the discourtesy.

Lea's overriding impressions of that session were its coldness and its jealousies. He sensed the peace terms had already been agreed upon by England, France, and Italy and that the real job of the conference was to present them as palatably as possible to the United States and the smaller European nations. He believed that the conference betrayed not only those who had died for freedom, but also the living who would have to abide by the decisions at Versailles. The sacrifices, the sufferings, and the sorrows humanity had endured were discounted, and human rights were considered secondary to property rights.

Upon Lea's return from the theater one evening, he found pinned to his pillow an order to report to the Department of Paris the following morning. Promptly at nine he presented himself before General W.W. Harts, commander of the American forces in Paris, who ordered Lea to report immediately to G.H.Q. at Chaumont. Having anticipated that order, Lea had already ascertained that the next train left Paris at 10:00 P.M., and about three hours later, he arrived at Chaumont. He reported at nine o'clock, January 26, 1919, to the inspector general's office where he waited in the anteroom all morning.

Colonel J.C. Johnson arrived shortly after 12 to take Lea's statement about his trip into Holland. Then began an interrogation conducted for many hours each day for several weeks. Not only was every aspect of the trip to Amerongen examined and recorded, but inquiries were also made concerning various incidents in Lea's life, civilian as well as military. At the start Lea assumed full responsibility for the trip. He stated the officers and the enlisted men acted under the order of their superior officer and did not know the object or the destination of the trip until shortly before the arrival at Amerongen.

The investigation centered around three points. The first was whether General Order, No. 6, issued January 8, 1918, pertaining to leave of officers and enlisted men, had been violated. Paragraph seven stated that neutral countries could not be entered without permission having been obtained from G.H.Q. and was obviously intended to apply only to enlisted men. The next paragraph of the order, however, clearly removed all ambiguity, as it expressly stated that officers on leave could, with permission of their brigade commander, go anywhere except to Paris, for which permission must be granted by G.H.Q.

Lea maintained there was no conflict between the two paragraphs. Furthermore, in instance of conflict between parts of an instrument, the latter, as the last expression of intent, controlled the former. His position was sustained a few days later. Lea had won the first round, and later he would recall further interrogation:

> The second important question was the use of a government car on leave. That matter was approached as a grand climax to the investigation. For several questions I could sense the inspector general leading up to it. Finally he blurted out, "You will not seriously insist, Colonel Lea, you had the right to use a government car on leave."[16]

Lea pointed out that the *Manual of Court Martial* allowed an officer under investigation to call witnesses. To prove the widespread use of government cars by officers on leave, he demanded to have summoned every officer of the A. E. F. who had custody of a government car.

> I stated my first witness would be the Commander in Chief of the A.E.F., General John J. Pershing, who had recently motored to Nice on leave in his government car. The next would be the judge advocate general, who had motored to a prize fight the night before in his government car. The third would be the inspector general who had questioned me and who had taken a pleasure trip in his car the day before....
>
> Finally the inspector general smiled and said, "The inspector general is satisfied the witness had the right to use a government car on leave."[17]

Clearly, the decision of round two was in Lea's favor. The investigation had passed its climax, but still it dragged on. Lea was told by a captain in the decoding section that a cable had been received stating that some high civil official had requested that, if Lea could not be court martialed, the investigation be prolonged so he could not return to the states with his regiment.

The next day Lea was told by a brigadier general that the kaiser had preferred charges "that a party of American officers, headed by one Senator Colonel Luke Lea, had appeared uninvited at the castle of his host, Count Bentinck, and had made him nervous."[18] The brigadier general then stated Lea could only be court martialed by a general court and that he would insist that Lea be given his constitutional right to face his accuser, and therefore would demand that the kaiser be summoned immediately.

Lea considered that information his cue to make opera bouffe of the whole investigation. He immediately went to the inspector general in charge of the investigation and said that he had been informed that the kaiser had preferred the heinous charge that he had made His Imperial Highness nervous. Lea then stated that it had been the ambition of every American soldier to make the kaiser nervous. While thousands claimed to have done so, Lea wanted to establish proof of this claim on his part. If the brigadier general would prefer the kaiser's charge that a group of American soldiers headed by Luke Lea had made him nervous, Lea would plead guilty to the charge. He would serve whatever sentence a court martial might impose for that terrible crime and after the sentence was completed he, as the only soldier who had been proved to have made the kaiser nervous, would go on the vaudeville stage at $1,000 a week which stipend he would split with the brigadier. Lea's offer spread throughout G.H.Q. at Chaumont, and the investigation became a subject of innumerable jokes.

Finally the third point in the investigation was touched upon. The officer conducting the investigation said apologetically:

> I must ask you regarding one other matter, though it seems absurd to do so. Still it is in the list of the Kaiser's complaints. What do you know about an ash tray of the Kaiser's that was taken from the library table at Count Bentinck's?[19]

Lea answered he had heard about it but had declined to discuss the matter. All he knew was hearsay. The inspector general agreed as to the incompetency of Lea's testimony upon this point. After a few pleasantries they shook hands and the long investigation was formally over.

As Lea walked to his hotel for lunch with Captains MacPhail

and Henderson, who had also been ordered to Chaumont but not interrogated, he surmised the disappearance of the kaiser's ashtray would be raised again. He told MacPhail of the questions about it and said, "Mac, I have changed my ideas on this subject. I want you to retain me as your counsel and tell me every fact about the ashtray."[20] McPhail complied. He had succumbed to the common American proclivity of souvenir hunting and had pocketed a bronze ashtray of little intrinsic value, but with the kaiser's monogram, as a momento of the trip.

They had just finished lunch when an orderly appeared and presented the compliments of the inspector general, who asked Lea to report to his office immediately. Lea was there in ten minutes. The general requested Lea to be sworn again, after which he asked him to relate all he knew about the missing ashtray, as his testimony although hearsay might provide a helpful lead to its whereabouts.

Lea replied:

Mr. Inspector General, if you had asked me that question this morning I would have necessarily been forced to answer it. At lunch I became Captain MacPhail's counsel, since you stated you were through with me as a witness. MacPhail has told me all the facts of the incident and I cannot answer your question as it is all privileged being between lawyer and client.[21]

The general then summoned Captain MacPhail and questioned him about the matter. To each question MacPhail responded, "On advice of counsel I decline to answer." The investigation finally ended that afternoon. Again the inspector general and Lea shook hands and parted.

A few days later Lea was awakened about two o'clock in the morning by an insistent knocking at the door. The caller identified himself through the keyhole as Charlie Franklin of Gallatin, Tennessee, and a field clerk stenographer to Judge Advocate General W.A. Bethel of the A.E.F.

Lea jumped out of bed and flung open the door.

Franklin quickly explained the object of his visit. The previous day, General Pershing had returned to Chaumont and had requested from General Bethel the entire record of Lea's trip into Holland. Later Pershing had conferred with Bethel about an hour, and then Franklin was called. Bethel, in Pershing's presence, then dictated a letter to be delivered to Lea.

Franklin said he had transcribed the letter too late the previous day for it to be delivered to General Bethel for formal approval and that he had been trying all evening to find Lea. Lea eagerly read the letter and was delighted with it. It praised his frankness in relating the facts of the trip but spoke of the visit as "amazingly indiscreet."

Since the long investigation had failed to establish that any army regulation had been broken or that the neutrality of Holland had been violated, that mild reprimand from General Pershing was the army's official disposition of the incident.[22]

Several months after their return to the States, Lea was having lunch in Washington with General Bullard, Commander of the Second American Army in France under whom he had served during the latter part of the war. He recalled:

> Suddenly General Bullard turned to me and asked, "What did John Pershing say to you about your trip to see the Kaiser?"
>
> "General Pershing," I replied, "wrote that the trip was 'amazingly indiscreet'."
>
> "Oh, hell! I don't mean what General Pershing said officially. What I want to know is what did John Pershing say to you personally about the trip?" interrupted General Bullard.
>
> "General Pershing never spoke to me about it personally," I answered.
>
> "Well, I'll tell you what John Pershing really thought.... [He] said to me, 'Bullard, I am a poor man, but I'd have given a year's pay to have been able to have taken Lea's trip into Holland and to have entered the castle of Count Bentinck without invitation'."[23]

By the time the investigation was finally concluded, the 114th had already left Lemans where it had been deloused and was en route to St. Nazaire to sail for home. Lea and the other officers who had been detained at Chaumont by the investigation were scheduled to go to Lemans and then to St. Nazaire, but if they did so they would not reach the port of embarkation in time to sail with the regiment. Red tape was cut. The officers were ordered to proceed directly to St. Nazaire and arrived in time for Lea to resume command of the regiment. He was also placed in charge of all the troops aboard the *U.S.S. Finland.* As the ship weighed anchor about noon on March 10, a mighty cheer rose from 2,700 American throats. In minutes they were headed out to sea for America and for home.

Three days before they reached land, Colonel Lea received a wireless that his wife had died. Slowly he comprehended the dreadful news. How could Mary Louise have died? Her last letters had been full of joyful anticipation of his return. He had faced death constantly at the front, but it was she who had died.

For hours he strode around the deck that night. Around and around he circled in the darkness. Reese Amis was one of the first to hear the sad news. He matched his stride to the colonel's and walked with him around the ship's deck. Sometimes they strode in silence. Then Lea would talk of his wife, his love for her, the impossibility of imagining life without her.[24]

The *Finland* reached Hampton Roads the night of March 22 and docked at Newport News early the following morning. Granted a few days leave, Lea went immediately to the Hotel Warwick (*The Nashville Tennessean* 24 March 1919). Reunited there with his son, Luke, Jr., and his father-in-law, Percy Warner, he learned the details of Mary Louise's death.

She had been quite well, her heart overflowing with joy that her husband was soon returning safely to her. She was excitedly expecting word of the date of his arrival. Suddenly late Saturday afternoon, March 8, she was taken gravely ill. She called to Luke, Jr., to phone the doctor quickly. He carried out her instructions then rushed to her room where she was in bed. She had suffered an aneurysm and had died before Doctor von Ruck could get there.

Before the *Finland* had docked, Tennesseans had besieged the War Department with requests to permit state troops to parade in the large cities rather than going directly to Fort Oglethorpe to be mustered out of service. Permission was granted. The 114th was the first large unit to return to the state, and its reception was tumultuous beyond all expectation (Amis, *History of the 114th Field Artillery* 94-95).

The regiment, traveling on a special train in three sections, left Newport News on March 28. It reached the Tennessee state line the following morning, and at every station they were welcomed by a large crowd. Knoxville, the site of their first parade, was gaily decked with flags and bunting, and a half-holiday had been declared in honor of the 114th's return. More than 30,000 persons lined the route of the parade and cheered themselves hoarse. After the parade, the women of Knoxville served a delicious supper at long tables arranged in roped-off streets.

After the festivities the men returned to the train, which left early Sunday morning for Nashville, where it proceeded to the siding adjacent to Centennial Park. As the first section pulled in about four o'clock in the afternoon, every whistle in the city blew full blast in welcome to the returning soldiers. After instructions were issued regarding the parade the following morning, the men were dismissed and allowed to mingle with the large crowd of friends and relatives who had gathered to greet them.

The next morning, business came to a virtual halt as Nashvillians and folk from surrounding towns turned out en masse to participate in the official homecoming. The crowd was estimated variously from 100,000 to a quarter of a million, but it was agreed that it was the largest ever gathered in Nashville. The regiment was formed at the Parthenon in Centennial Park to hear the welcome address by Governor A.H. Roberts.

As E.C. Faircloth, chairman of the homecoming committee, led Colonel Lea forward, the men of the regiment let out a cheer that could be heard blocks away. Then the huge crowd broke into applause, and it was several minutes before the colonel could begin speaking. Every few sentences he was interrupted by cheers as, on behalf of the regiment, he thanked the citizens for their warm welcome.

He had words of high praise for the men of his regiment and declared they wanted to be regarded as citizens who had done their duty and not as wards of the government. Lea's voice was steady, but tears came to the eyes of many of his listeners as he said:

The one emotion uppermost in our hearts is the fact that we are home again—home again with those we love. (*The Nashville Tennessean* 1 April 1919)

Then began the parade led by Colonels Lea and Gleason riding side by side on handsome horses. The regiment marched through Vanderbilt campus where three of the units had drilled 21 months previously, then to town, around the public square, up to Capitol Boulevard and through the Victory Arch, erected for the occasion, to the foot of the state capitol grounds. The streets were decked in flags and streamers rippling in the strong breeze and the entire city was flooded with bright sunlight. All along the route back to Centennial Park, the crowd waved and cheered. At several points the police had difficulty restraining the happy mob from completely enveloping the soldiers who smiled as they were pelted with flowers.

The Red Cross emergency canteen service provided a sumptuous feast at the Hippodrome. Sixty tables, laden with roast turkey, salads, cakes, and coffee, were arranged throughout the brightly decorated auditorium. At a signal that the soldiers had arrived, the canteen girls lined the center aisle between the tables. At the entrance of Colonel Lea, cheer after cheer rang out and the beating of the metal trays carried by the girls was deafening. The colonel, holding the hands of his two young sons, smiled to the left and to the right as he marched to the head table (*The Nashville Tennessean* 1 April 1919). After dinner, the street was roped off for dancing. The celebration continued until the soldiers' special train left Nashville after midnight.

The troops were brought April 3 into Chattanooga where they again received a tumultuous welcome.

Demobilization at Camp Forrest, Georgia, proceeded rapidly. The final physical examinations were given, service records straightened out, payrolls compiled, and discharges issued. The regiment was formed for the last time. Colonel Lea praised the men for the valiant service they had rendered to their country.

The men were then mustered out. With the exception of a few who had to remain in the hospital for medical treatment, they were all out of the service by the night of April 8 (Amis, *History of the 114th Field Artillery* 96).

The 114th Field Artillery no longer existed as a unit. However, its name and the splendid record it made were a permanent part of the military history of the United States. It would continue always to be a cherished memory of the men who composed that volunteer regiment. As long as there were soldiers to assemble, until the mid-1980s, they would hold reunions and swap stories of the stirring days of the Great War. As long as Colonel Lea lived, he was invited to the reunions and when he was unable to attend, "his boys" would send him greetings. The passage of time would never erode the strong ties that bound together the comrades in arms. Future events would not lessen the admiration, respect, and affection that often bordered on hero worship in which the men held their colonel, and he would retain forever a genuine interest in them.

Chapter Eight
A Power to be Reckoned With

Even before he returned from overseas, in the spring of 1919, there was speculation about Luke Lea's political future. A Memphis newspaper the preceding November had stated unequivocally that he would be the new political leader in Tennessee, the only uncertainty being whether he would run for the Senate or for the governorship, his election to either being practically assured. Well-known across the state before the war, Lea, by fighting on the battlefields of France, the article concluded, would have the support of the majority of the nearly 100,000 Tennesseans who had served in the armed forces.[1]

Lea allowed his name to be used by Lieutenant Theodore Roosevelt, Jr., to call the convention of foreign veterans in St. Louis, May 8-10, 1919, at which meeting the American Legion was founded.[2] Spokesman for Tennessee and an influential floor leader, Lea was a member of a committee that met daily to work out organizational problems. The only Tennessean to be named to the 34-member national executive committee, Lea served on the Legion's national finance committee. He also was chairman of organization and nominations for the Tennessee state convention, held in Nashville in October. Lea's participation became less active as the future of the American Legion became assured, but his interest in its affairs continued, and it was a source of satisfaction to him that he had been instrumental in the establishment of the Legion both on the national and on the state levels.

In June 1919, Lea assumed the day-to-day management of *The Nashville Tennessean* and *The Evening Tennessean,* the latter having been launched in 1918. While he was in the Senate and the army the newspapers had gone deeply into debt. Forty thousand dollars had been deposited to their account the day he left for overseas. That amount was all he thought could possibly be needed during his absence, but the money was gone in less than six months.[3] His efforts to get the papers on a sound financial basis soon bore fruit, and in a short time the publishing company was earning more than operating expenses and fixed charges.[4]

In October 1919 the printers, who were being paid $6 a day, about the national average at that time, demanded a bonus of an additional dollar a day. When their demand was not met, they walked out. All other employees, from Lea to the janitor went to the composing room, determined to make the presses roll.[5] Smiling and with his shirt sleeves rolled up, the colonel went wherever there was a snag and lent a hand. He ordered coffee and sandwiches brought in and stayed until the last paper rolled off the presses. As each man left, he said good night and thanked him for helping get out the paper.

Although the printers were striking illegally, Lea soon discovered that he had a battle on his hands. He considered that he was fighting on behalf of all publishers, and finally six printers broke the strike by going back to work the night of November 16.[6]

Throughout his publishing career, Lea was consistently a friend to labor. From the first issue of *The Tennessean* in 1907, the printers had been unionized. He refused later to join with his competitors in an open shop movement in Nashville, a decision that made him powerful and lasting enemies. When his competitors locked out the union printers and all but two of the small job offices were open shop, Lea could have dictated any pay scale he desired. Instead he dealt as liberally with the printers as he had formerly when the union was strongly organized.[7]

Lea was never able to refuse a job to anyone who had been in his regiment, and he placed in key positions many of his soldiers on whom he knew he could depend. Reese Amis, captain of battery C of the 114th, was put in charge of the editorial department. Nuch Brown, who had been captain of battery E, was made circulation manager. Walter Siegenthaler, Lea's office boy who had been fired by James Allison, was reemployed and put in charge of supplies and purchases. When Brown was transferred to advertising, Siegenthaler moved up to circulation manager, a position he was was to occupy for nearly 50 years until he retired. Pete Charlet, who had been in headquarters company, was employed in the cashiers office, made auditor, then became secretary-treasurer, which office he held as long as Lea published *The Tennessean.*[8]

Through the years the editorial staff of *The Tennessean* boasted such outstanding men as Blinky Horn, whose articles on sports were widely read throughout the South and who took over the slot from nationally known Grantland Rice, the paper's first sports editor; famed cartoonists Carey Orr, Joe Parrish, and Pulitzer Prize winner Tom Little; Fugitive and Agrarian poet, critic and distinguished professor of English at Vanderbilt University, Donald Davidson, who edited the newspaper's outstanding book page (*The Tennessean* 8 September 1974, "Fifty Years Have Come and Gone"); political columnists Joe Hatcher and Percy Priest; and chief editorial writer Jack Nye.

Lea was generous in his treatment of former political foes. When ex-governor Malcolm Patterson was in financial straits, *The Tennessean* in 1923 ran briefly a daily column, "Day by Day with Governor Patterson," for which the paper paid him $25 a week. Lea also wrote the editors of several county newspapers trying to interest them in carrying those syndicated articles.

Lea was fascinated with the running of a newspaper and made the final decisions on all matters. Problems that arose in advertising or circulation were taken to him. If the presses were late and the papers missed the mail train, he was informed of the fact, and he learned the reason for its occurrence.

The editorial policy was always set by Lea, and one of the foremost matters of public concern in 1919 was women's suffrage. Lea believed that women should have the vote, so *The Tennessean* strongly supported the 19th amendment, which was passed that year by Congress. By the following summer the amendment had been ratified by 35 states and rejected by eight. Ratification was needed by only one more state.

Governor Albert H. Roberts called a special session of the legislature for August 9, 1920, to act on the constitutional amendment. Hence, Tennessee became the pivotal state. Leaders favoring and opposing the measure converged on Nashville. Carrie Chapman Catt, long active on the national level in the movement for women's rights, was most persuasive in her arguments. The Senate quickly voted in favor of the amendment, but the House debated for several days before final approval. Governor Roberts signed the bill on August 24, and two days later with the president's signature, it became the law of the land (*The Tennessean* 21 August 1977).

After the war his mother had wanted Luke Lea to move to Washington and to let her help rear her two grandsons, but because of his business interests he never considered settling anywhere except Nashville. At the insistence of the Percy Warners, he decided that he and the boys would stay temporarily at Royal Oaks. The house was large and well staffed so their presence would inconvenience no one. The boys would have constant supervision, an ideal place to play in the large lawn, but most important of all, they felt quite at home with their grandparents and their Aunt Margaret and Aunt Percie, all of whom had spent much time with them both in Denver and Asheville.

Before he knew it was happening, Luke had become aware in a new way of Percie, the youngest Warner daughter. For as long as he had known her, she had had a strong claim on his affections, and she had always adored him.

After his and Mary Louise's marriage, they often had invited Percie to their house in town. Tall and willowy, she had grown into a striking young woman with hazel eyes. She had early developed a mind of her own and had no time for things she considered inconsequential.

Her mother, not wanting her daughter and her husband to be known as "Young Percie" and "Old Percy" or "Little Percie" and "Big Percy," started calling her as a small child "Miss Percie," a name that was used by young and old alike all of her life. She was blessed with an abundance of common sense, which was fortunate, because disliking school heartily and not being robust as a child, her formal education left much to be desired.[9]

Soon after her father bought her an automobile, in lieu of the debut party she did not want, Percie began driving the five local public health nurses on their rounds each morning. In that work she met Blanche Fensterwald, with whom she developed a warm friendship that became ever closer through the years. Two of the few young women in Nashville who had automobiles of their own at that time, they provided the nurses' only transportation.

As Percie spent more and more time with Luke her affection for him deepened into love, and before long they became engaged. Only members of the immediate family were informed of the forthcoming wedding. Dr. James I. Vance, minister of the First Presbyterian church, officiated at the simple home ceremony on May 1, 1920.

While they were on their wedding trip, the white frame cottage Luke had built for Mary Louise atop the highest point in Lealand was to be moved to the foot of the hill. However, it slipped its cable, crashed down the hill, and was completely demolished. Consequently, Luke and Percie spent the summer at Royal Oaks until they could find a home of their own. In August they moved into a lovely white clapboard house with a large yard on Iroquois Avenue. The colonel had a barn built for his sons' ponies and the two head of cattle that Luke, Jr., had purchased that spring.

Percie was supremely happy in her new role of wife. Luke's erratic schedule did not bother her. She was fortunate in having good domestic help, and she never allowed anything to keep her from being with her husband.

They both loved to ride horseback, and when he could get away from the office, they would ride together. Before their marriage she had gotten into the habit of driving him when he had to go back to the office at night or to a surrounding town on business. She learned to make arrangements on a moment's notice to accompany him on one of his frequent short business trips. Had she not thus fitted her time into his, she would have been with him a great deal less, and their marriage possibly would not have grown into such an unusually close relationship.

After the war, the United States had been plunged into a severe industrial recession. Luke Lea's practice of borrowing on what he owned in order to buy more property and securities made him particularly vulnerable to economic cycles of prosperity and depression. Usually overextended, he found it difficult during the early 1920s to make payments on his large indebtedness. However, it never occurred to him to take bankruptcy. He was confident that in time economic conditions would improve, and he would be able to work out his own matters.

He undertook to make monthly payments of $500 beginning May 1, 1922, to reduce his indebtedness to his mother, the bulk of which was money advanced him by his father during his father's life. In his will Overton Lea treated these advances, which amounted to approximately $103,000,[10] as Luke's share of his estate. In the three years since his return from the army, he had paid to his mother's account $35,500, which was more than the entire amount she had lent to *The Tennessean* while he was in France.[11]

With Luke being the only man in the family and the only member living in Nashville, family business often devolved upon him, which was a mistake for all concerned and had an abrasive effect on the relationship between mother and son. Having rented Lealand from his mother, he farmed it from his return to Nashville in 1919 through 1921. Percie was instrumental in making him realize that leasing Lealand was a burden that he had no moral obligation to continue, and that it was ridiculous for him to try to farm both Lealand and his own farm, LeaMead.

When Percie was expecting a baby, Luke realized that his growing family would need more room, so purchased in the autumn of 1922 a two-story red brick house on Howell Place just off Belle Meade Boulevard. Feeling splendid throughout her pregnancy, Percie nevertheless went to St. Thomas Hospital to have her baby, which somewhat scandalized her mother and sisters, who as was customary at that time had given birth at home. Baby Mary Louise was born on February 21, 1923, and in later years when explaining family relationships, she delighted in saying that she was named for her father's first wife.

The tide of public opinion running so strongly to elect veterans to public office combined with Lea's ability and national prominence made him an attractive vote getter. Champ Clark, an aspirant for the Democratic presidential nomination in 1912, was to remark many years later that had Lea been successful in capturing the kaiser, nothing could have kept him from being elected president.[12] There was discussion at an informal conference of some of Lea's friends on the Democratic national committee that he be the 1924 vice-presidential nominee, the third time he was considered as a possible candidate for that high office.[13] However, his various enterprises required his personal attention, so he declined to allow himself to be considered.

World War I not only marked the coming of age of the United States as a nation, but it also brought into sharp focus long-standing problems of the individual states. The increased acceleration of industrialization and urbanization gave rise to a progressive movement that endeavored to make state government more efficient and to provide much needed public services (Tindall, "Business Progressivism" 92-106; Lee, *Tennessee in Turmoil* XIII). Although no two locales were identical, the problems Tennessee faced were similar to those of southern states generally, and the solutions Tennessee devised were akin to those arrived at by its neighbors.

The South had continued to suffer the devastating effects of Civil War and Reconstruction well into the 20th century, and economically continued to lag behind the rest of the nation. The migration from farm to city was gradually creating in Tennessee, and in much of the upper South, a new power base. As the cities increased in size, they became more influential politically with a corresponding decline in the power of rural areas. However, even though manufacturing had grown steadily in Tennessee since the

Civil War and by 1890 had supplanted agriculture in the production of wealth, nearly three-fourths of all Tennesseans were still engaged in farming in 1920, and the state continued to be dominated by rural influences (Lee, *Tennessee in Turmoil* 3-4, 6).

The one-party system of the solidly Democratic South spawned factional politics built around personalities with constantly changing alliances somewhat akin to a feudal society. Both the Democratic and Republican parties in Tennessee were continually engaged in intraparty strife, which prevented the emergence of unified leadership on the state level in either party. The Democrats were divided into three main factions. Perhaps the most influential was headed by Luke Lea (Lee, *Tennessee in Turmoil* 10) around whom had formed a coalition of dry Democrats of which he had been the leader, forward-looking businessmen, and returning veterans. The second Middle Tennessee faction, the Nashville machine controlled by the Howse-McConnico-Stahlman triumvirate, was bitterly opposed by Lea. As McConnico became more intimately involved with the Nashville machine and differed with Lea on an increasing number of issues, their friendship which had been extremely close, began to cool and would, over the next several years, grow into bitter enmity. The third faction was the Edward H. Crump machine in Shelby County.

In Tennessee, as in most of the South, the Republican party was divided into the white supremacist lily-whites and the black-and-tans, a racially mixed group. The party machinery was controlled throughout most of the 1920s by national committeeman J. Will Taylor. The election of a Republican to the United States Senate or to the governorship would cause Taylor to have to share his patronage, so he was usually amenable to cooperating with the Democrats, particularly in close primaries (Lee, *Tennessee in Turmoil* 15).

In the early 1920s, the black population of the state moved in significant numbers from the farms to the cities, and the urban black vote became an important Republican bloc. Taylor was allied with Robert R. Church of Memphis, a wealthy black who was a member of the national Republican advisory board and who was credited with controlling the large Shelby County black vote. B. Carroll Reece, after his election as congressman from the first district in 1920, became a dominant figure in the lily-whites. He, too, for the same reasons as Taylor, would cooperate with the Democrats when expedient (Lee, *Tennessee in Turmoil* 15, 18).

The constitution adopted by Tennessee in 1870 vested the preponderance of power in the legislature, which, however, was unable to provide leadership that was desperately needed because of the high turnover of its members, its meeting only every other year, and its sessions being limited by law to 75 days. The state's main source of income was taxes on real property, but under its archaic revenue system some property, such as the railroads, had escaped equitable taxation for decades (Macpherson, "Democratic Progressivism" 12). The inability to tax income from securities made taxation increasingly unfair (Macpherson, "Democratic Progressivism" 12-13; Lee, *Tennessee in Turmoil* 7).

Most aspirants to the governorship, cognizant of the splintered condition of the Democratic party and sensing 1920 to be a Republican year, were hesitant to challenge the incumbent, Albert H. Roberts, who with the support of the Howse-McConnico-Stahlman faction had been elected in 1918. Even though Roberts had no opposition, he failed to receive the endorsement of the Democratic convention in May because of his handling of the tax problem. Shortly thereafter Colonel William Riley Crabtree, former mayor of Chattanooga, announced his candidacy, and taxes became the foremost issue of the campaign (Lee, *Tennessee in Turmoil* 21). Roberts was again backed by the Nashville machine, and Luke Lea threw his support to Crabtree.

Roberts won the primary, but in the 1920 Warren G. Harding landslide, he was defeated in the November general election by "Uncle Alf" Taylor, his revered and popular Republican opponent. Taylor had been a candidate for the governorship in 1886 against his brother, "Our Bob," in the famous campaign known as the War of the Roses.

The two years of Taylor's administration could scarcely be classified as much more than frustrating, with the Democratic legislature taking over more and more power from the Republican governor, the mild "Uncle Alf" (*The Nashville Tennessean* 10 Jan. 1971), who was beleaguered by strong opposition and intraparty disharmony (Lee, *Tennessee in Turmoil* 25). Beset by increasing debts and falling revenues, Tennessee had reached a crisis in which its schools stagnated and its highways were little more than mud trails. With a virtually powerless chief executive, a parochial legislature that controlled appointments and appropriations, and a confused and overlapping system of bureaucracy, the state government was unable to cope with the situation (Lee, *Tennessee in Turmoil* 26).

A wide-based movement advocating efficiency and economy in government had come into being by 1922. The preceding year a group of Nashville businessmen had commissioned Arthur E. Buck of the New York Bureau of Municipal Research to make a comprehensive study of the maze of state government. Committed to the necessity of overhaul, the Tennessee Manufacturers Association and the Nashville and Knoxville Chambers of Commerce together with several private citizens financed Buck's return to Tennessee in the autumn of 1922 to formulate a complete reorganization plan to be ready to present to whomsoever should be the victorious gubernatorial candidate (Lee, *Tennessee in Turmoil* 41).

Austin Peay of Clarksville was ready to make another bid for the governorship. He had spent the four years since his defeat in 1918 by Roberts in the Democratic primary working out a definite reform plan and getting support among various economic groups across the state (Macpherson, "Democratic Progressivism" 31). The other major contender was former governor Benton McMillin. Luke Lea backed Peay and the Howse-McConnico-Stahlman faction together with the Crump machine in Memphis supported McMillin (Lee, *Tennessee in Turmoil* 28-29).

The intense rivalry of the two Middle Tennessee factions made the campaign bruising, but Peay won by 4,000 votes. In the

November general election he won by a resounding victory against the Republican Governor Taylor. Peay's election was also an undisputed victory for the political faction headed by Luke Lea, whose influence was thereby increased (Lee, *Tennessee in Turmoil* 35).

Many new days had dawned in Tennessee politics, but none was brighter than the day Austin Peay was elected governor. A man of unusual ability and integrity, he was beholden to no one for financial backing as his wife had considerable means. He, therefore, had the freedom to do whatever he considered to be in the best interest of the state. He was definitely his own man and would always remain so, but because of their broad agreement on state policy, he would become more and more closely allied with Lea. According to Gordon Browning, who later was governor of Tennessee, Lea's opinion carried more weight with Peay than the opinions of any other ten men combined.[14]

Lea wanted nothing of a material nature for himself, but he was eager to help shape the sweeping changes the state was on the threshold of initiating. He was convinced the machinery of government needed to be modernized, the tax system revised, and the citizens provided the public services to which they were entitled. The influence of Lea's newspaper was substantial, and having served in the United States Senate, he was conversant with the legislative process. His statewide connections, formed through his political activities and his service with the 114th Field Artillery, would be extremely helpful in getting the administration's program adopted.

In his inaugural address on January 16, 1923, Austin Peay charged the legislature to establish fiscal responsibility and tax relief (Macpherson, "Democratic Progressivism" 46). The following day he sent to the legislature his famed state reorganization plan, which combined the 64 bureaus into eight major departments, whose chairmen were to be appointed by the governor. The plan further provided that a detailed state budget be prepared by the chief executive and presented to the legislature (Lee, *Tennessee in Turmoil* 41-42). Peay's program also included a comprehensive reform of the tax structure and several measures making government the protector of the people (Macpherson, "Democratic Progressivism" 46). The time being ripe for reform, Peay was able to get his far-reaching reorganization plan passed in less than a week by the overwhelmingly Democratic legislature.

The dawning of the automobile age made highways a top priority (Macpherson, "Democratic Progessivism" 193-94), the financing of which created immediate controversy (Lee, *Tennessee in Turmoil* 43). Peay proposed a pay-as-you-go system, whereby funds would be generated by current revenue including federal aid, automobile registration fees, and the leveling of a $.02 per gallon tax on gasoline, thereby placing the financing on those who used the highways (Macpherson, "Democratic Progressivism" 205, 206, 209, 213).

The great advances made during Peay's first term were unprecedented in the recent history of Tennessee. Despite its long tradition of decentralization, the state in that two-year period had become a leader in progressive administration reform. The success of the streamlined, budget-controlled executive agencies could be measured in dollars and cents. The large deficit had been turned into a small surplus, and for the first time in 15 years, payment had been made on the state debt (Macpherson, "Democratic Progressivism" 51). With no precedent to go by, Peay was free to work out the mechanics for exercising the functions granted to the executive branch by the reorganization act according to his concept that state government should function with honesty, efficiency, and economy and should be organized under a logical chain of command (Macpherson, "Democratic Progressivism" 115). His overall record of achievement was so outstanding that he was unbeatable in 1924.

Lea not only had an increasingly strong voice in the formulation of state policy, but he and the governor developed a deep personal friendship. Almost every week the Peays had Sunday night supper at the Leas' home. The colonel worked tirelessly to get Peay's programs enacted and his influence was such that he was a determining factor in directing the course charted by Tennessee in the 1920s. Because of his closeness to the administration, the colonel frequently became controversial as the status quo was disturbed and he often bore the brunt of the inevitable dissatisfaction resulting from executive decisions. However, as he was not running for office he was not overly concerned that he, too, was making many political enemies.

Peay's belief that government must serve the needs of the people dictated expansion of schools and highways. To produce additional income he proposed a ten percent retail sales tax on tobacco products which immediately stirred up great opposition. The Tobacco Merchants Association of the United States marshalled local tobacco interests and the anti-administration forces in an effort to defeat the proposal (Macpherson, "Democratic Progressivism" 267). Lea strongly favored the concept of a luxury tax, as opposed to a general sales tax, and was in large measure responsible for the high tax the administration proposed levying on tobacco. The bill passed, but it provided that the tax would automatically expire at the end of two years (Macpherson, "Democratic Progressivism" 160, 269). Because of his support of the measure, the tobacco industry ceased advertising in Lea's newspaper.

Lea urged Governor Peay in his second administration to go ahead with the proposed program of public improvements including $1 million for buildings at the University of Tennessee; $750,000 for improvements of state institutions; the completion of the War Memorial Building; the extension of the capitol grounds; construction of a supreme court and law library building and a national guard armory; and establishment of a crippled children's hospital.

Lea proposed that the state follow the sound financial practice of most successful corporations—the payment of capital investments over a long period of time. He further suggested that rather than separate measures being introduced for each expenditure, a general law be enacted creating a commission with authority to request the funding board to issue internal improvements notes maturing in no longer than five years.

Legislation was enacted in 1925 to acquire property adjacent to Reelfoot Lake in West Tennessee and in the Great Smoky Mountains in East Tennessee, thus beginning a system of state parks (Macpherson, "Democratic Progressivism" 65-66). Lea grasped the unlimited possibilities of a national park in the Great Smoky Mountains. Convinced that the land must be acquired at that time or the opportunity lost forever, he worked closely with Peay in guiding this project through the interminable and intricate steps from conception to completion and was persuasive in convincing legislators from other sections that the park would benefit the entire state.

After one of the bitterest legislative battles in the history of the state, Peay's general education bill was finally enacted, which upgraded the quality of instruction by standardizing the licensing and salary scale of teachers and establishing a statewide eight months elementary school term (Macpherson, "Democratic Progressivism" 276).

However, the 1925 legislature also passed an anti-evolution law that made it a felony to teach the theory of evolution in public schools. Peay was not in sympathy with the ban on teaching the theory of evolution but signed it for fear that his veto would jeopardize his general education bill. Moreover, he doubted that the statute would ever be applied. Within a few days, however, the Rhea County grand jury indicted John Thomas Scopes, a young biology teacher in Dayton, for violation of the "Monkey Law" as it became known throughout the United States (Folmsbee *et al*, *Tennessee—A Short History* 557-59).

Lea found public opinion, with the exception of a small group dubbed by itself the intelligentsia, to be overwhelmingly against Scopes. William Jennings Bryan, in several letters to Lea, displayed "all the enthusiasm of a debutante" over the approaching trial at Dayton.

The steaming courtroom was crowded with spectators, reporters, and photographers to watch the verbal combat in which attorneys Clarence Darrow and Bryan were locked. Scopes was defended gratis by the American Civil Liberties Union, and H.L.

Mencken was in Dayton to report the happenings to the entire country (*The Tennessean* 30 March 1975). Outside on the courthouse grounds, fundamentalist revivalists preached to the assembled crowd while vendors hawked religious pamphlets and souvenir monkey trinkets. Never wanting to miss any excitement, Lea motored to Dayton to attend the trial.

Scopes was convicted. Although he was denied a rehearing, he remained free as the case was ended on a technicality, and the "Monkey Law" stayed on the statute books. Bryan, hurt and depressed by Darrow's tactics and the ridicule of the national press, died a few days after the trial ended.

While the trial was underway, Governor Peay was convalescing from a chronic heart condition at a sanitarium in Battle Creek, Michigan. In a philosophical vein, he wrote Lea:

…but everybody, it seems, wanted to talk to me about that abominable Dayton trial until I was discourteous and unobtrusive as a dog with a bone. How I would like to pull the ears of those boys who invented that jamboree. I see that some of the boys are breathing quicker and longing for the political track. Let them go to it. The end of the rainbow is not there—it is far away. How life repeats. We long for the baubles like children catching fireflies. My own opinion is that anything may be expected to happen.

Our best-laid plans are never sure. Something may come along always at the most unexpected moment like this evolution business and sweep aside everything. I am suffering over those two death cases at home [men sentenced by the court to be executed]. Those experiences make you sick to the core. Well, Luke, there are a lot of things I want to talk with you about. It is worth all it has cost being Governor two terms to know you and your wonderful family. Always we will wear each of you next to our heart.[15]

In pushing through his far-reaching reform and progressive measures, Peay had made the inevitable number of enemies. In the 1926 gubernatorial race, the opposition to the administration chose as their candidate Hill McAlister, who was serving his fourth term as state treasurer (Macpherson, "Democratic Progressivism" 68). McAlister's campaign was built around the promise to repeal the reorganization act and to decentralize state government. He pledged a curtailment of spending, the repeal of the tobacco tax, and the release of additional highway funds to the counties for local roads (Macpherson, "Democratic Progressivism" 238). In short, his goal was to undo all that Peay had fought to obtain (Macpherson, "Democratic Progressivism" 72). Peay's principal strength was among rural and small town voters, and McAlister, backed by the Nashville and Memphis machines, had strong support in the urban areas.

From this hard-fought primary, Peay emerged the victor by 8,000 votes (Lee, *Tennessee in Turmoil* 73). The heavy vote against him in Shelby County was offset by his receiving 68 percent of the vote in East Tennessee. Peay had given that Republican sector of the state its fair share of roads and schools, had worked untiringly toward establishment of a park in the Smoky Mountains, had been a staunch supporter of the University of Tennessee at Knoxville, and was sympathetic to that section's demand for development of its water power.

In the general election Peay defeated his Republican opponent, Walter White, superintendent of Rhea County public schools, by a margin of nearly two to one, even carrying East Tennessee, thereby for the first time breaking the Republican hold on that section (Macpherson, "Democratic Progressivism" 331). He also was the first governor since Isham G. Harris (1857-1862) to be elected to a third term in succession.

After winning the nomination to the state Senate from Lincoln and Marshall Counties, Henry H. Horton decided to run for speaker. He wrote Lea on August 19 to solicit his support. Lea replied the speakership was a decision for Governor Peay to make and suggested he take the matter up with him. When the legislature convened at noon on the first Monday in January 1927, Horton was elected speaker of the Senate of Tennessee.

Late in the winter, Governor Peay suffered a severe heart attack. The legislature adjourned for six weeks for him to convalesce. During that time North Carolina made available $2 million for the acquisition of land for the park. When the Tennessee legislature reconvened, the administration introduced a bill in the Senate that would authorize a bond issue for the same purpose (Macpherson, "Democratic Progressivism" 337).

The opposition to the park increased its efforts to attempt to defeat the project. The anti-administration faction claimed the park bill was a political pay-off for support of the governor in the 1926 election, and the *Banner* termed the park "ridiculous" and "preposterous" (Lee, *Tennessee in Turmoil* 61).

Having proved its worth many times over, it seems strange years later that the establishment of this park was strongly opposed by anti-administration forces and that only through adroit political compromise did it become a reality. After a hard fight the legislature passed the park bill in April 1927 (Macpherson, "Democratic Progressivism" 341), and on July 8 of that year the federal government announced it would accept for development as a national park the designated 427,000 acres (Macpherson, "Democratic Progressivism" 345). Thus the long battle to preserve that mountain region was at last won, but it would be February 1930 before the National Park Service received titles to the first parcels (Macpherson, "Democratic Progressivism" 345).

During his third term, Peay not only got legislative approval for the renewal of the vital tobacco tax but, despite strong opposition, succeeded in having his entire education plan adopted. The 1927 legislature passed two measures that virtually completed the state highway program. Peay succeeded in building roads without incurring a huge bonded indebtedness (Macpherson, "Democratic Progressivism" 246), and the highway system was one of the state's greatest bargains with its value far surpassing its cost. Its benefits were immediately apparent in the development of the state and in the attraction of tourists (Macpherson, "Democratic Progressivism" 247).

However, the legislature, still trying to get control of highway funds, also passed a bill raising the gasoline tax by one cent, the proceeds of which would be divided equally among the 95 counties for the building and maintenance of roads not included in the state system. Peay immediately vetoed the bill, characterizing it a waste of the taxpayer's money (Macpherson, "Democratic Progressivism" 242-43). If the administration's highway program was to remain intact, it was imperative that the governor's veto be sustained.

Lea explained the situation to Congressman Gordon Browning who agreed to use his influence with state Senator Dorsey Bramley of Carroll County to persuade him to vote to sustain the governor's veto. Finally Bramley acquiesced provided Browning took responsibility for his vote. That night a chair was in the aisle by Bramley's desk. Before the roll call began, Browning walked onto the floor of the chamber and sat in the chair. When Bramley's name was called, he pointed his arm at Browning as he voted. The governor's veto was sustained.[16]

On October 2, 1927, Peay was stricken with a cerebral hemorrhage, and three hours later died without regaining consciousness. Acutely aware that the governor's death was a great loss to the state, Luke Lea was one of the eight personal friends who bore Austin Peay's body to its final resting place in Clarksville (*The Nashville Tennessean* 4 October 1927).

Chapter Nine
The Dream Expands

Luke Lea was usually working on a variety of matters at the same time, and as an idea matured in his mind, changes in the original concept developed. Ever projecting into the future he, in a sense, lived before his time. Many of his dreams that at their inception seemed utterly fantastic have come to be accepted as commonplace, such as super highways spanning the continent.

Others are still unrealized such as the memorialization of Tennessee's three presidents by a plaza in Nashville of needed public buildings, widened boulevards, and beautification of the Cumberland River. The Nashville Exchange Club of which Lea served as president in 1925-1926 spearheaded the plan,[1] which had not gotten off the ground before the depression of 1930 made it impossible for it to be carried out. Lea did not give up on the idea, however. Years later he tried unsuccessfully to revive interest in carrying out a much more elaborate memorial.[2]

Other projects in which he was greatly interested have come to fruition but without his being closely identified with them, such as the Great Smoky Mountains National Park, in the establishment of which he was instrumental by helping members of the Tennessee legislature grasp its unlimited potential, and the American Legion in the founding of which he played a prominent role.

Lea, one of seven civilians appointed by President Coolidge to the Board of Visitors to the Naval Academy for 1928, always retained a profound interest in the men who had served their country in the time of war. *The Tennessean* consistently advocated the veterans bonus or adjusted compensation legislation. Chairman of the committee that considered that matter when the American

143

Legion was founded in 1919, Lea left to Congress the amount and the method by which relief would be given as he was confident Congress would handle the matter justly.[3] One of his blind spots was his quixotic belief that without inducement people would be fair even though the action might be costly, and time and again he was surprised when persons were not.

Plans for a soldier's memorial in Nashville had been initiated shortly after the end of World War I. Lea advocated a handsome structure with a wide plaza in the area of the state capitol. The War Memorial Building, dedicated on September 21, 1925, has proved a distinct asset to the business section of the city. Always one to think in grand terms, Lea had hoped that both President Coolidge and General Pershing would be among the notables present for the dedication, but neither was able to come, and it fell to Lea to receive the structure on behalf of Tennessee's soldiers.

Two years later the Ladies Battlefield Association erected a statue on the site on Franklin Road where Confederate General John B. Hood and Union General George H. Thomas met at the Battle of Nashville on December 18, 1864. When the monument was dedicated on November 11, 1927, it attracted nationwide attention as the first monument to commemorate soldiers both of the North and the South and their sons and grandsons, who, fighting side-by-side in World War I, had cemented through their sacrifice the united sections of this nation.[4] Again neither Coolidge nor Pershing was able to attend, so Lea was drafted to give the address.

Lea was notified on December 1, 1922, that he had been awarded the Distinguished Service Medal

...for exceptionally meritorious and distinguished services...during the St. Mihiel and Meuse-Argonne offensives....[5]

Many years after his death, another tribute, and one that he would have appreciated deeply was the Nashville organization of veterans of World War I being named the Luke Lea Barracks.

Expansion was the mood of the optimistic twenties, and no one exemplified the confidence of that era more than Lea. A gambler in the sense that he was willing to stake a down payment today on a property that he believed would increase in the future, he continually invested in real estate. Besides the large acreage he was developing in Belle Meade, he owned several blocks of property in downtown Nashville, the value of which in 1925 he figured was approximately $800,000.[6]

The more properties Lea acquired, the more complicated his financial affairs became. He chartered a new corporation almost every time he bought another property. A separate company facilitated the trading of a particular piece of real estate in that other properties he owned were not a part of that transaction. Acquisitions were often financed by issuing mortgage bonds against the real estate purchased. These bonds, to be retired as the property was sold, were readily acceptable at banks with which Lea did business (McFerrin, *Caldwell and Company* 70). Also, in keeping with accepted practices of that time, proceeds from the sale of one property would frequently be used to buy another property. Consequently, although owned by separate corporations, the different properties were often interrelated and dependent one on another. As long as the economy was strong and expanding, this procedure created no problems more serious than a scarcity of liquid assets, but built into this house of cards' financial structure were the seeds of its destruction.

Aware that demand would increase for parking space in downtown Nashville, Lea borrowed $50,000 from National Life and Accident Insurance Company in 1925 to build a parking garage on property he owned on Seventh Avenue between Church and Commerce. This was the first ramp-type garage for public parking in Nashville.

After two or three stories had been constructed on the Bennie Dillon building on the corner of Seventh and Church, it was discovered that the structure extended 12 or 18 inches onto the property owned by Lea. Knowing how costly it would be to tear down and rebuild that side of the building, Lea could have charged an exorbitant price for those inches of land. Instead they were sold at the median price of three real estate appraisers not connected with Lea or with Dillon.[7]

As a chess player calculates the effect of possible moves, Lea contemplated numerous ways tracts of land could be used in various combinations, and in his constant trading of real estate he usually considered many transactions simultaneously.

During the latter 1920s *The Tennessean* papers were doing well financially, and Lea valued at $1.25 million the Tennessee Publishing Company.[8] Its total bonded indebtedness was $385,000 consisting of $110,000 American Company bonds, which had been assumed by the Tennessee Publishing Company when it purchased the property of the American Company and two secondary bond issues, amounting to $275,000.[9] *The Nashville Tennessean,* with the Associated Press wire service, and *The Evening Tennessean,* with the United Press wire service, were two distinct papers as to news, editorial and feature content and with only a portion of advertising duplicated.[10] The circulation of *The Tennessean* papers continued to increase and the influence they exerted was manifested by the public's having approved at the ballot box the great majority of candidates the papers supported during the 1920s.

As *The Nashville Tennessean* became one of the most widely read papers in the state, Lea dreamed of expanding. He would buy various newspapers as their acquisition became possible and forge them into a great chain. Through those papers, his influence could be increased to help his state and his region develop their latent potential.

Lea was interested in 1926 in buying the *Kansas City Star*, which became for sale following the death of its publisher. He went to Kansas City to negotiate in person and, according to John Erwin of Washington, left thinking he had bought the paper, having put in a bid reputed to be around $10 million (*Kentucky Messenger,* 19 May 1927). However, the *Star*'s trustees, in Erwin's opinion, were determined not to allow the control of the newspaper out of local hands and managed to be presented a higher offer, which was promptly accepted.

Disappointed that he had not been able to buy the *Kansas City*

Star, Lea began looking for other newspapers. During the autumn of 1926, he commenced negotiations to acquire the Memphis *Commercial Appeal* from the estate of its former editor, C.P.J. Mooney and other stockholders. Established in 1894 by the consolidation of three papers, the *Commercial Appeal* had a circulation of over 150,000, at that time the largest in the South (*Globe Democrat* 16 May 1927). The Memphis *Evening Appeal* began publication on December 1, 1926, with the Commercial Publishing Company being formed to publish both morning and afternoon papers.[11]

Lea secured in January 1927 an option to buy the papers, but he needed financial backing. He initially contacted Halsey Stuart, which Chicago firm suggested that Caldwell and Company, recently organized by a young Nashvillian, participate in the undertaking. The purchase of the *Commercial Appeal* was the impetus that brought together Luke Lea and Rogers Caldwell.

Connected with his father in the insurance business, Rogers Caldwell came to believe that a Southern bond company dealing in Southern municipal bonds would be a profitable venture. Therefore, he established Caldwell and Company in September 1917. From its inception Caldwell and Company purchased bonds under depository agreements, which provided that funds from the sale of bonds would be left on deposit with banks agreeable to Caldwell and Company until the money was needed to pay for actual construction on the projects being financed. However, these deposits were needed as working capital if Caldwell and Company was to expand (McFerrin, *Caldwell and Company* 5).

To solve this problem, the Bank of Tennessee was chartered in 1919 with a capital of $200,000 and a capital surplus of $50,000. Completely owned and controlled by Caldwell and Company, it occupied the same offices and had the same personnel. Its customers were limited to the municipalities and later the businesses financed by Caldwell and Company (McFerrin, *Caldwell and Company* 5-8).

The creation of investment trusts by investment banking houses and also by many banks was an important development of the bull market of the twenties. Following the lead of older and larger houses, Caldwell and Company chartered under the laws of Delaware on August 9, 1928, its investment trust, Shares-in-the-South, Incorporated (McFerrin, *Caldwell and Company* 81).

The base of Luke Lea's political power long had been *The Nashville Tennessean* and *The Evening Tennessean*. These papers were published by the Tennessee Publishing Company, of which Luke Lea was president and his son, Luke Lea, Jr., was business manager. This was solely a Lea enterprise. At no time did Caldwell and Company have any financial interest in it. Furthermore, at no time did either Luke Lea or Luke Lea, Jr., own any stock of, or hold any position in, Caldwell and Company or the Bank of Tennessee.

Both Luke Lea and Rogers Caldwell were interested in state political affairs and, as they became associated in business, their relationship developed into friendship. Frequently they lunched together, usually at the Hermitage Club in downtown Nashville. They both enjoyed horseback, often riding together Sunday morning at Harpeth Hills Hunt Club. Both were in the habit of inviting various people to join them, and even persons who cared little for riding would accept so they could boast of having ridden with the colonel or Caldwell.[12]

The fact that Luke Lea and Rogers Caldwell were jointly interested in several business undertakings caused in time the Lea interests and the activities of Caldwell and Company to become one and the same in the minds of the public. That error of lumping together all the enterprises of Luke Lea and all the enterprises of Rogers Caldwell because of their joint interest in some matters did injustice to both. Those who in the future lost money in a Caldwell controlled enterprise, and their number was legion, held Lea also responsible for the loss. Also many of the political enemies Lea had made through the years, and as long as he was a power to be reckoned with their number inevitably increased, became unfriendly toward Caldwell.

To purchase the Memphis *Commercial Appeal,* Luke Lea and Rogers Caldwell chartered Southern Publishers, Incorporated,

April 22, 1927, under the laws of Delaware to hold the stock of the Memphis Commercial Appeal, Incorporated. At that time the laws of Delaware were most favorable to corporations, so it was not unusual for them to be chartered in that state. Luke Lea and Caldwell and Company each bought half of the 1,000 shares of common stock. Lea, who would have the entire responsibility for publishing any newspapers Southern Publishers would acquire, was elected president of the new corporation at a salary of $50,000 a year (McFerrin, *Caldwell and Company* 88).

The following month Luke Lea and Rogers Caldwell entered into a contract with the Howell family to acquire *The Atlanta Constitution,* one of the South's most influential dailies. The contract stipulated that the Howells were to sell the Nashvillians 3,025 shares of the 5,000 shares of stock of the *Constitution* for $1.05 million, but if an audit showed the profits of the first three months of 1927 to be less than recorded on the books of the newspaper, the purchase price would be reduced accordingly.[13]

On the basis of an audit that showed first quarter profits substantially smaller, Lea and Caldwell tendered approximately $54,000 for the controlling interest in the *Constitution*, which offer was unacceptable to the Howells. Lea and Caldwell brought suit for the performance of the contract but becoming convinced in September that they could not win the case, withdrew without going to trial. Unable to agree with the Howells on a purchase price they ended their efforts to acquire the *Constitution* (*Editor and Publisher* September 1928).

Lea had begun negotiations with A.F. Sanford to buy the *Knoxville Journal* in January 1927. In addition to the newspaper, its building, and 980 shares of stock in the East Tennessee National Bank owned by the Sanford family were included in the discussions.[14] After many months negotiations were concluded and the sale became effective on March 31, 1928. Lea then had a newspaper in each of the three grand divisions of the state.

Full and unbiased coverage of news had been the policy of Lea's papers since he entered the publishing field (*The Nashville Tennessean and the Nashville American* 26 September 1910).

However, as with most newspapers, their editorial stance reflected the political opinions of the publisher. Consequently when he acquired the Republican *Knoxville Journal*, it became a Democratic newspaper.

One day during the early part of 1927, when in Knoxville on *Journal* business, Lea stopped by the newly organized Holston National Bank and met its charming and competitive president J. Basil Ramsey.[15] They chatted only a few minutes, but each man was impressed with the other. Shortly thereafter, Lea told a friend of Ramsey's that he and Rogers Caldwell were in a position to buy a one-fourth interest in the Holston National Bank.

Its board of directors were of the opinion that it would be to the bank's advantage for Lea and Caldwell to own a one-fourth interest, and that it would be better for the board to sell sufficient amounts of stock to comprise the block to sell to Lea and Caldwell, rather than to go outside to other stockholders. Lea's purpose in buying into the bank was to make an investment which would bring in money that in turn could be invested elsewhere. Ramsey's objective was to secure new business and to build up his bank. Hence, it was a mutually advantageous arrangement for Lea, for the bank, and for Caldwell who was expanding his financial operations.

Lea and Paul J. Kruesi, a Chattanooga manufacturer, both decided to run for the class B directorship of the Federal Reserve Bank of Atlanta, made vacant by the death in 1927, of Captain W. H. Hartford of Chattanooga, whose term did not expire until December 31, 1928 (*American Press* January 1928). To be eligible for the position, a person could not then, and still cannot, be an officer of a bank.[16]

The sixth district of the Federal Reserve was composed of Tennessee, Mississippi, Alabama, Georgia, and Florida. On the nominating ballot Lea received 75 votes and Kruesi got 42. Within a week 14 banks which did not vote in the nominating ballot had pledged their support to Lea which would give him a strong majority.[17] Kruesi conceded defeat on September 27 (*The Atlanta Constitution* 28 September 1927).

Because of Lea's connection in various enterprises with Rogers Caldwell, who was a banker, Lea was in years to come labeled by the press so often as a banker that it came to be widely believed as true. Lea, however, was never involved in the management of any bank. His being a director of the Federal Reserve Board of Atlanta attests to this fact.

Lea purchased bank stocks, as he did real estate, for an investment. In May of 1928 he, Rogers Caldwell, and Edward Potter, Jr., of Commerce Union Company, purchased 51 percent of the capital stock of the Manhattan Savings Bank and Trust Company, considered to be the strongest small bank in Memphis. By this extension of its banking interests into Memphis, Caldwell and Company became a dominant influence in Tennessee banking (McFerrin, *Caldwell and Company* 72).

Its large volume of slow and doubtful accounts caused the Union Planters Bank and Trust Company, one of the three largest banks in Memphis, to be in a rather unsound condition toward the end of 1928. Aware that its thorough reorganization (McFerrin, *Caldwell and Company* 72-76) was desirable, the three Nashvillians who had purchased control of the Manhattan, together with Frank Hayden, an officer of the Union and Planters, and William White, executive vice-president of the Manhattan, offered to reorganize the ailing bank.

The offer was accepted. James E. Caldwell of Nashville, through the Fourth and First National Company, joined the group and the six men formed Bank Securities Corporation on February 25, 1929. The cash deposited to increase the Union and Planters Bank's net worth put it in a sound financial condition, and the West Tennessee Company, a subsidiary of Bank Securities Corporation, was formed to liquidate its slow assets, and over time progress was made in that endeavor.

The approximately $8.37 million required by this reorganization plan plus a projected cash profit to the promoting group of over $800,000 was expected to be raised by the sale of Union Planters stock. Lea was not responsible for the sale of any stock, nor was he ever an officer or director of Union Planters. His sole interest in its reorganization was the profit he stood to make on the stock. However, because of a weakened market, this stock was not taken up as quickly as anticipated. Neither Lea nor the other organizers of Bank Securities realized the projected profit.

The commitment to racial equality was still in the future in the South, and Lea's attitude toward blacks was molded by the time and place in which he lived. Keenly aware, however, of their needs, he worked for the improvement of their condition, a prime requisite, he believed, being better education. Toward that end he contributed of his time and ability as a member of the Board of Trust of Fisk University to which he had been elected in 1912.

During the late 1920s Lea lent a building he owned on Seventh Avenue to the newly formed Junior League of Nashville, of which his wife was a charter member. As a result of his generosity the Nashville League was the first in the South to have a clubhouse.

Lea grasped the advantages that would be obtained from the merger of two large Nashville companies, Morgan and Hamilton with Werthan Bag Company. Many believed this an impossibility, but Lea persevered, and from the transaction, one of the largest in Nashville up until that time, he acquired a block of stock in the highly successful new company, which became Werthan Industries.[18]

Lea's varied interests knew no geographical bounds. He had long been deeply concerned about the plight of the farmer and about high taxes because he believed that throughout history excessive taxation had been the major cause of revolution. He tried unsuccessfully to interest Henry Ford, in the summer of 1921, in becoming head of an association for tax relief.[19] Lea's papers state his opinion that national taxes could be cut in half through disarmament, efficiency in administration, and reduction of interest by retirement of liberty bonds, and that state and local taxes could be reduced materially by elimination of duplication in governments and services. Therefore, he advocated the city and county becoming co-extensive, a change that would occur locally some 40 years later when the governments of Nashville and Davidson County would be consolidated into one Metropolitan government. Lea's papers also reveal that he tried to interest industrial leaders in giving to the capitals of the various states parks that would bear the donors' names.

As early as 1913 when Lea was in the Senate and recognized the great asset Rock Creek Park was to Washington, he had conceived the idea of setting aside for a park some of the original Belle Meade plantation acreage, then owned by his Belle Meade Park Company.[20] In order to arrange his holdings so he could make a gift of land to the city, it was necessary to retire all the Belle Meade bonds and to issue lien notes in lieu thereof.[21] Arrangements also had to be made with his mother to swap certain pieces of property to which she held deeds for other pieces of equal or greater value, so that he would have an unencumbered tract to give.

At a called meeting of the Board of Park Commissioners on September 17, 1926, Lea made the following offer: a 325-acre tract of which the Belle Meade Park Company owned a three-fifths interest, the other two-fifths being owned by the Nashville Railway and Light Company; and four other tracts totaling 543 acres which he owned outright, making a total of 868 acres. This acreage lay between Page Road and Highway 70, a mile farther from downtown than Belle Meade Country Club.

The board immediately voted to accept his offer and Colonel and Mrs Lea deeded the property to the city of Nashville on January 10, 1927.[22] The only stipulation on this gift was that it should always be used as a public park.

Both Mrs. Lea and her father Percy Warner were insistent that the park be named Luke Lea Park. Lea, however, did not want to request that his gift bear his name and the park remained unnamed when Percy Warner died unexpectedly on June 18, 1927.

After his retirement as president of the Nashville Street Railway and Light Company, Warner as chairman of the park board had devoted increasing time to the development of parks for the city. Associated in many enterprises through the years, Luke Lea and Percy Warner transacted business as contemporaries, yet the younger man relied on the wisdom and judgment of the older one for whom he had a filial affection and respect. Wanting to honor his father-in-law, Lea requested the park board to name the park after Warner, which it unanimously voted to do.[23] A few months later the board named one of the highest points in the park Luke Lea Heights in recognition of the donor. That point overlooks the main entrance gates and the city of Belle Meade.

It is a fitting memorial to Percy Warner, who also envisioned a magnificent park and gave liberally of himself to develop a city park system, that this large wooded acreage should bear his name. However, what Mrs. Lea foresaw as the result of the park not being named for her husband came to pass, in that the identity of the donor was forgotten by the general public and the gift was credited to the man whose name the park bears.

Few of its citizens have been as generous to Nashville as was Colonel Lea, and Mrs. Lea was determined her husband should have some recognition for having given to the city the initial acreage of Percy Warner Park. Financially unable to erect a marker commemorating his public-spiritedness, she conceived the idea of the officers in his regiment doing so. At a reunion of the six battery commanders and their wives in 1949 she broached this plan and they immediately undertook the project.

At the dedication ceremonies in the spring of 1950, a large crowd, including the governor of Tennessee, Gordon Browning, who had been captain of battery A in Lea's World War I regiment, gathered in the brilliant sunshine. Young Luke Lea III helped unveil the granite monument erected inside the entrance gates in front of the flagpole in the álle. The bronze plaque is inscribed:

In Memory of
COLONEL LUKE LEA
1879-1945
So that posterity might enjoy the benefits of a public park preserved in its natural beauty, in 1927 Colonel Lea gave the original tract of 868 acres of this land to the city of Nashville requesting that the park bear the name of his father-in-law Percy Warner.

Erected by officers who served under Colonel Lea in the 114th Field Artillery during the first World War.

Ella Cocke and Overton Lea, parents of Luke Lea.

Luke Lea, in a style popular for children in Victorian America.

Lealand, home where Luke Lea was born and spent his childhood.

The legendary varsity football team of the University of the South, 1899. Manager Luke Lea sits second from left in the back row (wearing hat).

The Tennessean's offices on Nashville's Fourth Avenue. Upper left: J.H. Allison; lower left: E.F. Caruthers; upper right: Luke Lea. (Photo from *The Linotype Bulletin*, 1916.)

Luke Lea about the time of his marriage to Mary Louise Warner.

Mary Louise Warner Lea (Mrs. Luke).

The "baby senator" (cartoon from the *Knoxville Journal and Tribune*, 10 February 1911).

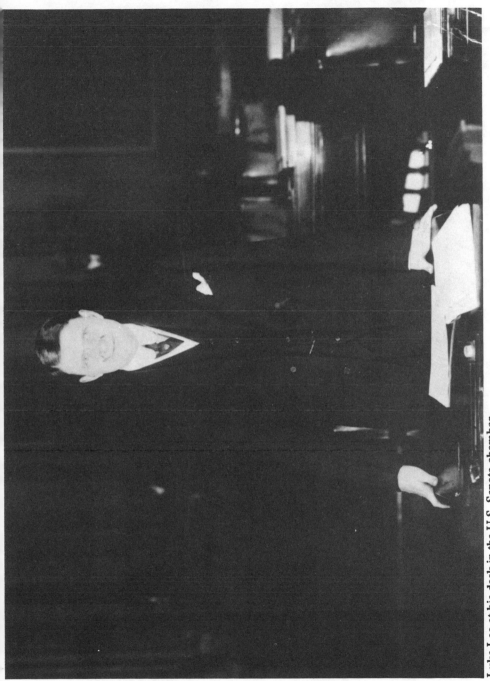

Luke Lea at his desk in the U.S. Senate chamber.

Colonel Luke Lea, 114th Field Artillery.

Colonel Luke Lea astride a horse supplied by the Rothschild stables, France, 1918.

The soldiers who tried to kidnap Kaiser Wilhelm. Front row left to right: Captain Larry MacPhail, Colonel Lea, Captain Thomas P. Henderson, Lieutenant Elsworth Brown. Back row: Sergeant Dan Reilly, third from left, Sergeant Owen Johnston, and Corporal Marmaduke Clokey. The man second from left, though unidentified, is presumed to be Egbert Hail, who accompanied Lea to Amerongen Castle.

Luke Lea and Percie Warner about the time of their marriage, with his sons Percy and Luke Lea, Jr.

Three generations: Percy Warner, Luke Lea, and Luke Lea, Jr.

On the stump (Photo courtesy of Laura Lea Knox).

Awaiting a court decision. Left to right: Percy, Mrs. Lea, Luke Lea, Luke, Jr.

The North Carolina state prison at Raleigh.

FRIENDS WELCOME COLONEL LUKE LEA WITH BANQUET

Approximately 300 old friends of Col. Luke Lea welcomed him home to Nashville again Saturday night at a banquet in the Noel Hotel. The colonel was officially greeted at the banquet by Mayor Hilary E. Howse.

Judge J. D. B. DeBow was toastmaster.

MAYOR HOWSE GREETS COLONEL LEA

Above, Homecoming: Friends welcome Lea at a banquet at the Noel Hotel; below, Nashville Mayor Hilary Howse (left) greets Lea. (Man in the middle is unidentified.)

Luke Lea in his later years.

Dedication of a marker, 1950, given by officers in his regiment, commemorating Colonel Lea's gift to the city of Nashville of the original 868 acres of Percy Warner Park. Luke Lea Heights rises in the background.

Chapter Ten
Zenith of Political Influence

The death on October 2, 1927, of Austin Peay, the first strong chief executive of the state in decades, created a power vacuum (Lee, *Tennessee in Turmoil* 75). Henry H. Horton, speaker of the state Senate, automatically succeeded to the governorship. He was 61 years of age, not strong physically, and the speakership was his first position on the state level. He pledged himself to carry out the policies of his predecessor, but possessing neither Peay's exceptional ability nor a strong base of support, Horton lacked the strength to fill the position into which he had been suddenly thrust.

Needing advisers the new governor leaned heavily on Luke Lea (Lee, *Tennessee in Turmoil* 81). Lea had never intended being drawn into state affairs on the day-to-day level. Convinced, however, it was essential that the programs initiated by Peay be carried through, the colonel was willing to shoulder the increased involvement. Coupled with his crusading spirit was his vision to see what needed to be done and supreme confidence in his ability to get the job done better than anyone else. Moreover, he loved the excitement politics engendered, the being at the center of the action.

The opportunity for foes of the administration to attack Governor Horton was not long in coming. He had been in office only a little over four months when he asked for and received the resignation of Highway Commissioner C. Neil Bass, who was succeeded by Colonel Harry S. Berry.

The *Nashville Banner* was quick to see in this action a ready-made issue with which to attack not only the governor but also its archenemy, Luke Lea. In fact, a more ideal issue could hardly be imagined. Lea was quite influential with Horton and was a friend of Rogers Caldwell, who wanted to sell his company's brand of bitulithic rock asphalt, called "Kyrock," to the state. The *Banner* sought to make Lea the target of blame from all angles. With adroit handling, Kyrock could be made the reason for the governor's firing of his highway commissioner, and with luck, the firing could even be made an issue in the August primary.

The *Banner* on the following day printed on page one that rumor had it Bass was removed from office because he had not awarded Caldwell's Kentucky Rock Asphalt Company a bid on a highway project in West Tennessee (*Nashville Banner* 15 February 1928). Editorials in the same vein continued almost daily.

Lea had endeavored to keep comment on the highway controversy out of the editorial columns of his newspapers. The *Banner*, however, continued to harp on the dismissal, and a page one editorial on February 27 demanded to know why "Luke Lea and Horton fired Neil Bass." The next day *The Tennessean* countered with a front page editorial signed by Lea:

> The daily attacks by the *Banner*, formerly made upon Governor Peay, have broken out afresh upon Governor Horton. . . .
> The *Banner*, angered at Governor Horton because it cannot control him is continually "straffing" him, and without provocation has for a period of twelve days daily attacked me.
> I WISH TO REPEAT THE STATEMENTS I MADE SEVERAL WEEKS AGO, THAT I HAVE NOT NOW AND NEVER HAD AT ANY TIME ANY FINANCIAL INTEREST OF ANY KIND IN ANY ROAD MATERIAL OR IN ANY FIRM OR COMPANY THAT DOES BUSINESS WITH THE STATE OF TENNESSEE, WITH THE SOLE EXCEPTION OF NEWSPAPERS IN WHICH THE STATE OCCASIONALLY INSERTS LEGAL ADVERTISING.
> I neither requested nor demanded the removal of Commissioner Bass nor the appointment of Col. Harry Berry as his successor. My sole relationship with Col. Berry has been that both of us served in the same artillery brigade in France during the World War. . . . (*The Nashville Tennessean* 28 February 1928)

The feud between the two newspapers erupted again in what came to be one of the state's bitterest gubernatorial primaries.

Horton, whose campaign was based on carrying out the programs started by Austin Peay, was challenged by Nashvillian Hill McAlister, who had run unsuccessfully against Peay two years previously on a platform to repeal the state Reorganization Act and other reforms. Still adamantly opposed to Peay's policies, McAlister had always been allied with the anti-Lea political faction. His strategists sought to keep the attention of the voters riveted on the state's use of Kyrock. At every opportunity McAlister reminded the voters that Kyrock was sold to the state by Caldwell and Company's Kentucky Rock Asphalt Company; that Luke Lea and Rogers Caldwell had several joint business ventures; and that they had great influence with the incumbent governor, Henry Horton. No mention was made of the fact that when rock asphalt was specified for highway construction it was cheaper, because of the freight charge, to purchase it from Kentucky Rock Asphalt Company than to buy the identical grade of material from a concern more distant from Tennessee.

The third candidate, former state Commissioner of Institutions Lewis Pope, was generally regarded as having no chance of winning but was unusually vitriolic, particularly in his accusations against Horton. His daily attacks on the governor were based largely on the charge that the support of Rogers Caldwell and Luke Lea constituted a "sinister influence."

Lea believed Tennessee had stagnated for decades prior to Peay's election as governor in 1922. During his term sound business practices and taxes levied upon tobacco and gasoline had converted an annual deficit of more than $1 million into a surplus, and at the same time most state programs had been enlarged. Lea was convinced that never in its history had the state progressed as rapidly and upon as sound a basis as it had the past five and a half years. He understood that only through victory at the polls would the legislation be enacted necessary to insure continued progress. Therefore, he was willing to exert all his influence for the election of Horton.

The base of Lea's political strength had always been *The Tennessean* and the rural voters. He had fought and been opposed by the Nashville and Memphis machines, except during brief periods of armed truce. He kept in his head an accurate count of the number of votes each county could reasonably be expected to cast and maintained personal contact with key people in each county. The men who Lea relied on to carry counties for his candidate would support almost any man he asked them to because they liked the colonel personally and over the years had come to trust him.[1]

As the campaign progressed, Horton was hurt in East Tennessee by the Kyrock issue. Lea clearly understood that the highway department could be of tremendous political assistance to the administration and was Jacksonian in his belief that, when qualified, persons who had supported the administration's building of roads and bridges, rather than its opponents, should share in the financial benefits accruing from their construction. However, since he had no financial interest in any building materials, he never profited monetarily from their construction.

As the election neared, activity at the colonel's office increased. Phones rang; people streamed in with reports and left with new instructions. At the center of all the excitement was the colonel, smiling as he shook hands, expressing his appreciation to one man, and confidently predicting victory to another.

Monday preceding the primary a group of ten or 12 key men from across the state met with Lea in Nashville. They were determined not to let Crump steal the election. All were aware of the large number of votes in Shelby County he controlled through agreements with Memphis black leader Robert Church (Lee, *Tennessee in Turmoil* 70). After lengthy discussion, Lea decided the best way to defeat Crump was to employ the Memphis boss's own strategy. It was agreed not to report the returns from ballot boxes that they were confident would give Horton a large majority until after Shelby County had reported its vote. They would simply outwait Crump.

Finally election day, August 2, arrived. In Memphis the *Appeal* papers gave cameras to their reporters with instructions to photograph blacks being shuttled to the polls. Nine reporters were beaten and driven from voting places and their cameras smashed or confiscated by the police and allies of the Crump machine. Three reporters were thrown into jail briefly in what the August 11 issue of *Editor and Publisher* termed a flagrant violation of the constitutional and traditional right of freedom of the press.

The story that later made the rounds of political circles (*The Tennessean* 16 May 1978) was that Frank Rice, one of Crump's right-hand men, phoned McAlister's headquarters in Nashville and asked what majority, on the basis of the early returns, was needed from Memphis to insure McAlister's victory. Rice reputedly was told that a 20,000 majority would be ample. Accordingly, Shelby County reported 24,069 votes had been cast there for McAlister and 3,693 votes for Horton.

Lea had figured correctly that McAlister would carry Memphis by about 20,000 votes and Nashville by approximately 7,000. After Shelby County had announced its vote, results began to be reported from counties that had given sizeable majorities to Horton. When the ballots were finally all counted, Horton had carried 83 counties and had won the nomination by approximately 5,000 votes.

In later years Rice was frequently quoted as saying in effect, "We learned never to go to bed early. We could have delivered a 40,000 margin as easily as the 20,000" (*The Tennessean* 16 May 1978).

Tennessee would occasionally go Republican in national elections, but except in rare instances, such as Taylor's being elected governor in the 1920 Republican landslide, state offices were filled by Democrats. The real contest was among contending Democratic candidates, and winning the Democratic primary in August was tantamount to winning the general election in November. Predictably the Republican aspirant for the governorship in 1928, Raleigh Hopkins, was easily defeated by Horton.

Lea realized that he was making political enemies, but what he considered the continuing progress of the state had been assured for two more years by Horton's victory. In retrospect it is interesting to wonder if the colonel ever imagined the lengths that would be gone to in the future to strip him of power and influence by the men he had a large part in defeating at the ballot box.

Shortly after the election, Lea wrote Horton that the greatest obstacle that he had had to overcome was lack of loyalty in several of his departments, especially the engineering department. Although Lea had established the policy when Tom Rye was governor and continued it during the administration of Austin Peay not to request the appointment of any one to a state job, the colonel nevertheless thought it absurd to have in a position of responsibility a person who opposed the policies of the administration.[2]

Even though Lea was not as vitally interested in politics on the national level as he was on the state, his prominence in state affairs made him a factor, nevertheless, in Tennessee's stand on national matters. At the convention in Houston the end of June, the Democrats nominated Al Smith, and Herbert Hoover was the Republican nominee. *The Tennessean* on June 30 commented editorially:

...although, for reasons stated, Governor Smith was not our original choice for the nomination, on another ground we welcome his selection as the Democratic standard-bearer because it will for the first time enable the people to put to the acid test our oft proclaimed declaration of religious tolerance...there are great issues in this campaign.... We believe that the triumph of the Democratic party is necessary for the preservation in their original purity of our cherished institutions....

Understandably difficult as it was for a staunch prohibitionist to embrace a "wet" candidate, when Smith came to Tennessee in October, Lea boarded his train in Chattanooga and accompanied him to Nashville for a speaking engagement. The next morning *The Tennessean* came out strongly supporting Smith, and Lea personally contributed $6,500 to his campaign fund.

The controversy between *The Tennessean* and the *Banner* in the gubernatorial primary carried over to the presidential campaign. Stahlman accused the Lea papers of being lukewarm to

Smith because of Lea's alleged ownership of electric power stock and financial assistance from street railway interests. Lea denied the charge and countered that Stahlman was supporting Smith, not because of his stand on the water power issue, but because of a deal with Crump: Stahlman would support Smith in exchange for Crump's delivery of Shelby County to Stahlman's candidate for governor, Hill McAlister. However, in spite of the support of Al Smith by both newspapers Hoover carried Tennessee.

When the Tennessee legislature convened in January 1929, it was immediately apparent that the battle between the administration and the opposition forces would be rejoined with renewed vigor. Crump wrote McKellar, "We will whip them before it is over, for there will be no cessation of hostilities for seventy-five long days" (Lee, *Tennessee in Turmoil* 100).

In an effort to lessen Crump's power, a bill co-sponsored by Democrats and Republicans was introduced, which would decrease the size of the Shelby and Davidson delegations and increase the representation of the Republican areas in East Tennessee. That redistricting plan, for which rightly or wrongly Lea got much blame, stirred up so much opposition that it was dropped (Lee, *Tennessee in Turmoil* 102).

The General Assembly rejected almost every administration proposal with the exception of the highway program, which was adopted with only slight changes over minimal opposition. The only other important administration victory was the choice by the Democratic caucus of Grover Keaton, a staunch supporter of Horton, for the West Tennessee seat on the State Board of Elections Commission (Lee, *Tennessee in Turmoil* 101). The administration thereby finally gained a majority on the board, making it possible for an anti-Crump slate of county officials to challenge the long-time boss of Shelby County. Furthermore, by virtue of the increased power given the chief executive by the Reorganization Act, Horton would be able to appoint a Shelby County criminal court judge who would have the power to investigate Crump's alleged connection with vice rings in Memphis.

Crump realized the state was in a position to destroy his influence in Shelby County (Lee, *Tennessee in Turmoil* 104). In addition he was reluctant for his activities to be scrutinized by an unfriendly judge. In order to survive, Crump made an accommodation with the administration faction. In return for the appointment of his men to the county election commission, Crump would support Horton in the 1930 election, and the Shelby delegation would support the administration sponsored measures in a forthcoming special session of the legislature (Lee, *Tennessee in Turmoil* 104).

From a decade of constant battling for control of the state, the political faction headed by Luke Lea emerged the undisputed victor. Lea's statewide political influence coupled with the power of his newspapers in the three major cities made him, in the opinion of many, the most powerful man in the state. His position seemed unassailable. However, some people, on principle, opposed any one person's having that much power, and Lea's political enemies, whose numbers were ever growing, bided their time.

By July 1930 Lea was engrossed in organizing Horton's campaign for reelection. His newspapers devoted a good deal of editorial space to attacking their Scripps Howard competitors in Memphis and Knoxville that supported L.E. Gwinn for governor (Lee, *Tennessee in Turmoil* 100). Lea's detailed knowledge of the political situation in each county enabled him to pinpoint trouble spots as indicated by his memorandum to Bob Claggett, who was in charge of running the *Knoxville Journal*:

I believe Knox County would be lost today despite the belief of most of our leaders to the contrary....

The trouble areas in Knox, the best I can determine through the various channels are the following wards:

11th, 17th, and 18th—labor wards.

10th Ward, South—Eastern State Hospital employing practically all Republicans.

19th Ward and 15th—general, with state highway garage and maintenance crews being all Republicans having a lot to do with the trouble.[3]

Election day, Thursday, August 7, was a scorcher, and it was another political victory for Lea and Horton. The governor carried 75 counties and received the largest number of votes ever given a candidate in a Democratic primary.

Crump faithfully carried out the bargain he had made with the administration, and Horton racked up a 27,000 majority in Shelby County. Lea considered this the most remarkable political performance he had ever observed,[4] and indeed it was compelling evidence of Crump's tight control of the county. Having to kowtow to Lea in state politics, Crump contented himself by entering the national field. He won the nomination to the United States House of Representatives from Tennessee's tenth congressional district.

Major E.B. Stahlman, at age 87, died in August 1930 at his home in Nashville. His mantle fell to his grandson, James Geddes Stahlman, who for the past several years had taken an increasingly prominent role in publishing the *Nashville Banner*. Lea wrote a restrained editorial in the *Tennessean* papers about the death of his erstwhile political enemy:

> Death has its sting. Yet death does away the sting of life. In the face of death, prejudice and passion fade and in their place stands the warmth of universal brotherhood....
>
> Very positive in his views...Major Stahlman was a picturesque journalist and made strong friends as well as strong enemies, by the position he took on subjects of public interest and general concern.
>
> Major Stahlman's death will deprive the community of one of its leading and outstanding citizens, who took an active part in every phase of its life and will bring genuine grief to a large family connection and to a host of warm and devoted friends. (*The Nashville Tennessean* 13 August 1930)

In contrast to the controversies of politics, Luke Lea's home life was unusually harmonious. A second daughter had been born on April 6, 1927, and named Laura for his older sister, Laura Lea Robertson, and a son was born on November 3, 1928, and named Overton for the colonel's father and brother. With the family growing, a larger home was needed, and Lea proposed to build on his LeaMead farm. However, Mrs. Lea, realizing it would be a problem getting children to school and domestic help to and from the streetcar line on Belle Meade Boulevard, did not want to live that far out in the country. After looking at several houses, they agreed on Boxwood which they purchased from W.G. Simmons. On the corner of Jackson Boulevard and Warner Place, the oblong, three-story, white, clapboard house was centered on a large lawn shaded by stately maples and tall oaks.

Lea enjoyed having friends around him. The Starnes—Alice, Cookie, and their daughter Mary—spent nearly every weekend at Boxwood, and Luke and Percy were encouraged to bring their friends home. Guests were included in whatever the family was doing and thereby put completely at ease. Lea often carried on business discussions into the evening, and when people came from out of town to see him, they frequently joined the family for dinner. Nothing alcoholic was ever served; *The Tennessean* had led the fight for prohibition, and Luke Lea lived as he had voted. Two or three times a month Bob Claggett came from Knoxville to see the colonel and would frequently stay overnight, as would George Morris, vice-president of the *Commercial Appeal.*

Late one afternoon Lea telephoned home he had invited about 25 people for dinner. The throng of unexpected company did not seem to worry Miss Percie. She understood that many of the gentlemen were from out of town, and it would facilitate matters if the discussion could be continued in the relaxed atmosphere of their home. Having a good-size family, frequent company and a staff of seven, she ran the kind of household where one or two extras for dinner at the last minute made no difference, but the meal planned for that evening could not be stretched that far. However, enough ham and eggs were somehow rustled up and everyone not only seemed to get enough to eat, but also to have a good time.[5]

Colonel Lea had no firm routine—except going to the office daily—his schedule being determined by the demands of that day. He had boundless energy and required little sleep. Often he would write late into the night, page after page with a dull pencil in his almost illegible scrawl. Sometimes he would arise early and work several hours at home before going in to the office. In good weather he and Miss Percie enjoyed riding horseback before breakfast. In winter, when he could manage it, he would leave the office early so they could ride in the afternoon. This would sometimes necessitate his going back to the office at night to sign his mail or check on some matter. Usually Miss Percie would drive him, and frequently she would go in to town and have lunch with him. Sometimes she would sit in on *Tennessean* staff meetings simply because she happened to be there.

At those meetings everyone had the opportunity to express his opinion, but it was Lea who made the final decision. It was extremely hard for him to delegate authority because he liked to be in the middle of each phase of every operation. Consequently, more decisions on a minor level were left up to him than he had time to consider thoroughly. Moreover, he had a dislike for detail, so much was left hanging.

As rapidly as profits were realized from *The Tennessean* and the myriad other enterprises with which Lea was connected, they were reinvested in other ventures. If making money was all that he wanted to do, he would have secured the large fortune he amassed. Perhaps because his family had always had wealth, money to him was a means by which to acquire more property, more stock, more newspapers. Success bred upon success. The bubble grew ever bigger as he plunged ever deeper into a growing number of business ventures.

Able to juggle numerous enterprises simultaneously, overextension was Luke Lea's Achilles' heel. To his great detriment he suffered also from myopic vision in that he would not see defects in people or in situations that he did not want to see. He disliked having his judgment questioned, and he had such supreme faith in himself that he seldom took advice. He relied on Reese Amis and Nuch Brown more than anybody else except Luke, Jr.[6] Moreover, he was a past master at not discussing a subject on which he did not wish to converse. He would listen courteously, then go right ahead, usually with a half smile, and do exactly as he had planned.[7]

Lea had realized for some time he needed more space and more privacy, so early in 1929 he moved his private offices to the second floor of the McGavock Building directly across the alley on Fourth Avenue from the newspaper. A few months later, Ted Hagerty, at the age of 23, went to work as an under-secretary for the colonel.[8] From that day on, her life was to be indissolubly linked with the Leas. As Irish as her name and a devout Roman Catholic, she was fascinated with the newspaper and loved the excitement that always surrounded the colonel. Quickly she moved up to be his private secretary, and before long she was entrusted with preparing financial statements for Lea's various corporations. Quite easily she fit into life at Boxwood, where she was a frequent overnight guest. She developed a genuine affection for each member of the household and they became devoted to her, fondly regarding her as almost family.

Shortly after the death of Senator L.D. Tyson, Governor Horton appointed Luke Lea to the Senate on August 31, 1929, to fill his unexpired term. Telegrams and telephone calls poured in congratulating the colonel on his appointment and urging him to accept this unsought honor.

Lea, in what was said to be without precedent in Tennessee, declined on September 1 to accept the appointment. His reasons for refusal he thus stated to Governor Horton:

The confidence expressed by your appointment of me to the vacancy caused by the death of the late Senator Tyson is deeply and genuinely appreciated....

Acceptance of public office is warranted by the conviction that it is the best avenue to serve.

In my case I am convinced that office-holding does not afford the greatest opportunity for civic work. I believe I can be of more service to Tennessee, working in the ranks as a private citizen in the great task that lies before the forward looking men and women of our state than by holding any office, even as exalted an office as United States Senator....[9]

Luke Lea's declining the Senate appointment has been variously described as the high-water mark of his prestige and the greatest mistake of his life. His not accepting that honor tended to confirm his often repeated assertion that his interest was indeed the advancement of the state rather than his own political fortunes.[10] Another reason he did not accept the appointment was that he could not afford to, either financially or time-wise, because the host of far-flung enterprises in which he was deeply involved demanded all his energies.

Those who considered his decision a tragic error believed that had he accepted the appointment he could have remained in the Senate the rest of his life, not only rendering great service to his state and to his country, but also avoiding the debacle that soon was to engulf him.

Chapter Eleven
The Bubble Bursts

The Central Bank and Trust Company
A few days after Luke Lea declined the appointment to the United States Senate, Wallace B. Davis, president of the Central Bank and Trust Company in Asheville, North Carolina,[1] sent P.M. Burdette, a former Tennessee newspaper publisher and later owner of the *Asheville Times*, to Nashville to interest Lea in buying the Asheville paper. Lea was not interested at the quoted price of $600,000. However, Burdette, portraying Davis as the most influential man in western North Carolina, arranged for Lea, when he would be in Washington the latter part of the month, to meet him.

The two men met at the Mayflower Hotel on Monday, September 23, 1929. Davis stated the *Asheville Times* was completely pledged to secure its indebtedness to the bank and must be sold. Lea reiterated he was not interested at $600,000. A few days later, Davis by telephone requested Lea to stop by Asheville en route home and intimated they could come to an agreement on the price of the *Times*. At that meeting Davis made only a slight reduction in its price but was most eager to secure, through Lea, an entree to Rogers Caldwell. Lea agreed to ascertain if Caldwell were interested in including the Central in his expanding banking operations.

The small, conservatively managed Central Bank and Trust Company, founded by Davis, overflowed with public deposits during Asheville's boom of the mid-1920s as had the city's other banks. Then Asheville's boom suddenly collapsed in the spring of 1928 as the market for its real estate abruptly ceased to exist. On

189

June 28 of that year bank examiners condemned as worthless more than $3 million of loans in the Central Bank. Davis made no attempt at concealment.

The Corporation Commission, which controlled state banks, after analyzing its examiner's report, instructed Davis to try to keep the bank open until Asheville's real estate regained its true value, making the bank solvent again. Therefore, the Central Bank, complying with that instruction, continued to receive and to solicit public deposits and to extend lines of credit already condemned by the examiners as worthless.

Caldwell was interested in the possibility of including the Central Bank in the Caldwell chain. A conference was scheduled the weekend of October 12, 1929. Also present were Edward Potter, Jr., president of the Potter banks in Nashville and a member of the group that had reorganized the Union Planters Bank and Trust Company in Memphis; and W.E. Norvell, attorney for Lea, Potter's banking interests, and Caldwell and Company. Within a week, a contract giving the Potter-Caldwell syndicate the right to reorganize the Central Bank was signed.

McCubin, Goodrich and Company and Otis and Company had tentatively agreed to underwrite the sale of stock in the reorganized bank. Representatives of the groups involved had an appointment to meet in New York on October 29, 1929, the fateful day of the stock market crash. Negotiations collapsed.

Before the sun set on October 29, the biggest boom this country had ever known was ended. The business cycle downswing, begun several months previously, was intensified by the Wall Street crash, the effects of which although all-encompassing, were not immediately felt throughout the country. However, as money became increasingly tighter and economic conditions continued to worsen attempts were made with a growing sense of urgency to strengthen financial positions, to make holdings more liquid.

Wallace Davis endeavored during the winter and spring of 1930 to keep alive his association with Luke Lea and through him with Rogers Caldwell. Frequently Davis wrote requesting interviews with Lea—the bait always being the sale of the *Asheville Times*. When Caldwell's affairs had progressed to the point that the reorganization of the Central, if it could be accomplished on a sound basis, was feasible, he asked Lea to advise Davis of that fact. Lea scheduled a meeting early in May 1930 in Knoxville.

That evening Lea had appointments with J. Will Taylor, congressman from that district, and J.B. Ramsey, president of the Holston-Union National Bank in which Lea was a large stockholder, as well as with Wallace Davis. While waiting to see Lea in the reception room of his hotel suite, Ramsey and Davis introduced themselves, and the first transaction between those Tennessee and North Carolina banking interests was begun.

Davis' bank did much business with the City National Bank of Knoxville, Ramsey's competitor. While they waited to see Lea, Davis agreed to transfer his Knoxville account, with a balance averaging approximately $100,000, to the Holston Union, and Ramsey gave to the Central Bank a $100,000 line of credit at the Holston.

This agreement between Davis and Ramsey was a customary banking practice, and Luke Lea was not a party to the transaction.

Shortly thereafter Wallace Davis arranged for the Central Bank to borrow $300,000 from the Holston-Union.[2] The Central received $100,000 in cash and a $200,000 note of the Union Trust Company, in which Lea was a large stockholder. On that note the Central later secured additional deposits from the city of Asheville.

The next transaction between the Asheville bank and a Tennessee firm was the sale in the summer of 1930 by Nashville's Liberty Bank and Trust Company of a $50,000 note of Lea's Belle Meade Company to the Central Bank. The note, secured by Belle Meade Company's first mortgage bonds, was also used by the Central Bank to obtain additional city of Asheville funds amounting to $50,000.

Lea did not know that the Central Bank was financing itself through the sale of revenue notes issued by the city of Asheville and thereby securing the cash necessary to stay afloat. That information came to the surface only after the bank failed. The Central's financial statements showed that the bank had that amount of cash or notes on hand, and Lea accepted the condition of the bank to be as it was reflected in its published statement in the Asheville newspapers.[3]

As funds became needed during the summer of 1930 by various Lea interests, the Central Bank was asked to make the necessary loans, which the bank considered good business.

The Central was unable in July to pay its notes and to repurchase its securities that it had sold in Tennessee. Instead additional cash was needed. Believing Davis' reorganization plans sound, and already deeply involved with the bank, the Tennessee interests with which Lea was connected considered their best option was to renew the Central's notes and to render it further accommodation. Hence, the Memphis *Commercial Appeal* and the *Knoxville Journal* deposited $100,000 in the bank the latter part of July.

The financial situation by the first of August had become alarming. Money daily became tighter as credit continued to contract and depositor confidence weaken. The Tennessee interests that had become heavy creditors of the Central Bank that summer attempted to tide over their affairs until the return of normal conditions. Should the Central Bank fail indebted to the Holston-Union National Bank for over $600,000, it would undoubtedly cause a run on the Holston-Union. If the Holston-Union should close, Caldwell and Company would be affected because of Caldwell's close connection with the Knoxville bank. If Caldwell and Company, the largest investment banking house in the South, should close, it would pull down with it the Caldwell associated banks.

As Lea was a large stockholder in the Holston-Union, his assistance to the Central was not altruistic but was continued for self-protection. Hence, his daily average credit balance and that of the *Commercial Appeal* and the *Knoxville Journal* during August continued to be large.

On several days in the late summer and early fall of 1930, the Central came perilously close to being unable to meet its clearings, but neither Lea nor its other Tennessee creditors were informed of the extreme gravity of the bank's condition. Davis requested from Lea extra deposits on Saturday, August 30, the last business day before Labor Day. Even though heavy demands upon the *Commercial Appeal* and the *Knoxville Journal* were due September 1, Lea wired $150,000 to the Central through the Federal Reserve Bank. Davis arrived in Nashville on Labor Day to ask first Lea and then Rogers Caldwell for an additional accommodation of $300,000. On the next day, the bank had to pay large maturities to the city of Asheville, and until those notes were paid, the bank could not receive renewals from the city. Lea wired $160,000 to the bank, and Caldwell wired $130,000. Without that financial assistance on August 30 and September 2, 1930, the Central Bank, its records indicate, could not have met its clearings on those days and would have closed. At the end of September, Davis went again to Nashville and arranged to secure temporary deposits of approximately $300,000 from Lea to be made the first part of October.

Lea's four deposits on August 30, September 2, October 10, and October 11, totaling more than $600,000 enabled the Central Bank to remain open and gave its officers additional time to try to effect a reorganization. Ironically, it was on these transactions that Lea would be indicted the following year for defrauding the bank.

The condition of the Central becoming ever more acute, it issued during October approximately $781,000 worth of cashier's checks and drafts, which it sent to Lea in a desperate effort to attempt through him to raise much needed funds for the bank. Sometimes those checks and drafts were charged directly to Lea's account, thereby causing it to be greatly overdrawn. Often made payable in blank, most were delivered personally by employees of the bank to Lea in Nashville. Lea would then deposit them and wire the proceeds to the Central Bank (McFerrin, *Caldwell and Company* 158).

Lea had become increasingly aware of its desperate condition, but up until the day the Central Bank failed, he thought it was going to succeed in its reorganization. Not until later, however, would he learn that the bank examiners of North Carolina had found the Central to be in a precarious, if not insolvent, condition two years before he had any transactions with it, and that the bank had continued in operation with the knowledge and consent of the Corporation Commission.

When the Central Bank closed its doors on November 20, 1930, the loan accounts between it and the Lea interests practically balanced.[4] The assistance that he rendered the Central Bank by enabling it to remain open on at least four days of crisis, however, could never be balanced in any account. Moreover, the daily credit balance the Central had in addition to the accommodation it was rendered by the Lea interests is not reflected in any statement. During the last three weeks of August 1930, Lea's balance with the Central averaged nearly $46,000, and for the month of October it averaged a little more than $60,000.[5] Not only did Lea lend his money and his credit to the Central Bank, furnish it with cash with which to pay its checks on at least four different days, and enable it to secure nearly $500,000 of new money on notes of his companies, but he also accounted to the penny for every cashier's check, New York draft, certificate of deposit, and other securities sent to him to raise money for the Central. In addition, every note or obligation of his or any of his companies that found its way into the Central at any time did so with the approval, expressed in the minutes, of the discount committee, of the executive and examining committees, and finally the board of directors of the Central Bank.

The statement that Luke Lea defrauded the Central Bank of $1,375,000 was published in the press so often that the charge came to be generally believed. However, the bank could not have been defrauded of that sum in 1930—the only year Lea had any transactions with it—for the simple and later obvious reason that throughout that year the Central never had $1,375,000 or any substantial amount in cash of which to be defrauded.

The Bank of Tennessee

Early in November 1930, James E. Caldwell, president of the Fourth and First National Bank in Nashville and father of Rogers Caldwell, telephoned Luke Lea to request a conference.[6] As the two men sat facing each other, Caldwell asked what, in the colonel's opinion, would be the effect if Caldwell and Company failed.

Lea was much surprised at the question. In an effort to strengthen Caldwell and Company at the end of May 1930, Rogers Caldwell had negotiated a merger of that company with Banco-Kentucky, a holding company that controlled the National Bank of Kentucky at Louisville (McFerrin, *Caldwell and Company* 134).

Lea asked what the problem was. James E. Caldwell replied that the Bank of Tennessee, which was completely owned by Caldwell and Company, did not have the cash to meet expected withdrawals by the state and various municipalities. Lea asked how much money was needed to keep the Bank of Tennessee open. James E. Caldwell replied, $4 million.

Lea then stated that in his opinion if Caldwell and Company and the Bank of Tennessee failed, the Fourth and First National Bank would fail too. Caldwell disagreed. He believed the Fourth and First was in such a strong position that it could ride out the failure of Caldwell and Company. He stated that even though Rogers was his son, he could not lend that company or the Bank of Tennessee any more money. However, he thought that James B. Brown, president of both Banco-Kentucky and the National Bank of Kentucky, could deposit the needed $4 million in the Bank of Tennessee and thereby save that institution and Caldwell and Company. James E. Caldwell requested Lea to be the intermediary, and he agreed.

The colonel walked back to his office and asked his son, Luke, Jr., to drive him to Louisville right away. Lea had an extended conference late that afternoon alone with Brown. The colonel explained the situation in detail, and Brown agreed to make the desperately needed deposit.

The following day, James E. Caldwell reported to Lea that the promised deposit had not been received and requested the colonel to call Brown at once. Lea acquiesced and told Brown that unless the deposit was forthcoming, the Bank of Tennessee would unquestionably fail. Thereupon, Brown asked Lea to return to Louisville for another meeting early the next morning.

In that conference Brown said he had come to the conclusion that James E. Caldwell's Fourth and First Bank should deposit the funds necessary to tide over the Bank of Tennessee. Lea replied that the Fourth and First was not in a position to do so and that only Brown could save the situation. He further stated that if the Bank of Tennessee and Caldwell and Company failed, the National Bank of Kentucky would also fail. Brown disagreed. In spite of the merger of Banco-Kentucky with Caldwell and Company, he thought his bank was in a strong enough position to withstand the failure of Caldwell and Company. At length, however, Brown realized the desperateness of the situation, but could not make the vital loan until he obtained the approval of his board of directors the following morning.

Late that night after the colonel had driven back to Nashville, in telling Mrs. Lea about the conference, he said in a somber tone,

If the banks fail, my political enemies who have been on the outside ever since shortly after I came back from France in 1919 and are hungry for power, will do everything they can to get rid of me. There is even a possibility they will try to have me indicted regarding Governor Horton's campaign expenses. They will want him out of the way, too.[7]

At that time a state law prohibited a gubernatorial candidate from spending more than $10,000 on his campaign. While the letter of the law was not violated, its intent was often circumvented by friends making contributions without the candidate's knowledge.

The next morning the board of directors of the Bank of Kentucky refused to make the loan. The crisis had arrived. Later Brown would send some notes to Nashville, but by that time the notes were of no help.

Caldwell and Company

Rogers Caldwell's efforts early in November 1930 to put Caldwell and Company in a more sound position through the sale of its controlling stock of Inter-Southern Life Insurance Company fell through. Then it became generally known how dependent Caldwell and Company was upon the National Bank of Kentucky (McFerrin, *Caldwell and Company* 176).

Although the investigation by the Nashville Clearing House had found the condition of Caldwell and Company sound, and its loans in Nashville banks well secured, because of the unusual financial conditions nationwide, it was difficult to dispose of the company's securities at a fair price. With the consent of Caldwell and Company, the clearing house therefore appointed Nashville business leaders Paul M. Davis, C.A. Craig, and T.D. Webb to conduct the affairs of the company and to conserve and protect the interests of its creditors (McFerrin, *Caldwell and Company* 177).

The committee on November 5 requested state superintendent of banks D.D. Robertson to make an immediate examination of the Bank of Tennessee. The examination indicated that it was not advisable for that bank to continue operation. A petition was filed in chancery court on Friday, November 7, asking for liquidation of its affairs. Following the granting of that petition, the superintendent of banks, as then provided by law, was named receiver for the bank. Funds of the state of Tennessee on deposit in that bank when it closed were estimated by Attorney General L.D. Smith at "something like $3 million" (*The Nashville Tennessean* 9 November 1930).

No institution was an island unto itself. When a bank closed its doors, a chain reaction was set in motion, the end of which no one could foresee. Conferences lasted long into the night as feverish efforts were made to try to reorganize in a last attempt to salvage whatever was possible. The financial situation changed radically each day.

Prior to the closing of the Bank of Tennessee, the Fourth and First National Bank had been negotiating to take over the American National Bank. However, the failure of the Bank of Tennessee so weakened the Fourth and First, that within a week it was absorbed by the American.

The condition of Caldwell and Company had deteriorated to the point that receivership was inevitable. Preferring voluntary receivership, the company had one of its bond buyers file on November 13 in the federal district court at Nashville a bill asking for the appointment of a receiver (McFerrin, *Caldwell and Company* 180). Nashville attorney Lee Douglas was then appointed receiver and Caldwell and Company ceased to exist. Sending shock waves throughout the entire South, its collapse brought down many banks and insurance companies and financial losses to persons who had invested in its securities.

The Liberty Bank and Trust Company
and Other Nashville Banks

That same day, the Liberty Bank and Trust Company did not open its doors. It went into voluntary liquidation by order of its board of directors.

R.E. Donnell, president of the bank, stated that action had been taken because of heavy withdrawals, but that bank officers believed that the institution was solvent and with careful management the depositors would be paid in full. The bank's affairs were turned over to the state superintendent of banks for liquidation (*The Nashville Tennessean* 14 November 1930).

Donnell personally supervised the work in an effort to have the bank reopened. His friends believed that a week of that herculean task broke his spirit, which in turn caused him to commit suicide.

Two weeks previously when Lea had heard there was a run on the Liberty Bank, in which he was a large stockholder but was never an officer nor a director,[8] he had instructed E.P. Charlet, secretary-treasurer of the Tennessee Publishing Company, to deposit immediately a check for $20,000 in the bank. Lea hoped if people who were withdrawing their money saw that somebody had the faith to make a deposit of that amount, perhaps it would stop the run. After Charlet made the deposit, he had stood in the bank and watched the run continue. Lea's deposit had not lasted 15 minutes.[9]

The raging financial storm continued to take its toll. *The Tennessean* announced Saturday morning, November 15, that Commerce Union Bank, of which Edward Potter, Jr., served as president, had taken over the Tennessee Hermitage National Bank. This action was taken at the insistence of local bankers after a conference to consider a run Friday on the Tennessee Heritage.

The Holston-Union National Bank

Trying every way possible to keep his bank open, J.B. Ramsey made several trips to Nashville during the late summer and autumn of 1930 to confer with Luke Lea and Rogers Caldwell, both of whom were large stockholders. After Caldwell's difficulties became known, Tennessee's banking department began withdrawing state deposits from banks in which he had an interest. Several large companies also began withdrawing by wire their deposits—White Truck wanted to withdraw $1 million at one time.

At a meeting called by Ramsey of the presidents of all Knoxville banks, plus the state examiners, he stated that if they came to his rescue, they would also be saving their own banks. They refused, however, to put up the money necessary to keep the Holston-Union open so Ramsey voluntarily closed his bank on November 30 without it ever having had a run.

In Knoxville, as elsewhere across the country, it was demanded that financiers responsible for the debacle be indicted. It ceased to be a novelty for a bank president to commit suicide. The *News-Sentinel*, the competitor of the *Knoxville Journal*, sent a reporter to see Ramsey with the offer to make him a hero if he would give evidence sufficient to indict Luke Lea.[10]

Kentucky Banks

In the late summer of 1930, E.W. Bryan of Central City, Kentucky, asked Lea to help facilitate a merger of the First Bank and Trust Company and the City Bank and Trust Company of Hopkinsville along the lines of the merger of the Manhattan Savings and Union Planters Bank in Memphis and the Holston

National and Union National Bank of Knoxville.[11] Bryan stated a considerable amount of money could be made from the merger and that consolidation would strengthen both institutions.

Interested in the merger of the Kentucky banks as an investment, Lea was instrumental in successfully concluding their consolidation into the First City Bank and Trust Company of Hopkinsville. Additional capital was put into that institution by the issuance of its stock together with the stock that was purchased to enable the banks to be merged.

Bryan was of the opinion in October 1930 that several other small banks in Kentucky could be acquired. He and R.E. Donnell, president of the Liberty Bank in Nashville and a party in the merger of the First City Bank and Trust Company of Hopkinsville, wrote a letter outlining the situation to Wallace B. Davis, president of the Central Bank and Trust Company. Since neither of them knew Davis personally, they requested Luke Lea, Jr., to sign the letter.[12] Due probably to lack of judgment because of his youth, he complied. Written October 9, 1930, it stated that a Mr. Reynolds, who owned the controlling interest in two banks in Greenville and one in Central City, wished to retire. The letter concluded:

> I believe we could pay a 300 percent cash dividend at Greenville and could buy control of the bank with an investment of $60,000, and with nearly $1,000,000 in bonds on hand we could sell a good part of them and substitute our issues instead. (McFerrin, *Caldwell and Company* 79)

Even though written by Bryan and Donnell concerning the possibility of the merger of Kentucky banks that never occurred, that letter would be read the following year at the trial of the Leas and Davis in connection with the failure of the Central Bank.

After the failure of Caldwell and Company and the merger of the Fourth and First National Bank with the American National Bank in November 1930, the officers of the First City Bank and Trust Company of Hopkinsville went to Nashville and stated to Colonel Lea that unless he gave them the stock he had in that bank for the amount the stock was pledged, they would not open the bank the next morning.[13] Not wanting the bank to fail, he gave them the stock for that amount, thereby wiping out any profit he stood to make from the merger.

The whole country soon became embroiled in economic chaos. A fight for survival ensued. Little cash was available. Lines of credit could no longer be extended. The over-expanded economy collapsed like a balloon that had been pricked. Fifty to 60 banks closed every week. More than 500 failed in one month. In the aftermath of the collapse of financial institutions, depression spread over the whole United States with a paralyzing weight that crushed beneath it many businesses and individuals.

Chapter Twelve
Ensnared

The financial crisis had political overtones in Tennessee as it did throughout the United States. The anti-Lea faction was quick to recognize in the crash their chance to destroy the colonel's influence and bombarded him with litigations. This coalition was masterminded by, he believed, Paul M. Davis, president of the American Bank, with the legal expertise furnished by K.T. McConnico, a prominent leader in the Nashville machine, who Lea believed had aspirations to become the boss of Tennessee, but whose ambitions had been thwarted by election of the candidates for governor supported by Lea.[1]

Lea came to believe that Davis had harbored deep resentment toward him since the success of the prohibition movement had forced Davis' in-laws, the Shwabs, out of the whiskey business in Tennessee. The bitterness aroused by Carmack's murder in 1908 had intensified this feeling, because of Lea's connection with Carmack and Davis' sympathies with the Coopers by whom Carmack was killed. Another factor was rivalry in the newspaper field. In 1912 Davis became secretary-treasurer of a newly established Nashville daily, the *Nashville Democrat,* which had ceased publication in 1913. Furthermore, Davis and the Caldwells were competitors in the banking field, and because of the friendly relations between Lea and the Caldwells, this rivalry was also directed toward the colonel.

Even though the American National Bank had absorbed the Fourth and First, there was talk that it remained in a precarious, if not insolvent, condition. In November 1930, Davis ordered news of a lawsuit damaging to him and his bank withheld from publication in the Nashville newspapers. He succeeded in keeping the story out of the *Banner*, which was reported to be heavily in debt to his bank, but he failed to prevent it from being published in *The Tennessean*.² It was at that point, Lea believed, that Davis determined to try to destroy him and to impeach Henry Horton as governor of Tennessee. With Lea out of the way, Davis would be able to suppress adverse news, and with an ally in the governor's chair, he would be able to secure badly needed state deposits for his bank.

Later that month Lea received word, reputedly from Davis, that if *The Tennessean* henceforth were operated on a basis friendly to Davis and his institutions, and if he were furnished the information necessary to impeach Horton for having spent more than the legal limit of $10,000 in his campaign for governor, *The Tennessean* would be left alone.³ Lea naturally rejected that proposition.

The *Banner*, circumspect in its reporting while the financial storm raged and the situation was in flux, began running on November 20, 1930, publicity concerning Caldwell and Company or Luke Lea almost daily on page one. *The Banner* charged on November 26 that the "Lea-Caldwell banks" had been favored by the state in its deposits. The Bank of Tennessee and the Holston-Union National Bank of Knoxville were described as magnets that had attracted great sums of highway funds. The cry arose that everything that had gone wrong in Tennessee was the fault of what was termed the "Lea-Horton-Caldwell machine." To many persons, "Lea-and-Caldwell" became one word and was synonymous with questionable financial practices and the loss in failed banks of public and private funds.

Later after the bitterness of that era had subsided, it would be difficult to comprehend the intensity of the fight launched against Luke Lea. The financial affairs of companies in which he was interested and his transactions with defunct banks, particularly the Central in Asheville, the Holston-Union in Knoxville, and the Liberty Bank in Nashville, were subjected to hostile scrutiny. Deposits of state funds in the Holston-Union and in Caldwell controlled banks were investigated apparently in an endeavor to impeach Horton and to make Lea and Caldwell criminally liable for the loss of the taxpayer's money.

Three lawsuits, instigated Lea surmised at the behest of Paul Davis, were filed on December 10, 1930. One was an attempt to place the Tennessee Publishing Company in the hands of a receiver; another was an effort to place Southern Publishers in receivership; and the third was an action to recover approximately $166,000 that Lea was alleged to have gotten from the Liberty Bank and Trust Company by irregular methods, which suit was never brought to trial.

The lawsuit asking a receiver for the Tennessee Publishing Company, publisher of *The Nashville Tennessean* and *The Evening Tennessean*, filed by the Minnesota and Ontario Paper Company, charged that the publishing company owed more than $94,000 on past due bills and more than $17,000 on bills immediately due. Although the assets of the Tennessee Publishing Company were believed to exceed its liabilities, many creditors were pressing for payment. Unless a receiver were appointed, the bill concluded, suits most likely would be filed and publication of the paper might be suspended with disastrous results to all creditors (*The Nashville Tennessean* 11 December 1930).

The other lawsuit filed December 10, 1930, requested a receiver for Southern Publishers, the holding company that owned the Memphis *Commercial Appeal* and the *Knoxville Journal*. When Southern Publishers was organized to purchase the *Commercial Appeal*, 50 percent of the stock was issued to Lea and the other 50 percent to Caldwell and Company. According to the colonel, he and Rogers Caldwell had a verbal agreement that neither would dispose of his half without first giving the other an opportunity to buy that interest.

Several weeks previous to the filing of that lawsuit Frank Rice, one of Ed Crump's most trusted lieutenants, had appeared unexpectedly at the Lea home. Coming right to the point, Rice said:

Mr. Crump has learned that Rogers Caldwell has put up his half interest in the *Commercial Appeal*, and thought you might be hard up for ready cash, so he sent me to Nashville to give you this.[4]

Crump's emissary reached into his inside coat pocket, took out an envelope, and handed it to Lea. The silence in the room was broken only by the ticking of the mantel clock as Lea took the envelope. As the colonel's eyes quickly ran over the enclosed cashier's check, the visitor said: "Mr. Crump knows you will want to buy Caldwell's interest in Southern Publishers and hopes $50,000 will be of help toward that end."

A few seconds passed as Lea continued to stare at the check in astonishment. Then he handed it back without a word.

Why had not Rogers let him know that he was going to have to pledge his half, Lea mused. With a little warning, he probably could have raised the money necessary to buy Caldwell's stock. Perhaps he still could, but once it became generally known that Caldwell no longer had his interest Lea had no doubt that his political enemies would try to keep him from gaining control of the remaining 50 percent of Southern Publishers stock. His train of thought was interrupted by Rice reiterating that no strings were attached to Crump's check. However, accepting it was completely out of the question to Lea. Were he to do so, he would in the future be beholden to Crump. It would be a sell-out.

Amendments to bills in both the Tennessee Publishing Company and Southern Publishers receivership suits were filed in chancery court on December 16. Chancellor James B. Newman decreed that the Tennessee Publishing Company suit would be heard first. The day after he had taken it under advisement, the North Carolina Corporation Commission, in charge of the assets of the defunct Central Bank and Trust Company, together with the city of Asheville filed an intervening petition seeking to be made a party in the suit.

Shortly before the Central Bank closed, November 30, 1930, Wallace Davis demanded that the colonel pay all of his obligations held by the Asheville bank. Davis' Asheville attorneys associated Nashville attorney K.T. McConnico with them for the collection of these notes. It was in this way that Lea's political opponents in Tennessee learned that he had any obligations with the Central Bank.[5]

Lea replied that if the Central Bank redeemed its obligations to his interests, then he would make arrangements to pay in an orderly way his obligations to the bank. Before arrangements either to offset or to pay any of its obligations to Lea's interests had been made, the Central Bank and Trust Company closed.

The only obligation of the publishing company to the Corporation Commission of North Carolina was a $6,000 unsecured note, which the commission held as an asset of the defunct Central Bank and Trust Company. Lea wished to pay into the court $6,000 with interest plus attorney's fee of ten percent. Despite this tender, McConnico, as representative of the defunct Central Bank, had joined in the effort to put Lea's main newspaper property in the hands of a receiver on this $6,000 note, even though receivership would destroy the value of the Tennessee Publishing Company bonds, $60,000 of which were held as collateral by the Central Bank.[6] Lea then employed an Asheville law firm to work out a settlement which was tentatively agreed to by the Corporation Commission. However, it failed to be accepted, so Lea reasoned that his political opponents in Tennessee did not want a settlement made.

The receivership suit against the Tennessee Publishing Company was denied on December 23. In a two-column box on page one of *The Nashville Tennessean*, three days later, the Leas expressed their gratification and pledged to continue to publish all the news, favorable or unfavorable. A Lea relative was to complain in the future that from the headlines it was hard to tell which local newspaper was published by the colonel and which paper was bitterly opposed to him.

The receivership suit filed against Southern Publishers by M. & O. Paper Company, the Nashville Trust Company, and D.D. Robertson, receiver for the Bank of Tennessee, charged Luke Lea and Rogers Caldwell, owners of Southern Publishers, with conversion and misuse of funds of the *Commercial Appeal* (*The Nashville Tennessean* 11 December 1930). As receiver for the Bank of Tennessee, Robertson held for the benefit of creditors of that defunct bank 500 shares or one-half of the capital stock of

Southern Publishers, Inc., pledged to that bank by Rogers Caldwell.

Before the suit was heard, D.A. Fisher, Inc., a Memphis insurance firm, requested receivership of the Appeal newspapers. The petition stated that although the papers were solvent, the Nashville lawsuits had so impaired the credit of Southern Publishers that publication of the papers might be jeopardized. The petition was granted.

The same day Knoxville concerns S.B. Newman & Company, M.B. Flenniken & Company, and Pryor Brown Transfer Company filed a receivership suit against the Knoxville Journal, Inc., owner and publisher of the *Knoxville Journal*. That petition, too, was granted (*The Nashville Tennessean* 13 December 1930). After lengthy charges and denials, Chancellor Newman granted the receivership of Southern Publishers on December 23. He stated that the holding company no longer had a function since both the Memphis *Commercial Appeal* and the *Knoxville Journal* were in the hands of receivers; and also that it had no source of income but would continue to incur an annual debt of $50,000 for officers' salaries unless the receivership was granted (*The Nashville Tennessean* 24 December 1930).

Soon after receivership of the Tennessee Publishing Company had been denied, counsel for the Minnesota and Ontario Paper Company announced their intention of making another application for receivership. Therefore, they asked to take a discovery deposition of E.P. Charlet, secretary-treasurer of the Tennessee Publishing Company. Lea considered this proceeding a fishing expedition. In addition to the avowed purpose of seeking information about the solvency of the newspapers, he thought attorneys for the M. & O. Paper Company, at the urging of Paul Davis,[7] hoped to uncover evidence of transactions that had benefitted any of the companies with which he was affiliated or that had contributed to Governor Horton's campaign. Therefore, Lea tried to prevent counsel for M. & O. from getting into any matters that did not pertain to *The Tennessean*.

Charlet testified that he knew of no suits likely to be brought against the company; there was no judgment against the company; no salaries were in arrears; since the filing of the suit two payrolls had been met fully and promptly; the publishing company owed Lea more than the advances made to him; certain advertisers had refused payment because of the poor quality of some of the paper furnished by M. & O.; through agreement between the publishing company and its creditors, payment of certain accounts had been postponed, thereby rendering its assets greater than its liabilities (*Nashville Banner* 29 January 1931).

That spring while Charlet's deposition was being taken, the colonel and Luke, Jr., went to Chicago for a conference with E. W. Bakus, former president of the M. & O. Paper Company and one of the three receivers appointed after it went into receivership on February 28. The Leas worked out with Bakus the identical agreement that the paper company had rejected prior to bringing suit the preceding December. The case was then dropped, indicating that the litigation, as the colonel had maintained, had been politically motivated.

The American National Bank held $210,000 of the Tennessee Publishing Company's debenture bonds, which were among the assets of the Fourth and First American National Bank when those two banks merged in November 1930. The Canal Bank and Trust Company of New Orleans had a $200,000 note of Lea's secured by $250,000 par value debenture bonds of the Tennessee Publishing Company. No bondholder could bring action except for default. Nevertheless, shortly after the adjournment of the Tennessee legislature in July 1931, an attempt, instigated Lea was informed by the American National Bank, had been made to get the bondholders in united action to file suit seeking receivership.[8]

Although camouflaged as an attempt to protect the property, the underlying purpose of this effort to place the Tennessee Publishing Company in receivership, Lea surmised, was to destroy the property, so that the bondholders could take possession of *The Tennessean* papers.[9] At once Lea attempted to work out with the bondholders an agreement for the protection of the Tennessee Publishing Company. Although these negotiations were suspended when the Leas went to North Carolina to stand trial the following month, Lea secured what he considered a positive agreement with Davis that no action would be taken during that period toward filing a receivership suit.[10] In return Lea pledged that during that time no action harmful to the bondholders' interest would be taken, and that no statement detrimental to the American National Bank concerning its condition would be published by *The Tennessean*.

Immediately after the bank closures Lea had begun to try to work out an orderly payment of his debts, necessarily extending over a period of time. Usually overextended, he was especially vulnerable to the depressed economic conditions. He owned few properties outright and mortgage bonds of one were pledged on the purchase of another. Collateral securing his obligations, although adequate at the time and approved as such by the institution to which it was pledged, had decreased in value. Often when he was unable to pay his notes when they fell due, his creditors sued for nonpayment and demanded his collateral be sold at deflated prices, thereby stripping him of much property.

LeaMead farm was lost through foreclosure proceedings early in 1931 because Lea considered other matters more pressing than retaining the farm. The need for cash became so acute so quickly that on December 5, 1930, he had to assign the loan value on two policies he had with Kansas City Life Insurance Company to Commerce Union Bank.

The economy continued to worsen. As interrelated as were Lea's multiple interests, refinancing any property was contingent upon securing the agreement of several parties. Every time one situation would be almost worked out, negotiations in another would break down. In order to devote his entire energies to trying to work out his own affairs, Lea resigned from the many boards on which he served. He also realized that he had become controversial, and he in no way wanted to embarrass his friends or be where he was not welcome. Even though he had given most of the land for the club and the golf course, his resignation from Belle Meade Country Club was accepted.

In the late spring of 1931, Mrs. Edward Ward Carmack insisted that Lea buy the stock in the Tennessee Publishing Company owned by her husband who had been editor of *The Tennessean* at the time of his death. The par value of the stock was $150,000, but it was not worth nearly that much in the depressed market. To avoid the suit she threatened to bring if the stock were not purchased, an arrangement was worked out. Several weeks elapsed, however, before Mrs. Carmack and her son notified Lea that they wanted him to carry out the proposed agreement. By that time he was unable to do so. Should he agree to buy the stock or exchange personal property for it, the bondholders of the Tennessee Publishing Company might consider it a violation of his agreement with them and start receivership proceedings.[11]

As Lea's attention became increasingly demanded by his legal difficulties, his son, Luke, Jr., shouldered more and more the daily responsibility of running the newspapers. Despite the financial and legal problems of the publishers, *The Tennessean* papers managed to keep their lead in circulation and in time would begin to regain their place in the advertising field (*Publishing Service Magazine* 6 October 1932).

While Lea was struggling to keep his newspapers from being put into receivership, the *Nashville Banner* constantly reminded the public that state money had been on deposit in banks that had closed. In a page one editorial on December 19, 1930, it called on the incoming General Assembly to enact legislation that in the future would safeguard deposits of public monies. Over the next several days, the *Banner* reported that citizens' groups across the state were demanding action.

Whether the governor would be impeached depended to a large extent on the leadership of the incoming legislature. Scott P. Fitzhugh of Memphis, a Crump man, was elected speaker of the Senate (*The Nashville Tennessean* 7 January 1931), and Pete Haynes was elected speaker of the House. A probe of the financial structure and operations of state affairs was immediately launched (*The Nashville Tennessean* 9 January 1931) by legislative investigating committees dominated by anti-administration members. The first order of business was to examine the system of depositing state funds in Tennessee banks, particularly in defunct banks in Knoxville and Nashville, which involved about $6 million (*The Nashville Tennessean* 17 January 1931).

Transactions of the state with banks in which Lea and Caldwell were interested were closely scrutinized, while a myriad of state deposits in other failed banks were not examined. In addition to finding evidence by which the governor could be impeached it was the purpose of this legislative investigating committee, Lea was convinced, to try to find some wrongdoing by him and by Rogers Caldwell in order that they might be indicted.

The probe, given front page coverage daily in both Nashville papers, dragged on week after week, its political overtones becoming ever more obvious. Crump had been quick following the failure of Caldwell and Company to disassociate himself from Horton and to seize the opportunity to attempt to gain control of the state for which he had battled for the past decade. It was at this time that great personal bitterness developed between Lea and Crump.

Almost the entire session of the probe on February 19 was devoted to Lea's personal banking with the Liberty Bank and Trust Company. Attempts, made almost daily, to prove that state monies had been deposited in Caldwell banks through the influence of Lea, failed to verify such allegations.

The Highway Department was the first department to be closely scrutinized. Although Harry Berry maintained that he was fired as commissioner because he refused to travel 100 percent with Luke Lea, Berry stated he had been advised by Lea to purchase through competitive bidding in the open market, which he had done and which had resulted in substantial savings.

As the climax of the bitter fight approached, Crump was in Nashville to conduct personally the drive for the voting of impeachment articles (*The Nashville Tennessean* 24 May 1931), and Lea assumed charge of the effort to defeat them.[12]

The first article was introduced in the House on Friday, May 29. That article was based on an alleged conspiracy between

Horton, Lea, Caldwell, and others to permit the use of state funds for individual favor and profit (*The Nashville Tennessean* 24 May 1931). Eight additional articles were introduced when the House reconvened on Tuesday, June 2. After much behind the scene jockeying for votes and two days of debate on the House floor, Article I, an omnibus measure including practically every charge in the other articles was brought to a vote on June 6. On the roll call 58 members voted against and 41 in favor. The defeat of this article by the decisive margin of 17 votes signaled the end of the impeachment effort. When the House reconvened, Tuesday, June 9, the remaining articles of impeachment by tacit agreement were called up in a group and voted down without discussion (*The Nashville Tennessean* 10 June 1931).

The defeat of the anti-administration forces was attributed variously to poor judgment, greed, backfiring of the attempt to pressure the independents on the committee, and the failure of the hand-picked probe committee and auditors selected by Crump (*The Nashville Tennessean* 7 June 1931) to find evidence of misconduct that he had loudly proclaimed had taken place. Some thought the decisive factor was Lea's out-maneuvering Crump by figuring out what in all probability would be the Memphis boss's next move and beating him to the punch.[13] Exhaustive as had been the search, neither evidence to impeach Horton nor to indict Lea had been found. Approximately $90,000 had been spent, and the state had been practically immobilized during the long probe; yet little had been accomplished in a positive way.[14] It would be difficult, however, to overestimate the political significance of the impeachment.

The effort to remove Horton from office having been unsuccessful, it was Paul Davis, Lea was convinced, who then tried to secure indictments against him in Davidson County.[15] Criminal court judge Charles Gilbert ordered Davidson County Attorney General Richard M. Atkinson to file a conspiracy indictment against Lea and his son in connection with the defunct Liberty Bank and Trust Company. After investigation, Atkinson told the court no evidence had been found to support such a charge, whereupon Judge Gilbert relieved Atkinson of his duties in that matter and appointed Seth Walker (*The Nashville Tennessean* 26 July 1931), who was allied with the anti-Lea faction, as Attorney General pro tem to carry out the judge's orders.

The Davidson County Grand Jury on August 10 returned misdemeanor indictments before Judge Gilbert charging Luke Lea and Luke Lea, Jr.; E.P. Charlet and R.B. Mosely, both employees of the Tennessee Publishing Company; J. Basil Ramsey, president of the defunct Holston-Union Bank in Knoxville; and W.S. Chappell, cashier of the defunct Liberty Bank and Trust Company in Nashville, with conspiracy to defraud the Liberty Bank of $150,000 (*The Nashville Tennessean* 11 August 1931).

Despite all the agitation, kept before the public by the *Nashville Banner*, to indict Lea in Nashville, he was never charged in his native Davidson County with a felony. Even with a special Attorney General appointed to obtain the indictment, the severest accusation that could be brought against him was a misdemeanor (McFerrin, *Caldwell and Company* 209).

The 22 acts cited in that misdemeanor indictment covered the same transactions listed in the civil suit filed against Lea and the other co-defendants by D.D. Robertson, receiver of the defunct bank, on December 10, 1930, to recover funds Lea was alleged to have gotten from the bank by irregular methods. Most of those transactions were negotiations of loans by various corporations with which Lea was connected. The hostile language of the indictments, by whom they were prepared, and under what conditions they were returned, as well as their ultimate dismissal lent credence to Lea's contention that they were politically motivated (*The Nashville Tennessean* 11 August 1931).

After the first attempt in December 1930 to put *The Tennessean* papers in receivership had failed, Lea had received another message reputed to have been sent by Paul Davis: Unless information to impeach the governor of Tennessee for exceeding the $10,000 legal limit in his campaign was provided, criminal prosecutions against Lea would be instigated.[16] That demand the colonel also rejected.

Lea was convinced that Davis then, through the influence of his brother, Norman, a member of the Disarmament Committee under Herbert Hoover,[17] secured indictments the middle of March 1931 by the federal court in Greeneville, Tennessee, against him, Rogers Caldwell, and J. Basil Ramsey in connection with the failure of the Holston-Union National Bank of Knoxville. In two of the indictments, the three were charged with conspiracy to violate national banking laws, while the third indictment charged the actual violations to Ramsey.

These indictments against Lea subsequently to be dismissed by motion of the government, came as a great surprise to him, and his distress over them was increased by his knowledge that the disagreeable publicity would adversely affect other members of his family. The indictments grew out of the purchase of stock in the East Tennessee National Bank.[18] In addition to buying the *Knoxville Journal* in March 1928, Lea and Rogers Caldwell joined ten citizens of Knoxville in purchasing from the Sanford interest, which owned the newspaper, 980 shares of stock in the East Tennessee National Bank.

Lea was to pay $9,800 in cash and to give his note of $20,000 to the Sanford interest. Caldwell was to do likewise. Both Lea's and Caldwell's checks were deposited to their account and paid upon presentation. They were informed by the bank that the ten Knoxville people had paid their amounts into Lea and Caldwell's account, and a check for $98,000, signed by Lea and by Caldwell was drawn on that account. The check was certified by the cashier of the bank. Lea and Caldwell did not know until later that in the confusion resulting from the consolidation of the Holston National Bank and the Union National Bank the amounts to be paid by the Knoxville people were not deposited until several days later. As Lea understood it, every bit of the money was paid by the Knoxville people, and there was no loss in any way. The violation was only a technical violation as far as the certification of the check was concerned, and this violation was only on the part of the officer of the bank who certified the check.[19] Knowing that he was innocent of any wrongdoing, Lea was not worried about this case criminally, but he was afraid that it might hamper his refinancing plans or damage his personal credit.

As he had done business with the Canal Bank in New Orleans, his opponents investigated the possibility of indictments being brought against him there. When Huey Long got wind of their purpose, he sent word that they were not going to wash their dirty linen in Louisiana and gave them until daylight to get out of the state. No suits were brought against the colonel in Louisiana.[20]

Chapter Thirteen
The Law's Disgrace

In the wake of bank closures that swept across the nation, a special Buncombe County, North Carolina, grand jury was appointed the end of January 1931 to probe the failures of the Central Bank and Trust Company and other banks in that area (*Nashville Banner* 28 January 1931). During the spring several officials and directors, including Wallace B. Davis, president of the Central, were indicted. Then Luke Lea, Luke Lea, Jr., and E.P. Charlet, secretary-treasurer of the Tennessee Publishing Company, together with Davis, were indicted on March 16 by the Buncombe County grand jury for violating North Carolina banking laws.

The colonel was convinced that it was his political enemies in Tennessee, through K.T. McConnico, attorney in civil matters for the receiver of the Central Bank in Asheville, who instigated this criminal action.[1] Lea called Albert L. Cox in North Carolina to request a copy of the indictment and to ask his opinion of the situation. In World War I, Cox had commanded the 113th Field Artillery composed chiefly of North Carolinians and had served with Lea in the 55th Field Artillery Brigade.

Cox reported back to Lea that there was absolutely nothing to the indictment. He then offered his services gratis to represent the Leas, but Lea, of course, would not accept.

Because the Leas were not in North Carolina at the time of any of the acts alleged in the indictment, neither the state of North Carolina nor the State of Tennessee could legally at that time issue the necessary papers to compel their appearance in North Carolina. Lea's family, his friends, and his attorneys all pled with him not to accept service on the indictment, to refuse to stand trial, and later, when the bitterness resulting from the failures had died down, to demand a trial. They pointed out that when people lost money through the closing of a bank, they wanted someone charged and punished. In that hostile atmosphere they questioned whether a fair trial would be possible.

Lea's lawyers were in agreement that if the governor of North Carolina sent extradition papers, Tennessee Governor Henry H. Horton was legally bound to turn them down. However, the consensus was that Horton's refusal to honor Lea's extradition during impeachment proceedings, then in progress, could possibly inflame opinion further against the governor and result in his removal. Lea thought that the North Carolina indictment was timed to produce that result.[2] It was suggested by some of the attorneys that Horton should be encouraged to honor the request for extradition and then for the Leas to go into federal court and show that they had not been in North Carolina and therefore were not subject to extradition.

Lea listened courteously as each person spoke. Absolutely certain in his own mind that he had done nothing wrong, he then expressed his vehement opinion that it would look bad, or as if they were guilty, to stand upon some legal technicality. Living under the stigma of false accusations was repugnant to him. The best course, he believed, would be to meet the charges head-on. His confidence in complete exoneration could not be shaken. He was determined to go and vindicate himself immediately. Luke, Jr., wanted to do what his father wanted, and whatever the colonel decided was agreeable with Pete Charlet.

The Leas and Charlet went to Asheville to make bond on March 27. Shortly after they had submitted to its jurisdiction, North Carolina changed the manner of selecting a jury where a change of venue was sought. Under the new law the judge could on his own motion designate the county from which the trial jury would be selected. Chapter 308 of the Public Acts of 1931 also empowered the judge to set the procedure by which that jury would be chosen, rather than its being drawn from a box by a child under the age of ten.[3]

Luke Lea, Luke Lea, Jr., E.P. Charlet, and W.B. Davis were again indicted on April 21, together with J. Charles Bradford, cashier of the Central Bank, for conspiracy to defraud the bank of $1 million.

With so many litigations pending—*The Tennessean* receivership proceedings, the Liberty Bank case, and countless civil suits—it was necessary for Lea to retain a battery of lawyers. L.E. Gwinn, a prominent Memphis attorney, whose specialty was criminal law, was brought in, and the detailed preparation of the North Carolina case was entrusted to him. Albert Cox, whom Lea thought it would be awkward not to retain, was lead attorney. In hindsight, the Leas came to believe it was on Cox's advice that many erroneous decisions were made. Attorneys who practiced in Asheville were needed, so Louis M. Bourne and his partner, A. Yates Arledge, were retained. Nashville attorneys Giles Evans and J.G. Lackey, preparing the defense of various litigations in Tennessee, offered to go to Asheville to be of assistance.

Several cases were tried in connection with the failure of the Central Bank and Trust Company. Wallace Davis was convicted on May 16, 1931, of publishing a false report as to the condition of the bank in the Asheville *Times* on September 24, 1930. It was brought out during that trial that the liquid assets of the bank had been diminishing since 1928, and that, although aware of that condition, the Corporation Commission had allowed the bank to stay open. Many North Carolinians were concerned whether that state department which oversaw banking had been lax in the performance of its duties and consequently shared the responsibility for the bank's failure. However, the court ruled that the purpose of the Davis trial was to investigate the actions of the officers of the bank, not the alleged negligence of the Corporation Commission (Illich, "The Case of Colonel Luke Lea" 11-16).

The Leas arrived in Asheville early Monday, July 27, the day they were to go on trial. Seeing for the first time Judge M.V. Barnhill, a tall, thin man with dark hair and sharp features, they did not know that at a house party the last weekend in May he had offered to bet that Lea would be convicted in his court.[4] It was common talk among North Carolina lawyers that Governor Max Gardner had appointed Barnhill to preside over the special term of court to hear cases growing out of bank failures with the understanding that he was to bring in convictions.[5]

While the Leas, Charlet, and Davis were awaiting trial in the courtroom at Asheville, the grand jury brought a new set of indictments and served them on the defendants on North Carolina soil. The indictments for which they had prepared were quashed, and over their vigorous protest, they were ordered to stand trial immediately on the new indictments.

According to newspaper grapevine, K.T. McConnico had advised the North Carolina interests he represented to bring weak indictments against Lea. Knowing the colonel as well as he did, McConnico believed that if the indictments were mild enough for Lea to think he would be acquitted, he would go to North Carolina to answer the charges. McConnico, reputedly, further advised that after Lea got to North Carolina those indictments could be quashed, and new ones with teeth could be brought on which he could be forced to immediate trial.[6]

Solicitor Zeb V. Nettles said the new bills were necessary to avoid questions of legality of the former grand jury and were, with few exceptions, duplicates of the original. The principal differences, he contended, were that the name of bank cashier J. Charles Bradford, a defendant in one of the original bills was omitted in the new indictment, although he was still accused of being a co-conspirator; that the words "and others" were added in several instances to allow the state to present evidence covering many phases of the Lea organization (*Asheville Times* 27 July 1931; *Asheville Citizen* 28 July 1931); and that the unnamed conspirator was the late R.E. Donnell, president of the defunct Liberty Bank in Nashville.

The defense contended that the new indictments differed radically from the old ones and that the object in Bradford and Donnell, the first in a mental institution and the other dead, being named co-conspirators was to make competent statements purporting to have been made by them, which statements would have been incompetent as hearsay except as declarations of co-conspirators.[7]

At the same time another indictment was returned charging for the first time the Leas, Charlet, and Davis with the substantive crime of misapplication, which was a statutory offense, thereby making that indictment obviously different from the original.

Attorneys for the defendants feverishly worked late into the night preparing defense of the new indictments. Shortly before six o'clock the following morning, L.E. Gwinn was stricken with the first of three gastric hemorrhages and was rushed to Mission Hospital. Doctor Bernard R. Smith appeared in court to testify that Gwinn would have to be confined to bed for at least ten days— actually he would not return to court until near the end of the trial.

In denying the motion for delay of trial for two weeks, Judge Barnhill remarked that the defendants had "engaged six or eight attorneys for this case, and it is not the fault of the court that you preferred to depend entirely upon one man" (*Asheville Times* 28 July 1931).

Judge Barnhill also dismissed the defense's motions to quash charges of conspiracy and embezzlement. The state elected to try the four men on six counts of conspiracy as alleged in one bill and on the blanket charge of misappropriation, misapplication, and embezzlement of more than $1 million of the bank's funds and credits as alleged in the second bill of indictment (*Asheville Citizen* 29 July 1931), and over the strenuous objections of the defense, the prosecution was allowed to consolidate the two bills of indictment for trial at that term of court.

Motions of the defense for a bill of particulars on both bills of indictment were granted (*Asheville Times* 29 July 1931), but two days passed before the state filed the bill consisting of 52 items, totaling over $2 million, with some of which transactions the Leas had no connection.[8] Records of the transactions in which they had been a party, the details of which would be impossible to recall with accuracy from memory, were in their files in Nashville; yet their trial on these items was already under way.

Having denied the defense's request for a change of venue,

Judge Barnhill dismissed the regular jurors and directed Sheriff Jake Lowe of adjacent Haywood County to summon a special venire of 125 citizens for jury service (*Asheville Times* 28 July 1931). Jurors chosen from another county in order to insure an impartial trial was more semblance of fair play than substance. The failure of the Central Bank had precipitated the closure of Haywood's Bank of Clyde, so feeling there was bitter against persons charged with wrecking those banks. Several men who would be chosen as jurors had what little money they possessed in the Bank of Clyde, and their deposits were tied up for a year until the bank reopened.[9] Moreover, these rural folk from depressed economic circumstances and not too highly educated did not have an understanding of complicated financial transactions, concerning which, as peers of the defendants, they would sit in judgment.

After the jury was selected Judge Barnhill invoked for the first time the state's new alternate juror law, providing for a relief juror in the event any of the regular jurors should be forced to leave the box.

The defendants pleaded not guilty to the new indictments consisting of seven counts.

Count 1. Issuance of $300,000 of certificates of deposit on October 8, 1930.

Count 2. Reissuance of the same certificates of deposit on October 23, 1930.

Count 3. Issuance of $50,000 of certificates of deposit on September 27, 1930.

Count 4. Issuance of $30,000 of cashier's checks on October 8, 1930.

Count 5. Issuance of $100,000 of cashier's checks on October 8, 1930.

Count 6. Issuance of New York drafts amounting to $100,000 on October 14, 1930.

Count 7. Fifty-two items involving City of Asheville anticipation revenue notes, cashier's checks, New York drafts, certificates of deposit, bonds, overdrafts, and notes discounted. Included in the fifty-two items were the six items charged in the first six counts of the consolidated indictment.

The transactions on which the indictments were drawn indicated that the prosecution made no distinction between Luke Lea and the Caldwell interests. Although Lea was never an officer, director, or employee of either the Central Bank or the Bank of Tennessee or Caldwell and Company he was being tried for some transactions solely between the North Carolina bank and those two Tennessee institutions. Defense counsel objected, as they were to do many times, but the prosecuting attorneys continued to lump together all Tennessee interests and to hold Lea as the responsible party.

The state of North Carolina would attempt to prove: Luke Lea had induced the Central Bank to make improper loans; that he had substituted poor paper for good collateral; that the bank issued to Lea hundreds of thousands of dollars worth of certificates of deposit made payable in blank; and that Lea was allowed to settle an overdraft of thousands of dollars with his personal note after he already owed hundreds of thousands of dollars to the bank.

The defense would attempt to prove: they had committed no banking violation; that every transaction with which they were connected was routine business procedure and was approved by the proper authorities; that when the collateral was put up it was sufficient and was so approved; that its deflated value was due to the worldwide economic depression, not to any willful act of Lea's to defraud; and that in the six-month period Lea maintained an account at the Central, he had deposited more than $1.6 million and that sometimes his balance was in excess of $90,000.

The prosecution, emphasizing that accounts of the Lea interests were frequently overdrawn, charged that the bank's liquidating agent held $382,000 of Lea's notes and $443,000 were held by the city of Asheville, which received them as partial collateral for large deposits the city made in the Central Bank. In an effort to show Lea admitted his indebtedness as opposed to the state's contention that his transactions with the bank were fraudulent, defense counsel pointed out Lea had made a written offer to settle his more than $800,000 obligation to the North Carolina Corporation Commission and the city of Asheville by paying $40,000 in cash and the balance over a 20-month period. Lea's first offer to settle his indebtedness had been made in December 1930, the month after the Central Bank closed and before criminal action had been instigated against him. A second offer had been made in February 1931, and a third offer in March

(*Nashville Banner* 1 May 1931), each of which had been rejected. *The Nashville Tennessean* stated Tuesday, August 4:

The Tennessean papers are not represented officially at the trial in Asheville of Colonel Luke Lea, Luke Lea, Jr., and E.P. Charlet, by a staff correspondent, but by the world-covering Associated Press and United Press....

It is felt *The Tennessean* papers' staffs could cover the hearing accurately and impartially, regardless of undeniable personal feeling, but to give readers double assurance that they may always rely on *The Tennessean* papers to print the news fairly and impartially, the editor relinquishes in favor of the press associations. You may depend upon your *Tennessean*, morning or evening to PRINT THE NEWS as it has throughout these proceedings.[10]

As soon as court was adjourned on Saturday, August 8, both Leas, with the permission of the trial judge, flew to Nashville. Lea considered he had a definite agreement by Paul Davis, president of the American National Bank in Nashville, that during the North Carolina trial, no action would be taken toward filing a receivership suit against the Tennessee Publishing Company.[11] Nevertheless the colonel had received the previous day a telegram from bank chairman P.D. Houston, ordering him to deliver the stock of the Tennessee Publishing Company to the officers of the bank within 48 hours or face a receivership suit.[12] Luckily the expiration of the 48 hours came at the end of the week.

At Houston's home the following morning, Lea issued an ultimatum. The perilous financial condition of the American National Bank would be published the next day in *The Tennessean* papers unless Houston gave him assurances by one o'clock that day that neither the Canal Bank, whose agreement Lea had procured, nor the American would launch any hostile litigation against the Tennessee Publishing Company as long as its bonds they held were not in default. After conferring with representatives of the Canal Bank, Houston gave Lea the assurance he sought.[13] For the second time Lea believed he had secured a definite agreement with the officers of the American National Bank. He and his son then flew back to Asheville and were present when court convened the following morning.

The prosecution charged on August 12 that Wallace B. Davis sent to Colonel Lea $875,000 of bonds of the Central Securities Corporation for which notes were to be signed by several different persons as the bank was not allowed to carry a note for more than $225,000 by one maker. It would not come out until much later that this transaction in no way benefited Lea. Rather he was asked and undertook to handle those bonds for the benefit of the Central Bank.[14]

It was further charged that Lea never returned nor paid for $214,000 of bonds, but on cross-examination, the witness admitted that Lea had tried to return them after the bank's failure, but they had not been accepted because of the impending receivership against Central Securities. Counsel for the defense then produced the bonds in court, thus strengthening their contention that Lea's transactions with the bank were legitimate and that he admitted his indebtedness to the Central but denied any fraud.

Of the $875,000 of bonds sent to Lea in October 1930, for which the state alleged the Central Bank had never received payment, cross-examination of several witnesses disclosed that $286,000 of the bonds were returned immediately and $375,000 were returned at a later date. Hence, all $875,000 were accounted for.

On the stand Monday, August 17, accountant W.S. Coursey, special investigator for the prosecution, stated that he considered the Central Bank was insolvent before it had any transactions with Lea. It was a matter of public record that the North Carolina bank examiners had found the Central Bank to be in a precarious if not insolvent condition two years before Luke Lea had any dealings with it, yet he was charged with wrecking it. Coursey further testified he had never heard of another incidence of certificates of deposit and cashier's checks having been issued in blank. However, the Central apparently had so desperately needed the money, it issued them in blank and sent them to Lea to handle in any manner he could and to wire it the proceeds.

Shortly before the state rested its case on August 19, Lea's attorney, Albert Cox, strongly urged him not to take the stand in his own defense.[15] Cox said one of the prosecutors had told him that the state had not been able to make a case against Luke, Jr., and in Cox's opinion it was always a mistake for the defendant to take the stand when no case had been made against him. Cox also stated that the prosecutor knew that the colonel could handle himself on the witness stand, but thought that Luke, Jr., because of his youth, could be rattled and that the state could tear his testimony to shreds.

Both Leas were insistent they go on the stand, as they knew they had done nothing wrong. Mrs. Lea pleaded with her husband to take the stand. If anything could refute the false accusations and untangle the maze of legal technicalities in which they were being enmeshed, it would be his lucid and compelling presentation of the facts. Wallace Davis and his lawyers opposed putting on proof,[16] as he had made a poor witness in his previous trial.

Reiterating the folly of gambling the certainty of Luke, Jr.'s, acquittal for the satisfaction it would give the colonel to obtain public vindication by going on the stand and explaining how he actually kept the bank open rather than break it, Cox finally stated that if his advice as lead attorney were not followed, he would have to withdraw from the case. His argument in regard to Luke, Jr., was the determining factor. Never would the colonel do anything to jeopardize the freedom of his beloved son. Therefore, Lea changed his mind and decided they would not offer proof in their own defense.[17]

Thus the Rubicon was crossed. The constitution and laws of North Carolina provide that the failure to take the stand by defendants cannot be held against them. Theoretically this is true; practically it is not. With feeling in Asheville as bitter as it was at that time against the defendants, the outcome of the trial probably would have been no different had Luke Lea taken the stand. However, the fact that he did not was a serious mistake, as it diminished the weight of the federal questions involved in the case on which an appeal to a higher court could be made.

The decision of the defendants not to put on proof brought the trial to a sudden climax on Thursday, August 20. The defense was allowed seven hours for its summation, while the prosecution was limited to five.

The courtroom, which seated approximately 1,000, was jammed with many persons standing for concluding arguments on Saturday. In his zealous efforts for conviction, Solicitor Nettles fanned to white heat the prejudice against the nonresidents by stressing the amount of the defunct bank's loans to them. Special prosecutor L.P. McClendon, referring to defense assertions that Davis had sought aid from Lea to save his tottering bank said: "Oh, yes, he was a powerful man. He came over here from Nashville just to save the bank. Do you believe that?" (*The Nashville Tennessean* 23 August 1931).

When court convened on Monday, Judge Barnhill charged the jury for five hours. As amazingly long as was his charge, its severity toward the defendants was even more unusual.

Even under such a trying circumstance, Lea did not lose his sense of humor. As Barnhill finished charging the jury, Luke leaned over and whispered in his wife's ear, "The judge has pleased me very much in one respect." To Mrs. Lea's astonished question, "How?" the colonel replied smiling, "He didn't advocate electrocution."[18]

The case went to the jury at 4:30 P.M. The wait began.

After the jury had been out 18 hours, it filed back into the courtroom about 10:30 Tuesday morning. They had reached no decision, and the foreman asked for further instructions, whereupon Judge Barnhill for 45 minutes delivered what Lea considered a terrific assault on the defendants.[19] The jurors then retired for further deliberation.

Nerves were stretched almost to the breaking point before the jury returned to the packed courtroom that hot August afternoon. The jurors stood as the verdict was read, count by count.

Count 1. Luke Lea, guilty.

Mrs. Lea, momentarily showing the strain of the past weeks, seemed on the verge of crying as she heard her husband

pronounced guilty. Quickly she gained control of herself but her
knuckles were white as she continued to grip her husband's hand
(*The Raleigh Times* 25 August 1931).

> Luke Lea, Jr., guilty.

Buoyant throughout the trial, the young man clapped his hand
over his mouth as the foreman pronounced the word "guilty."

> Wallace B. Davis, guilty. E.P. Charlet, not guilty.

Count 2. All defendants, not guilty.
Count 3. All defendants, not guilty.
Count 4. Not submitted to the jury because allegations included in the fifth
count.
Count 5. Luke Lea, guilty. Luke Lea, Jr., guilty. Wallace B. Davis, guilty. E.P.
Charlet, not guilty.
Count 6. Luke Lea, guilty. Luke Lea, Jr., guilty. Wallace B. Davis, not guilty.
E.P. Charlet, not guilty.
Count 7. Luke Lea, guilty. Luke Lea, Jr., guilty. Wallace B. Davis, guilty. E.P.
Charlet, not guilty.

There was no demonstration in the courtroom as spectators
listened in silence to the verdict. At its conclusion, tears were
trickling down the cheeks of three jurors (*The Raleigh Times* 25
August 1931).

Mrs. Lea was stunned by Luke, Jr.'s conviction. They had
been assured by Albert Cox that the prosecution had told him the
state had made no case against Luke, Jr. For that reason they had
decided not to put on proof, and now he stood convicted along
with his father. Heartsick though she was that her husband had
been found guilty, she had come to realize as the trial progressed
that he had little chance of being acquitted. Because of the intense
bitterness following the collapse of the Central Bank, it was, in her
opinion, impossible at that time in that place for any one charged
with conspiring to defraud the bank to get an impartial trial.[20]

The same opinion would be expressed later by attorney Arthur
Garfield Hayes:

When a bank fails, does anyone believe the banker can get a fair trial? Senator Luke Lea of Tennessee, proprietor of important newspapers, engaged in every variety of big business, a man of wealth and influence, was indicted in North Carolina, charged with conspiracy to wreck a bank. The bank in question was an old one, apparently reliable, and entrusted with millions. When it failed, havoc came to the town. Accused with Lea were his son, Davis, the president of the bank, and others, all caught within the web of an alleged conspiracy. Motion for change of venue was denied. Shortly before the trial, one of the defense attorneys was stricken with gastric ulcers and sent to a hospital. In spite of this an adjournment was denied. The defendants were tried, found guilty and sentenced to long terms in prison. I am not arguing the question of guilt or innocence; I merely suggest that under conditions such as these a fair trial was impossible. (Hayes, *Trial by Prejudice* 14-15)

On the first count the Leas and Davis were found guilty of conspiring on October 8, 1930, to defraud the Central Bank through the issuance of $300,000 worth of certificates of deposit payable to the Bank of Tennessee. This was a transaction solely between the Central Bank and the Bank of Tennessee.

Prior to Caldwell and Company opening for the day, those certificates of deposit were temporarily left in the safe at *The Tennessean* office while the employee of the Central Bank who was delivering them to Caldwell and Company went to breakfast. That fact was seized upon to connect Lea with the transaction. Because of the bitterness McConnico had against Lea, he was more interested in the colonel rather than in Caldwell being indicted.

After the trial many facts would gradually come to light. John Thrash, a deputy sheriff of Buncombe County, would make an affidavit in 1934 that part of his duties during the Lea-Davis trial was to take messages to and from Solicitor Nettles to Gatlinburg to K.T. McConnico, a lawyer from Tennessee; that McConnico was deeply interested in the case and sometimes during a single day communicated many times with Nettles by telephone and by messenger; that McConnico stated in terms of great bitterness his determination to have the Leas convicted.[21]

Count five charged the two Leas and Davis conspired to defraud the Central Bank through the issuance of $100,000 of cashier's checks dated October 8, 1930. It was proved at the trial that the Central Bank on that date issued ten cashier's checks in the amount of $10,000 each payable in blank. Luke Lea cashed five of these checks and wired for the account of the Central Bank, through the Federal Reserve Bank, $50,000. The remaining five cashier's checks were returned to the Central Bank by Charlet on October 13 and cancelled by the Central Bank on October 14 without any payment thereon. The record showed that the Central Bank did not lose one penny through these cashier's checks. Instead of conspiring to defraud, Luke Lea gave his credit to the Central by cashing the checks and letting the bank have the benefit of the funds therefrom (*Publisher Service Magazine* 17 November 1932).

The Leas alone were convicted on count six which charged conspiracy in the issuance by the Central Bank of $100,000 of its drafts on the Central Hanover Bank and Trust Company of New York. Judge Barnhill set aside the verdict on that count as it charged conspiracy of which the Leas could not have been guilty, he held, except in conjunction with an officer of the bank.

The seventh count charged the Leas and Davis not with conspiracy but with the statutory and substantive crime of misapplication. In permitting the state to amend this count, the trial court held that the state could not convict the defendants of conspiracy but could only convict them of misapplication; yet the crime of misapplication in North Carolina, as in other states and by federal statute, is not a common law offense. It is created by statute and applies to only four classes of people: bank directors, bank officers, bank employees, and bank agents. It was not even charged in the trial that either the colonel or Luke Lea, Jr., was ever a director, officer, employee, or agent of the Central Bank, because neither of them ever was. Yet they were convicted of a crime, defined by statute, that could be committed only by a person thus connected with a bank.

With the exception of $45,000 city of Asheville anticipation revenue notes, which Caldwell and Company had failed to remit to the Central Bank from $305,000 notes issued, the other items in the seventh count involved cashier's checks, New York drafts, certificates of deposit, overdrafts, and notes discounted. It was proved by the state's witnesses and the records of the bank that every cashier's check, certificate of deposit, New York draft, and overdraft was either promptly paid for or surrendered and cancelled without the payment of one cent by the Central Bank. The only obligation that the Leas owed the Central was for money borrowed by loans, each of which was approved by the examining and executive committees of the bank. The discount of the notes representing the loans to the Leas was so regular that Judge Barnhill said that if the notes were all that were involved in the bill of particulars, the court would set the verdict aside.[22]

The defense's motion for a new trial was overruled. Notice of appeal was then given, and the defendants were granted ninety days to make their appeals. In his recommendation for sentencing, Solicitor Nettles stated that Luke Lea, Jr., because of his youth and the fact that he was working under his father's direction, should be fined and not imprisoned.

Late that afternoon Judge Barnhill passed sentence. All eyes were on the judge as he began reading. Davis was sentenced to two to three years on the first count; two to three years on the fifth count to run cumulatively with the sentence on the first count; and four to six years under the seventh count to run concurrently with the sentences under the first and fifth counts.

Luke Lea blanched as he heard himself receive a heavier sentence than the president of the bank. He was sentenced three to five years on the first count; three to five years on the fifth count to run cumulatively with the sentence on the first count; and six to ten years on the seventh count to run concurrently with the sentences under the first and fifth counts.

With heart pounding, he tensely waited to hear the fate of his son. Luke, Jr., was fined $10,000 on the first count; ordered to pay $5,000 to Buncombe County toward the cost of the trial on the fifth count; and fined $5,000 and ordered to pay $5,000 toward court costs on the seventh count.

The judge set appeal bonds for the defendants at $30,000 for

Colonel Lea; $10,000 for Luke Lea, Jr.; and $10,000 for Wallace B. Davis. The following morning Judge Barnhill changed the sentence of Luke Lea, Jr., by adding a prison sentence as an alternative to the $25,000 fine, with the stipulation that the sentence be suspended upon payment of the fine (*The Nashville Banner* 26 August 1931).

After the appeal bonds had been posted Colonel Lea made a vain effort to save his son from the stigma of a felony conviction. As the trial-worn father rose to his feet, the courtroom became hushed. In a voice filled with emotion, he said:

> Luke Lea, Jr. worked under my instructions and he should not be held criminally liable. I am willing to assume the fine and additional sentence, if only this verdict can be set aside as to my boy. I don't admit that I have done any wrong, but I do insist that these transactions were my own, not my son's.... (*The Nashville Banner* 27 August 1931)

Judge Barnhill replied he would suspend the sentence of Luke Lea, Jr., provided Colonel Lea would withdraw his appeal and begin serving his prison sentence at once (*The Nashville Banner* 27 August 1931).

The Leas could not believe the judge's words. He was offering Luke, Jr., provisional freedom—a suspended sentence would not absolve him of the felony connection—contingent upon the colonel's admitting he was guilty, entering prison at once, and forfeiting his constitutional right to appeal the verdict of the court.

The father seemed on the verge of giving up his freedom in order to guarantee that of his son. Every eye turned toward Luke, Jr., who indignantly replied, "Absolutely not" (*Publishers Service Magazine* 3 November 1932).

The Leas left Asheville the following morning. When they reached home that night, the house was overflowing with countless friends and more than 100 employees of *The Tennessean*.

A page one editorial in *The Evening Tennessean* stated:

...Under order of Colonel Lea, who has asked no quarter and made no plea for public sympathy, there has been heretofore no comment in these columns as to the tragedy of last year's financial crash and its effect upon the lives and welfare of the publisher and his son.

In the absence of Colonel Lea, this rule is being violated, an action contrary to all tradition in the editorial department of *The Tennessean* papers, but one we feel to be justified by the circumstances.

The courts of North Carolina, or any other state, cannot shake the confidence, esteem and love in which Colonel Lea and his son are held by the workers in every department of *The Tennessean*.

To those who have been associated with such a leader as Colonel Lea over a long period of years, no judge or jury can overrule the evidence of their own knowledge that he is incapable of the law violations with which he has been charged.

Colonel Lea bears an honored name. To those who know the depths of his generosity, the steadfastness of his purpose, the courage of his convictions, and lofty code to which he has always adhered, that name has lost none of its splendor through the turn of events in Asheville. The same may be said of his son.

Many employees of *The Tennessean* have served with Colonel Lea on the field of battle. They found him a brave and just commander. He never asked his men to go where he would not lead. Bonds of friendship were established in France which never can be severed.

Others have served with him in peace, where the same spirit of leadership was evident. He has been a firm and fast friend in all circumstances, giving far more than he ever received.

It is impossible to see bared the innermost recesses of a man's soul, in time of victory, and defeat, and not know that soul's true worth.

It is because of this knowledge, and because of an abiding affection and unshaken confidence, that *The Tennessean* papers today welcome home Colonel Lea and his son.... (*The Evening Tennessean* 26 August 1931)

Chapter Fourteen
In Search of Justice

Sustained by a clear conscience that he had committed no wrong, nor even technically violated any law, and incensed by the verdict of the Asheville court, Luke Lea determined that his best course was to continue his legal fight to the finish.[1]

As the depression tightened its paralyzing grip on the United States, lack of money became an ever-increasing problem. Any one of several plans worked out by Lea might have put the Tennessee Publishing Company on an unassailably sound financial basis. However, the difficulty in raising money to meet the day-to-day obligations of the newspaper, coupled with the time and funds demanded to continue his legal defense, made impossible the concerted efforts necessary to secure long-range financing.

During the spring of 1932 the colonel's second son Percy was seriously injured in an automobile accident and Luke, Jr., was stricken with cancer. Even though there was no indication of spread when the malignant tumor was surgically removed, deep x-ray therapy was advised. Luke, Jr., entered Memorial Hospital in New York, now Sloan-Kettering, on May 13. The radium treatments, consisting of nine doses, were concluded on May 29.[2] Although optimistic about Luke's prognosis, the New York specialist stressed that the word "cured" could not be used until the patient had gone five years without a recurrence.

Tremendously shaken by the trial verdict and concerned about reports that the North Carolina Supreme Court was politically oriented—at that time it was customary for the governor to appoint his campaign manager to the first vacancy on the high court—the colonel still had confidence in the court's integrity. His attorneys were unanimous in the opinion that the case contained so many

233

errors that the Supreme Court would be compelled to reverse the lower court's decision.

At the hearing on the appeal, March 2 and 3, 1932, the state prosecuting attorneys charged that a monetary offer had purportedly been made to influence the jury in favor of the defendants.

Although not required to be there, Luke Lea was present at the hearing. Astounded by the accusation, and emphatically stating he had no knowledge of such action, he made an affidavit challenging the charge and calling for the fullest investigation. Every defense attorney also made affidavit denying knowledge of a bribery attempt. The investigation was not made.

Sometime thereafter Hurst Justice, foreman of the jury at their trial, contacted the Leas. He informed them that during their trial he had received an offer, purportedly to have come from one of their attorneys through a man by the name of Wiley Noland, of $1,500 if he could bring in a verdict of not guilty.[3] The foreman did not call this alleged offer of a bribe to the attention of the court while the trial was in progress but told some of the other jurors of it prior to their reaching a verdict.

Later the Leas would learn that Solicitor Nettles had attempted, though unsuccessfully, to link the colonel himself, rather than one of his attorneys, with Noland's bribery attempt.[4] Noland shortly thereafter was convicted of jury tampering for which he served a prison term. While ruling the jury in the Leas' trial had been tampered with, the courts of North Carolina refused to grant them a new trial!

The state Supreme Court found "no error" in their conviction, affirming on June 15, 1932 the lower court's verdict. The court held there were two theories in the Lea case: the prosecution's view that Lea had conspired with the bank president, Wallace B. Davis, to defraud the bank; and the defense's position that Lea had assisted rather than defrauded the bank. The jury took the former view, and the court ruled not to disturb the jury's verdict.

Chief Justice W.P. Stacy's opinion held that the indictments by the grand jury brought the case within the jurisdiction of the superior court of Buncombe County, even though Nettles lacked proof that the Tennesseans had been there at or about the time of the alleged offenses. The solicitor had been correct in his boast that although he knew neither of the Leas had been in Buncombe County at the time of the charges in the indictment, that the grand jury would return any indictment on a bank case that he requested without even reading it, and that the indictment, when returned, established venue.[5]

The North Carolina Supreme Court on June 20 refused the defendants' plea for reconsideration of its decision. In order for that court to affirm the conviction of the lower court, that high tribunal not only had to overrule its own decisions, but even more shockingly, had to change facts.[6]

On the appeal of a case containing a fatal error, the higher court was bound to reverse the verdict of the lower court. The record of the trial showed that over defense objection items not contained in the bill of particulars were introduced as evidence on numerous occasions thereby constituting a fatal error.

A letter written by Luke Lea, Jr., and presented at the trial had been damaging because it seemed to indicate what the prosecution charged was the defendants' scheme even though the letter concerned a bank in Kentucky and did not mention the Central Bank. This letter was dated October 28, 1930, five days after the date of the last act of conspiracy charged in the indictment. In the opinion handed down by the Supreme Court the letter was dated September 2, 1930, which was prior to any of the alleged acts of conspiracy. Attention was immediately called to this inaccuracy, which the court dismissed as a trivial clerical error. However, a stay of execution of sentence was granted July 5 pending a motion for a new trial on the grounds of newly discovered evidence.

Rogers Caldwell, whose legal matters had been sufficiently resolved for him to do so without jeopardy,[7] made an affidavit corroborating that the first count on which Lea and his son stood convicted was a transaction entirely between Caldwell and Company, the Bank of Tennessee, and the Central Bank and Trust Company; that the ten cashier's checks in the amount of $10,000 each payable in blank, the subject of the fifth count, were originally sent to Caldwell and Company, but upon his refusal to handle them, he was requested by the Central to deliver them to Luke Lea, who cashed five, wired $50,000 to the Central, and returned the remaining five cashier's checks; and that the 296 City of Asheville anticipation revenue notes, an item in the seventh count, had not been sent to Nashville at the insistence of Luke Lea as was charged during the trial but were sent by the Central Bank to Caldwell and Company, and Lea had neither any connection nor interest in the transaction.

As W.S. Coursey, the state's star witness at the trial, was more familiar than any other auditor with the records of the bank, Lea employed him after the trial to compile data on transactions between the Lea interests and the Central Bank for pending civil suits. At the time of Coursey's employment, Lea did not know that he would be able to use information Coursey uncovered in a motion for a new trial because the Herman Casey decision had not then been rendered.

Without contradicting his testimony at the trial, Coursey made an affidavit that the Central Bank was in a precarious, if not insolvent, condition for at least two years before the Leas had any transactions with it, and that they in no way contributed to its insolvency; that bank examiner D.M. Darden again reported to the Corporation Commission after his examination of the Central Bank as of July 3, 1930, that it was insolvent; that although the bank examiner's report was critical of many of the bank's loans, none of the Leas' were cited; that the bank's records showed that greater accommodation had been rendered to it by the Lea interests than that extended to them by the Central Bank; that $86,000 was the average daily overage balance in favor of the Central Bank during the six-month period the Lea interests had transactions with the bank, from May 16, 1930, to November 20, 1930, the day the bank closed; that the accounts of the Lea interests were the largest and most profitable in the bank; and that on two days the Central Bank would not have been able to remain open without the large sums wired to it by the Leas and their interests.[8]

In addition to Wiley Noland's attempt to bribe the jury, other astounding reports concerning the jurors and court officers gradually came to light. Contrary to court rules, the jurors, while the trial was in progress, were allowed to read newspapers that contained references to the Leas, visitors were allowed into the jury room, and on several occasions the jury was left unattended.[9]

Prior to their acceptance as jurors, P.F. Cook and W.C. Flynn had expressed their opinion that the Leas as well as Davis were guilty.[10] Before a verdict was reached several jurors stated that if any man voted for acquittal, he was no doubt being paid to do so, and that he better not go back to Haywood County; and after the verdict John Thrash, one of the deputy sheriffs guarding the jury, bragged about the influence he had exerted in bringing about a conviction.[11]

At the hearing on the motion for a new trial in the superior court of Buncombe County, the state of North Carolina attempted to discredit the new evidence in the affidavits by charging that Rogers Caldwell was an associate of Lea's and that W.S. Coursey had entered Lea's employ. After Coursey made those affidavits, he was not able to secure further employment in North Carolina, even though he had been classified by the court as an expert witness during the Leas' trial the preceding year. He moved to Fort Benning, Georgia, where he became treasurer of the Fort Benning Railroad.

The motion for a new trial was overruled by Judge John J. Clement, who held that there was no evidence to show misconduct of the jury, or that there was local prejudice against the defendants (Illich, "The Case of Colonel Luke Lea" 51). The court held the newly discovered evidence was contradictory to the evidence given by the state (Illich, "The Case of Colonel Luke Lea" 52), although the state made no effort to contradict the facts set forth in Caldwell's affidavit; and that Coursey's affidavit did not disagree with his former testimony.[12]

An appeal was then taken to the North Carolina Supreme Court, which dismissed it on the grounds that it was without merit.

A stay of execution of sentence was granted pending a decision of the United States Supreme Court on a motion for a writ of certiorari, then before that high tribunal, which refused on October 24, 1932, to review the Lea-Davis case. Informed of that adverse decision, Wallace Davis announced that he would give up the effort to maintain his freedom. Lea, however, went ahead with his announced plan to appeal to the United States Supreme Court for a review of North Carolina's denial of a new trial on the grounds of newly discovered evidence (*The Nashville Tennessean* 25 October 1932). That high tribunal declined on December 19, 1932 to review the North Carolina court's decision.

As soon as the North Carolina Supreme Court, then in session, was officially notified of the United States Supreme Court's final disposition of the case, it, in turn, certified down the decision to the lower court. The papers were received by the clerk of the Buncombe County superior court on December 23, and the case was put on Buncombe County's criminal calendar for January (Raleigh, *News and Observer* 23 December 1932).

Early that month, Lea's counsel asked recently elected Tennessee Governor Hill McAlister that if he honored the request for extradition and issued a warrant for the Leas' arrest, that date of removal be fixed for a period of at least 24 hours after they were taken into custody to allow them to test the validity of their extradition through habeas corpus. The purpose of a habeas corpus writ, which brought a person before the court, was to release that person from unlawful restraint. The governor had the power to designate in the warrant for arrest the date upon which the accused could be transported to the demanding state.

Counsel gave Governor McAlister written assurance that the Leas would remain in Tennessee to obey all legal processes that might be issued against them.[13] The governor, however, would give no assurance that he would grant 24 hours' grace.

The Leas had received information that a plot was afoot to take them by force to North Carolina.[14] As the method of return was not subject to inquiry, a demanding state was frequently able to take a fugitive into custody by catching him off guard or even by seizing him illegally (Illich, "The Case of Colonel Luke Lea" 62).

The long-standing opposition of the faction of the Democratic party controlled by the Nashville machine had become so bitter toward Lea since the bank failures that he believed he would not be able to get an unbiased hearing in the courts of his home county. Hence, it was decided that when the Leas learned the extradition papers were on the way from North Carolina, they would immediately go to rural Fentress County in northeastern Tennessee because Lea believed that prospects were more favorable in that district of a judge withstanding the terrific political pressure the colonel knew would be applied not to grant the writ of habeas corpus. The long legal battle waged by the Leas was criticized by some as an attempt to circumvent justice, but convinced of their innocence they were determined to continue their fight to maintain their freedom through every judicial channel.

North Carolina began on January 23, 1933, its extradition of the Leas. When they had failed to surrender in Buncombe County superior court under their conviction for banking law violations, Judge N.A. Townsend issued a warrant for their arrest. The Leas' attorneys notified Buncombe County Solicitor Zeb Nettles that their clients intended to resist extradition and to test through habeas corpus proceedings the right of North Carolina to enforce its conviction.

The governor of North Carolina signed the extradition papers the following day, and it was reported that Nettles would immediately proceed to Nashville (*The Nashville Tennessean* 25 January 1933). Believing Nettles en route Luke Lea and Luke Lea, Jr., quietly dropped out of sight. Their absence went undetected for a couple of days, then conflicting reports began to circulate as to their whereabouts.

During their stay in rural East Tennessee, the Leas communicated with their attorneys and their newspapers through Maxey Hewitt, an employee in the advertising department of *The Tennessean*.[15] In what he considered the best cloak-and-dagger fashion, Hewitt never called from the same telephone twice or made two calls in succession from the same town.

Almost a week elapsed before Solicitor Nettles arrived in Nashville on Tuesday night, January 31. The following day he conferred with K.T. McConnico and requested an appointment with Governor McAlister. The Tennessee governor's office then notified Henry E. Colton, one of the Leas' attorneys, that his clients would be given a hearing before action was taken on North Carolina's formal demand. The hearing was set for the next morning, February 2.

The Leas' attorneys based their pleas for the governor's refusal of extradition on the grounds that their clients were not fugitives from justice because of the uncontroverted proof that they were not in North Carolina at the time of the commissions of the alleged acts upon which they were convicted (*New York Times* 3 February 1933).

North Carolina's position was that the Leas, because they had waived extradition and stood trial in Asheville, were fugitives from justice. Guilt or innocence, they contended, was not a matter to be considered by the asylum state in the question of rendition (Illich, "The Case of Colonel Luke Lea" 66).

At the close of the hearing McAlister announced that he would take under advisement the voluminous records and exhibits of the case and the extradition hearing and would probably not make his decision until the following Monday, five days hence (*The Nashville Tennessean* 3 February 1933). As was expected, he honored North Carolina's request for extradition. The warrant he signed gave the Leas the 24 hours they had requested in which to file for a writ of habeas corpus. Nettles stated at that time he would not try to deprive the Leas of their right to seek that writ.

A few hours after the fugitive warrant for them was issued by Governor McAlister, Colonel Lea and Luke, Jr., whose whereabouts had not been known for almost two weeks, surrendered to J.M. Peavyhouse, sheriff of Fentress County. Although holding them under guard, he permitted them to move into the small, frame, two-story Mark Twain Hotel in Jamestown and to go about the building unmolested while waiting for the

North Carolina agents to come for them (*The Nashville Tennessean* 15 February 1933).

About two hours after they had been taken into custody, a petition for a writ of habeas corpus was presented to circuit Judge Henry D. Brown at Oneida, a small town in that judicial district.

Early the next day Judge Brown, stating he was incompetent to hear the petition, issued a writ demanding that the North Carolina officers and Sheriff Peavyhouse of Fentress County produce Luke Lea and Luke Lea, Jr., before Judge J.H.S. Morrison of Jamestown on Monday, February 13, on which date they would be given a hearing on their habeas corpus petition (*The Nashville Tennessean* 8 February 1933). Two days later, Judge Morrison announced that he would not assume jurisdiction of their habeas corpus petition. The Leas found themselves in the strange position of being under arrest and denied bond, but not in jail, and having a writ of habeas corpus, but no judge to hear it (*Nashville Banner* 11 February 1933).

In compliance with Judge Brown's writ issued the previous week, the Leas and their attorneys were in the courtroom at Jamestown on Monday, February 13, at ten o'clock for the hearing. All 250 seats were filled and people were standing. Suspense mounted as the minutes ticked by. The murmuring crowd kept glancing toward the door as they restlessly shifted positions. Finally when no judge had appeared by noon, the Leas returned to the Mark Twain Hotel. Their attorneys, foreseeing that possibly no judge would appear, had filed another petition on Sunday night before Judge Elijah G. Tollett of Crossville, who granted a writ returnable on February 28.

During this protracted waiting for the arrival of the North Carolina agents, local citizens, unaccustomed to the excitement caused by the presence of the Leas, crowded into the lobby of the small hotel and up the stairs to the hall above so as not to miss anything. The Leas did not know whether the same persons remained throughout the night or whether those left and others came. However, when they went to bed, men—some sitting in the few straight-backed, split-bottom chairs that lined the wall and others squatting on the floor—would be peering intently toward their rooms, and when they got up the following morning the hall would already be filled with silent, staring men.

The colonel's opinion that terrific pressure was being brought to bear on the judiciary was confirmed by the statement issued by E.H. Crump, then United States Congressman from Tennessee's ninth district, in which he bitterly attacked the Leas and the habeas corpus proceedings and threatened to impeach or abolish the office of any judge who heard the case (*The Nashville Tennessean* 13 February 1933).

Days passed and still the North Carolina agents made no attempt to arrest the Leas. Their strategy seemed to be not to serve the warrant for the Leas' arrest until it could be served in the jurisdiction of a judge who they had reason to think was in sympathy with the faction that was opposed to Lea. Before such a judge Lea believed an impartial hearing of his case would be impossible.

Late the afternoon of Saturday, February 18, J.G. Reagan, circuit court clerk of Fentress County, handed the Leas a copy of a letter from Judge H.D. Brown, who had originally granted them the writ of habeas corpus, stating the case was not before him for any purpose and that he was returning all papers. Judge Morrison, before whom the writ was made returnable, had already declined to consider the case. Both judges also declined the request of counsel for the Leas to certify their disqualification so that chief justice of the Tennessee Supreme Court, Grafton Green, might designate a judge to hear the Leas' petition (*The Nashville Tennessean* 20 February 1933).

Later that night Lea received information that he might be kidnapped in Cumberland County, which was in the jurisdiction of Crossville Judge E.G. Tollett, before whom the writ of habeas corpus was then pending. Furthermore, Roy Beeler, Attorney General of Tennessee, had been quoted as saying Tollett was without jurisdiction to issue the writ.

Lea called Maxey Hewitt into his room and said: "I want you to do one last thing for me. Figure out the back route to Clarksville and drive us there."

The colonel explained the situation to Sheriff Peavyhouse and the urgent need for haste, and he agreed to accompany the Leas to Montgomery County. It was decided that Mrs. Lea and daughter Mary Louise would remain behind and leave the following day.

When the colonel and his son did not appear for breakfast at the Mark Twain Hotel, word was flashed across the state that they were no longer in Jamestown. They had been safely in Clarksville for several hours before their whereabouts became known. The Leas went to Clarksville because Judge John T. Cunningham had indicated that if the case were brought before him, he would have to act on it, as jurisdiction was determined by where a person was or the location at which the event took place.[16] They also believed he would not be intimidated by political pressure.

Their attorneys issued a statement that the Leas were in Clarksville available for the service of any legal process. Two days after their arrival, Judge Tollett of Cumberland County recused himself in their plea before him for a writ of habeas corpus (*The Nashville Tennessean* 20 February 1933). As day succeeded day and still no word came from North Carolina, the Leas became increasingly convinced that the object in the long delay was to catch them off guard in a locale where they would not be able to file a habeas corpus petition before an impartial judge in the 24-hour period Governor McAlister had granted them. Hence, they determined their best option was to wait in Clarksville for the arrival of the North Carolina agents.

Chapter Fifteen
The End of the Legal Battles

Control of the government of Tennessee by 1933 had been seized by the faction of the Democratic party that Luke Lea had always fought. However, the officers of the American National Bank were keenly aware that he believed that institution insolvent, and apparently considered him a threat as long as he retained his Nashville newspapers.[1] Up until that time the journalistic canon that prohibited a newspaper from printing a bank was insolvent so long as it remained open had restrained Lea from publishing charges of the bank's unsound condition even though it was common talk on the street.

Lea believed that the officers of the American Bank considered it imperative that the bank's precarious position and the extreme measures employed to keep it open be suppressed in order that it could continue to receive deposits, so redoubled efforts to wrest from him control of *The Tennessean* papers.

The night of the failure of the East Tennessee National Bank in Knoxville, a correspondent bank of the American to which it was indebted approximately $500,000, *The Tennessean* had been called twice by a person representing himself as an emissary of the officials of the American banks. The caller requested, not only for the protection of those banks, but also in the best interests of the Tennessee Publishing Company and its officers, that there be no publicity concerning the failure of the Knoxville bank.[2] The caller stated that if *The Tennessean* papers would not publish that item of far-reaching consequence, neither would the *Banner* publish that news. Lea regarded those calls on January 30, 1933, not only as a direct threat but also as a challenge to the freedom of the press. To have suppressed such news would have been contrary to the policy of *The Tennessean* papers and a violation of honest journalism.[3]

By the end of February, the financial condition of the American National Bank and the Nashville and American Trust Company had become so acute that Paul Davis flew to Washington to try to secure additional loans from the Reconstruction Finance Corporation.[4] The R.F.C. reputedly refused to make the loans. Governor McAlister was then called and asked to declare a bank holiday in Tennessee,[5] which emergency measure he proclaimed at 2:00 A.M., Wednesday, March 1, 1933.

During the national moratorium, enacted five days later, the federal government determined which banks were sound enough to continue in operation. According to information received by Lea, Davis' banks were not on the list approved to reopen.[6] Norman Davis was said to have contacted W.R. Cole, president of the L & N and a member of the executive committee of the American National Bank, who succeeded in influencing Secretary of the Treasury William H. Woodin,[7] and on the list of national banks to reopen on March 14 after the banking holiday, was interlined the name of the American.[8]

Lea was convinced that it was Davis who, while fighting to keep his bank open, pressured C.O. Carpenter to file suit against the Tennessee Publishing Company. As receiver of the Holston-Union National Bank, Carpenter held as collateral 28 debenture bonds of the publishing company. The notes on which the suit was brought had been extended by agreement and Carpenter had written a few months previously that he was so impressed with the management of *The Tennessean* that he considered himself justified in allowing the publisher time to work out the financial problems of the newspaper.[9]

It had taken three attempts over a period of two years to put *The Tennessean* newspapers into receivership, but the end came with stunning suddenness.

Couched in such language as to deny the Tennessee Publishing Company a hearing on the application for receivership, the suit was filed Friday, March 3, 1933 after court had adjourned and heard in the chambers of federal Judge John J. Gore, who was reported to be heavily indebted to the American National Bank.[10]

Two of the main grounds on which the receivership was asked were that the newspaper might not be able to make its sinking fund payment, which would be due one year from that time, and that the newspaper might not be able to pay its bond coupon interest, which would be due in two months.[11] On the date of receivership, however, *The Tennessean* was not in default in either payment, and the money to pay the bond interest when it came due was in the bank. For a property to be put into receivership because at some future date bond interest might not be paid was a radical departure from the established legal code.

The Leas, pinned down in Clarksville in their fight to avoid extradition to North Carolina and lacking funds for another costly legal battle, did what little they could to regain *The Tennessean*. In the answer of the Tennessee Publishing Company to the bill of complaint filed against it by C.O. Carpenter, Lea stated it had become incumbent upon him, because of the many untrue and malicious charges set forth in the bill, and because of the fraudulent motives behind its filing, to reveal the facts.[12]

The true purpose of the bill, he stated, was to destroy the freedom of the press. By placing *The Tennessean* papers in receivership, censorship of the Nashville press could be achieved as control of the *Banner* had already been acquired, he charged, by its being heavily indebted to the bank.[13]

Although there was no default on the $210,000 of the debenture bonds of the Tennessee Publishing Company held by the American National Bank, that bank had attempted twice before to get the other bondholders to join in filing a receivership suit against the Tennessee Publishing Company.[14] The placing of the Tennessee Publishing Company in receivership was hence not a step required by present circumstances but was rather the culmination of two years' effort to wrest control of *The Tennessean* papers from Lea.

One of the allegations upon which the receivership had been granted was that *The Tennessean* papers could not continue to operate unless they were put into receivership. However, in the several weeks that had elapsed between the appointment of a receiver and the filing of the Tennessee Publishing Company's answer to the receivership bill, the newspapers had continued to be published with funds on hand on the date of the receivership, plus monies collected since that date on business resulting from the management of its former officers.[15]

The answer of the receivership bill further alleged that in an effort to destroy the property of the Tennessee Publishing Company, the coupon interest had not been paid when due on May 1, 1933, so that the bonds would be in default and the property could be foreclosed and bought in by the large bondholders for a nominal sum.[16]

The answer of the Tennessee Publishing Company had to be filed in the same federal court that had granted the bill requesting receivership, and hence, had little chance of securing favorable action. Also, with the local press then under the control of persons hostile to him, Lea's disclosures of what he perceived to be the motives for the receivership had slim chance of being publicized.

His newspapers gone and his influence eroded, Luke Lea continued to believe the best available option was to remain in Clarksville where he and his son could instantly initiate habeas corpus proceedings as soon as they were arrested by the North Carolina officials. He was convinced that the officers of the American Bank were attempting to prevent his being granted a hearing for fear that he would expose what he considered to be the condition of the bank.

Day after day they waited, from February 19 to March 14, when Buncombe County Sheriff Laurence Brown with four deputies finally arrived and arrested them.

Judge John T. Cunningham issued a temporary writ of habeas corpus, setting the following Monday, March 20, for the hearing. Denied bond the Leas were committed to the Montgomery County jail (*Nashville Banner* 14 March 1933).

In addition to the new question of extradition, the Leas'

petition for a writ of habeas corpus presented for the first time and at the first opportunity additional charges of jury tampering. Affidavits were filed stating that through the influence of the prosecuting attorneys the venire from which the jury at their trial had been selected was hand-picked to increase the chances of obtaining a conviction.[17]

Judge Cunningham ruled on March 20 that the Leas were entitled to bail and announced that on March 30 he would pass on further pleadings he allowed attorneys to file and decide what matters would be included in the arguments should a hearing be granted.

At that preliminary hearing on March 30, Judge Cunningham ruled that North Carolina's motion to prevent a hearing on a permanent writ of habeas corpus for the Leas would be decided on Tuesday, April 11. On that date he refused to grant the Leas a hearing through a permanent writ of habeas corpus, and quashed the temporary writ, issued March 14. Declining to hear evidence of misconduct, he reduced his decision to two questions: were the rendition warrants issued by Governor McAlister valid and were the Leas fugitives from justice? To both he ruled in the affirmative (*The Nashville Tennessean* 12 April 1933). Judge Cunningham then granted the Leas the right of appeal, and allowed 40 days in which to perfect the appeal to the Tennessee Supreme Court (*The Nashville Tennessean* 12 April 1933).

The case was argued on June 20, 1933. Because of the voluminous record and the importance of the questions raised, the spring term of the Tennessee Supreme Court adjourned without rendering a decision.

Meanwhile, realizing that it would not be possible to get back *The Tennessean* in the immediate future, Lea determined to start a new newspaper. The town needed it. That was his field. His paper would give him a chance to expose the acts of those who were demanding that he be imprisoned. The newspaper would supply the money he desperately needed to continue his legal battle.

He rented a warehouse at 160 Second Avenue, North, and bought machinery. The sale of stock and subscriptions was begun.

A small staff was hired to get the paper under way; the paper that was to be christened *Free Press* and was to be published morning, evening, and Sunday. However, due to the depression it proved hard to sell stock in a new paper. In addition, Lea's legal problems worked against the inception of a newspaper, as did the unavailability of a wire service.

Lea was aware that at times he was under surveillance, and he had reason to believe that his telephone was tapped. Returning home from a brisk walk one day, he noticed a man trying to conceal himself behind the shrubbery that bordered the country club grounds along Belle Meade Boulevard. When he got close enough to get a good look, he recognized the man. Much to the *Banner* reporter's discomfort, the colonel made straight for him, stuck out his hand and greeted him by name. Remarking that he must be uncomfortable behind the hedge, Lea invited him to come across the street and sit in the yard swing where he could not only relax but could also see better. Dumbfounded, the reporter could only stammer that he was not trying to watch Lea's comings and goings and weakly declined his offer of a glass of ice water.

The colonel recounted the incident at dinner that night. His son Percy and Laura McAlister, the governor's younger daughter, had many mutual friends and were going to the same party that evening. Percy suggested phoning and getting her to pick him up to see what the *Banner* reporter would do when he recognized the governor's car driving into Boxwood. However, his father vetoed the prank.

Colonel Lea and Luke, Jr., were notified to be present at the convening of the Tennessee Supreme Court, December 9. The court decreed that it could not rule on the guilt or innocence of the Leas, nor could it review the fairness or validity of the North Carolina court's judgments (*New York Times* 10 December 1933). By unanimous opinion it upheld North Carolina's right to extradite them even though it was divided as to the legal grounds for that action (Illich, "The Case of Colonel Luke Lea" 87). Counsel for the Leas gave notice of their intention to appeal to the Supreme Court of the United States.

So acute had become Lea's financial condition that he was not able to secure a loan to pay for the preparation of the transcript of the record, which had to be paid in advance. Every asset he possessed—his home, its furnishings, silver, china, and Mrs. Lea's jewelry—had already been put up as collateral for money borrowed for living expenses and his legal defense. He had been heavily insured, but the policies that had not been dropped because the premiums could not be paid had been borrowed on to the limit. Moreover, he and Luke, Jr., voluntarily had drawn no salaries for over a year prior to *The Tennessean* being put into receivership.[18]

Lea knew it was imperative that this last appeal be presented in the best possible manner. His future and that of his son hung on the court's decision. Loyal friends lent the necessary money, and Clarence Darrow and Arthur Garfield Hayes were retained to represent the Leas before that high tribunal.

In the petition filed on April 2 counsel for the Leas insisted that the writ of certiorari should be issued because the Tennessee Supreme Court had not only decided a question involving federal law, but had decided it contrary to decisions of the United States Supreme Court, which had held that a person was not a fugitive unless he had been present in the demanding state at the commission of the crime (Illich, "The Case of Colonel Luke Lea 97-98).

The Supreme Court of the United States declined on April 30, 1934, to pass on the validity of the Leas' extradition, thereby exhausting all legal resources available to them.

As payment of Luke, Jr.'s, fine would have been an admission of guilt, they had not wanted to exercise that option when money had been available. Moreover, they had been confident that they would be exonerated in the courts. Faced with immediate imprisonment, however, Lea's overriding concern was how to keep his son from being incarcerated. Every possible avenue was exhausted but to no avail. It would be bad enough to be behind bars himself, but the thought of Luke, Jr., being in prison was almost more than he could bear.

The decision of the United States Supreme Court was certified down to the Tennessee Supreme Court. The colonel and his son were notified to appear Wednesday, May 9, to answer such orders as the court would issue.

That, Lea knew, would be his last day at home for some time.[19] Never had he been prouder of Miss Percie than with head held high she preceded him into the courtroom packed with many of their friends.

As the members of the court filed in and took their places, not one looked at either the colonel or Luke, Jr. L.E. Gwinn rose, stated that his clients were present in obedience to the court's order, and announced he had no motion to make. Instantly former Governor A.H. Roberts, Tennessee counsel for North Carolina, was on his feet and moved that both Leas be delivered into the custody of the North Carolina officers.

As Sheriff Laurence Brown walked toward the defendants, both Leas stood. Brown gave the colonel a miliary salute and then leaned over to shake hands with Mrs. Lea, while several people grabbed the hands of father and son. The sheriff escorted Lea from the courtroom at a rapid pace, closely followed by Luke, Jr., with Deputy Frank Lakey. The hallway was crowded with friends who pushed past local police to shake the Leas' hands as they did double time along the corridor to the south entrance.

As Lea emerged from the capitol and started down the steps, a half dozen or more North Carolina officers drew their guns. The scores of well-wishers lining the capitol steps were astonished to see the formidable display of weapons—machine guns, automatic rifles, submachine guns, pistols, riot guns—flash in the warm May sunshine.

Mrs. Lea hurried down the capitol steps trying to catch up with her husband. As she reached the car in which he had been placed, she was brushed aside by a deputy holding an automatic rifle and not allowed to say goodbye. Sheriff Brown refused to answer her query as to the route they would take but was heard to say, in admonishing a reporter not to try to follow them, that they would spend the night in Asheville (*Commercial Appeal* 10 May 1934).

Mrs. Lea fought back the tears as she stood on the curb

watching her husband and Luke, Jr., subjected to the humiliating treatment usually reserved for dangerous criminals. A man asked what she planned to do. She answered that she was going to try to follow them, whereupon he handed her a $100 bill. Flabbergasted, she could only murmur her heartfelt thanks.[20]

The lead car, filled with armed deputies roared off, closely followed by three other cars. With sirens wailing the motorcade dashed through the heart of the city at a high rate of speed.

Caught off guard by this maneuver, the Leas, within five minutes after being delivered into custody, were rushed toward prison without being permitted to go by their home for pajamas and toilet articles.

The motorcade swerved off the direct route to North Carolina and headed north toward Kentucky. Lea then surmised the North Carolina officials had probably been warned by his political enemies that an effort might be made to intercept the motorcade on the highway and forcibly prevent their being transported to Raleigh.

Because of their 600-mile circuitous route, it was nearly midnight before they reached Asheville. Waiting were Mrs. Lea, Percy, and L.E. Gwinn, with whom Sheriff Brown allowed the colonel and Luke, Jr., a few minutes before they were taken to cells on the top floor of the courthouse.

Early the next morning at Lea's behest, Judge Thomas L. Johnson of Asheville, a special prosecutor at their trial, telephoned Governor J.C.B. Ehringhaus to request a stay for Luke, Jr., in order to make further attempts to raise $25,000 to pay his fine. The governor's refusal dashed Lea's last hope of his son retaining his freedom (*The Nashville Tennessean* 11 May 1934).

On their departure for Raleigh no machine or riot guns were in evidence. The deputies, apparently trying to make amends for their previous display of force, let Mrs. Lea ride in the automobile with her husband and Luke, Jr. They stopped at Statesville for lunch, and the guards allowed the Leas a table by themselves and handled the situation so no one else in the coffee shop knew they were prisoners.

During the all too short drive to Raleigh, the colonel and Mrs. Lea discussed plans for her during their separation. The officers were considerate enough to drive her to the Sir Walter Hotel, then the car hastened on to the prison, a forbidding red-brick fortress with iron bars on West Morgan Street at the edge of the business district. As the Leas entered those grim walls, they wondered with heavy hearts how long it would be before they could pass again through those gates.

Chapter Sixteen
Prison

When Luke Lea and his son entered the prison front office they were quickly surrounded by reporters.[1] In a statement issued through his attorney, L.E. Gwinn, Lea said:

> We enter prison sustained by the consciousness of innocence, and firm in the belief that when the exultations from legal victories are over and the passions and prejudices resulting from the failure of a bank for which we were not responsible have passed away, even those responsible for our conviction will be ready to make amends as far as possible for the injustice of a court decision that brings us to a North Carolina prison.... (*The Nashville Tennessean* 11 May 1934)

Lea's only request—that he and his son share the same cell—was granted, and they were assigned to cell 305 on the third block. Issued prison uniforms, they joined the line-up for supper on the long platform outside the dining room.

Each inmate had an aluminum plate, spoon, and cup. A piece of fried lard, referred to as "bacon," and four or five chunks of dough, euphemistically called "bread," were on the plate, and bowls of cabbage swimming in grease were on the tables. In the cups was a deadly sweet substance, labeled "coffee."

The meal was over in ten minutes, and the Leas returned to the cell block. Prisoners had to stand looking out of the bars of their cell until they were locked in. A bucket was the sole toilet facility. The Leas had been warned that new prisoners frequently were "hazed" by somebody stumbling and pouring the refuse on them as they emptied the buckets the next morning. To spare his son from that indignity, Lea determined he would carry their pail.

Lights went out at nine. Before Luke, Jr., got into bed he

kissed his father good night and said that he had never loved him more nor had greater confidence in him. Never had his son uttered the first reproof or regret. In spite of how low in the eyes of the world he had fallen, Lea realized he was still blessed beyond most men to have the love and devotion of a son like Luke, Jr.

Soon they found their cell crawled with bed bugs. Sleep finally came, but a little past midnight Lea awakened thinking for a moment he was at home. Then came the realization deeper than ever of their utter helplessness. The hardest battle of his life ensued. He knew he must force himself to sleep, or for the first time in his life he would be defeated. His manhood crushed, he would become one of those furtive creatures he had seen in the prison yard. He knew he dared not think of home or he would lose the battle. He must make himself sleep.

He started to count but would intersperse his chant of numbers with Marshal Foch's famous phrase, "the will to win."

Luke, Jr., awakened. Prison rules prohibited talking, but every now and then he would whisper the time. The prison bell struck one o'clock. The counting and the chanting of "the will to win, the will to win" went on. Two o'clock sounded and then three. The count became easier as thoughts of the past became less frequent and the chant of "the will to win" became more regular.

By sheer determination Lea forced himself to fall asleep sometime before four. The rising bell sounded at 4:45. Lea had little sleep but had won the battle of self-mastery.

Lea's anticipation of the visit they were to have that morning from Mrs. Lea, Percy, and L.E. Gwinn was somewhat dimmed by the thought of his wife's seeing him in stripes. Arriving with toilet articles, underwear, and fruit, she was, as he really knew deep within himself she would be, the same as ever.

Straight-backed chairs lined both sides of the long, narrow visiting hall. Prisoners sat directly in front of their visitors, and posted at each door was a guard with a gun. When the room was filled, it was difficult to converse, and privacy was nonexistent.

Late in the afternoon to their surprise and joy, both Leas were assigned to Ward 3 of the prison hospital, which was immaculately clean, contained eight beds and a bathroom, and a dining room in which with the other inmates they were to have meals.

Warden H.H. Honeycutt sent for Colonel Lea on May 24 and asked if he would like a position checking in material to fireproof and renovate the building. Lea welcomed the opportunity because within the main prison there was little work. At the end of the 60-day probation period inmates were classified, and many were then assigned to jobs at various state institutions (*The Nashville Tennessean* 11 May 1934). Lea was also designated timekeeper, and it made him cheerful just to hear the telephone ring in the little office. He was kept quite busy checking in supplies and assisting in unloading and stacking lumber and brick. Several times he was drenched to the skin when the trucks arrived during summer rainstorms. The heat and humidity frequently were intense. Once he drank too much water and contracted such severe cramps that he had to be hospitalized.

For some unexplained reason Lea, on June 9, was moved out of the hospital back to the cell block, which was dreadfully hot and buggy. The separation at night of father and son was a blow to them both. Not long thereafter he was relieved of his job checking in supplies and keeping time sheets. Later he learned from an employee of the highway department that he had been removed because he had kept too accurate records. Having been surprised when he entered prison at the sympathetic attitude of his fellow inmates, he was somewhat hurt on being informed by a fellow prisoner that his demotion had caused general satisfaction.

Shortly thereafter penal welfare officer Loomis Goodwin reprimanded Lea for having too much company, stating that if it continued he would probably be sent to the prison farm. Lea knew that at his age it would be hard physically for him to perform the strenuous work required there.

He was ordered shortly thereafter to report to the plant where automobile license plates were made. He was one of the few, if not the only prisoner, with academic training who was assigned to physical labor. He had expected this and had been preparing himself for it by a strict regimen of exercising, which he would continue. His assignment to manual labor, he reasoned, could only mean one thing: it was believed that he could not stand up under it. He was convinced that his political enemies in Tennessee were determined that he should not leave prison alive. Their continued fear of him was a compliment, but it also was a warning of danger. Both increased his determination to survive and to expose what he considered their illegal acts.

When in full operation the tag plant ran from 5:00 A.M. to 5:00 P.M., and turned out about 6,000 pairs of automobile license plates per day. On Lea's end of the machine, only he and one helper had no prior experience. He promised himself that it would never have to stop because he was behind. While not difficult, his job required complete coordination between the brain and both hands. Were the numbers pulled or placed incorrectly by the previous worker, everything would be out of kilter unless straightened out. Hour after hour he sweated through the monotonous grind. Then finished tags were packed into crates. The throwing of the crates up onto the truck would have been strenuous for a younger man, but Lea managed. On entering prison he had made up his mind to do as he had done in the army—ask no favors, perform all jobs assigned, regardless of how hard or how demeaning, as well as he was able and never to complain he could not do what was ordered.

When there was little work to do, after policing the plant and premises, the men would be assigned to whatever job was needed: going to the women's wing to fill sacks with rags left from making the inmates' uniforms, or shelling peas and shucking corn in the vegetable house.

Lea quickly came to understand how difficult it was for men without an education to rise above their environment and after a day of body-wracking labor to force themselves to do the necessary studying and thinking to improve their situation. He was determined not to sink to the low level of his present condition, but he had the advantage of education and the motivation that came from the conviction that he was the victim of a terrible injustice. He never became careless in diction or resorted to oaths.

He bathed and shaved every day and was as neat about his appearance as he had always been. Imprisonment he knew could break a man's spirit, or it could help teach him mastery of self, a lesson, perhaps, never completely learned.

The end of the 60-day probation period passed without the Leas receiving A rank. The elder Lea heard through the grapevine that the reason he had not been promoted to grade A when he became eligible was that it was thought in some quarters that he would escape if he became an honor prisoner. This notion he surmised came from the same source that advised machine guns when they were taken into custody in Nashville.

The thought of escaping had never crossed Lea's mind: he had never run from anything in his life. No one of his past prominence and present notoriety could possibly find safe asylum, and no sane person could really think that he would attempt to make a break for freedom, which could only lead to his being hunted down like an animal. But that excuse was probably as good as could be devised for keeping him from being promoted to A grade.

Efforts had been initiated at once to obtain Luke, Jr.'s release. After conferring with Governor Ehringhaus and Parole Commissioner Edwin M. Gill and obtaining practically all the letters they had advised, Mrs. Lea presented a formal petition on May 16, seeking Luke, Jr.'s immediate release so he could receive the medical treatment recommended.

The prison physician, George S. Coleman, sent Luke, Jr. into town to be x-rayed and had two doctors from Raleigh and two from Duke University to come to the prison to examine him. The father was alarmed by what one of the doctors thought he felt in Luke, Jr.'s stomach.

To have his son imprisoned was the harshest blow of all. Although he knew they were guilty of no wrongdoing, he knew he was responsible for Luke, Jr.'s being in prison. The fact that he had been stricken with a malignancy compounded his father's anguish. He was tortured by the fear that his son's future health, perhaps his life, would be affected by his not being able to have proper medical attention. His consuming thought was to get Luke,

Jr. freed. Each day started in hope that he would gain his freedom and ended in disappointment that he had not.

Lea had a hunch on Friday, July 27, that his son would receive his parole that day. Luke, Jr. arrived at the tag plant about four o'clock breathless from running. One look at his face and his father knew the news was good. Summoned to the warden's office, Luke, Jr. had been informed that Governor Ehringhaus had signed his parole and that he would be released the following morning. In addition to good behavior, his parole specified he was to report monthly for two years to Judge W.W. Faw of Franklin, presiding justice of the Tennessee court of appeals (*The Nashville Tennessean* 28 July 1934).

His son's release lifted a heavy burden from the colonel's shoulders. When all their efforts to maintain their freedom had failed, his greatest struggle had been to decide whether to permit Luke, Jr. to go to prison or to raise his fine in the only way that was then possible—to mature the little life insurance that he had left from the $2 million worth he had once carried. He came to the conclusion that Luke, Jr.'s life would be blighted were his freedom bought in that way and would incline him, should his burden ever become unbearable, also to take the easiest way out and follow in his father's footsteps.

The week following Luke, Jr.'s release, the colonel's son, Percy, was killed in an automobile accident. Returning to Nashville from Chicago on August 3 with the teen-aged winners of *The Tennessean*'s route carriers contest, Percy, the only person seriously injured, was thrown from the seat next to the driver onto the highway.

It was customary that prisoners be granted furloughs to attend funerals of their immediate families. North Carolina officials, however, were still apprehensive that Lea, if given the chance, might escape, or that his friends if opportunity arose would free him, so the request was not handled routinely. The governor at first opposed allowing Lea to return home[2] but finally agreed provided Tennessee officials guaranteed he would be returned to Raleigh immediately after the funeral and that they would defray all expenses incurred by the trip (*The Nashville Tennessean* 4 August 1934).

Lea was summoned to the front office and told that if he were allowed to attend his son's funeral he would have to be accompanied by an armed guard,[3] even though Tennessee officials had given the required guarantees and a group of *Tennessean* employees had agreed to be responsible for the expenses involved (*The Evening Tennessean* 4 August 1934). Lea's long-time friend Fred Seely of Asheville posted a $10,000 bond for the prisoner's prompt return.

Davidson County Sheriff L.A. Bauman and chief of the Tennessee Highway Patrol Benton McMillin, in compliance with the conditions set by the North Carolina chief executive, were dispatched to accompany Lea on his drive through Tennessee. At the state line the entourage was met by more Tennessee highway patrolmen. These elaborate precautions—humiliating and ludicrous—were borne in silence by Lea.

The house was filled with sorrowing friends when he arrived Sunday afternoon at Royal Oaks, the home of Mrs. Percy Warner, where his family was staying. The next morning Doctor Edmund P. Danridge, rector of Christ Church, celebrated Holy Communion for the family in the drawing room with Percy's remains. Several hundred friends gathered at Royal Oaks for Percy's services that afternoon and accompanied his body to Mount Olivet where he was buried next to his mother's grave.

Percy's holographic will dated March 1 of that year indicated to Lea that his son had a premonition of his approaching death. The three younger Lea children were the beneficiaries of his $15,000 life insurance policy.

The colonel was up before five the next morning to dictate some memoranda and to have a final conference with Luke, Jr. Accompanied by Miss Percie and daughter, Mary Louise, he started the trip back to Raleigh a little before eight.

As Lea re-entered prison, the turn of the key in the lock that barred him from freedom had the dreadful clang of doomsday. In addition to the rigors and isolation of incarceration that he already knew were the realization of his helplessness and the destitution of his family.

Through a company in which he was interested, Lea had participated that spring in the purchase of 104 Henderson County bonds. He had been assured of their genuineness by Charles W. Hewgley, a prominent Jackson attorney with wide experience in passing on the validity of municipal bonds; P.O. Roberts, the county judge who signed the bonds; an affidavit from Terry Wright, a Henderson County attorney from whom the bonds were purchased; and the judgment of W.N. Estes, who for many years had been in the municipal bond business and whose company handled the transaction (*The Nashville Tennessean* 10 June 1934).

A few months before he went to prison, Lea proposed to pledge to the Life and Casualty Insurance Company, which held the mortgage on Boxwood, $40,000 of Henderson County bonds, which he hoped to acquire. After Life and Casualty had made a careful check and was satisfied that the bonds were valid and would be good security, it had accepted Lea's proposal (*The Nashville Tennessean* 11 June 1939). The remaining Henderson County bonds Lea had purchased were to provide for his family in the event the United States Supreme Court refused to hear his case and he was sent to prison. On May 22, Estes visited Lea in prison to report that the bonds were forgeries.

Every last penny Lea had been able to scrape together he had put into those bonds because he considered their appreciation a certainty. He dared not think of how without them Miss Percie would manage for herself and the children.

Mrs. Percy Warner had planned to spend the summer in Honolulu with her other daughters and she invited Percie and the children to be her guests at Royal Oaks. Even though it was a bitter blow to Luke's pride to be forced to accept charity for his family, he and Percie were deeply appreciative of her mother's generosity.

Miss Percie asked their friend Stutson Smith for a job with his general insurance agency, and she went to work at once, which was another blow to Lea, but he realized it was necessary. Her success in selling insurance with no previous experience would be gratifying. However, little more than living expenses could be expected from that source. Moreover, she was needed in Raleigh to initiate efforts to secure the colonel's release.

Luke, Jr., struggled to carry through the plans he and his father had formulated for realizing what little money could be obtained from their remaining meager resources. Due to the lack of capital, however, he was not able to start the weekly newspaper about which he and his father had dreamed.

Shortly after his return from Percy's funeral, Lea was placed by the prison physician, Doctor George Coleman, in charge of the drug room. He finally was made an A prisoner on August 21, and at lunch break he surrendered his stripes in return for the white wash pants and shirt of honor grade inmates.

In addition to his exacting duties as head of the drug room, Lea was in reality Doctor Coleman's secretary. A card had to be made for each new prisoner as he was examined, routine shots tabulated, treatment of the sick recorded, drugs that were administered noted, and sundry records and reports compiled. The day began at seven o'clock in the morning and lasted until all records were completed, which was usually late afternoon with only a ten-minute break for lunch. Lea's hours varied according to the hospital's case load, but it was not unusual for him to work until eight or nine o'clock at night. Lea tried to the best of his ability to minister to the patients who were ill and to ease their pain both physical and mental. Innumerable times he sat all night by the bed of a desperately sick or frightened patient, holding his hand and trying to soothe him.

Quite soon it became Lea's heart-rending job to secure from a prisoner prior to electrocution the data for his death certificate. All he could do in those interviews was to give the condemned men cigarettes and to say a few words that he hoped would be of some comfort. Out of these experiences he became convinced that capital punishment must be abolished. If it were wrong for one person to take the life of another, it was equally wrong in his opinion for a court to attempt to right that wrong by taking that individual's life.

Lea adhered to a rigid schedule of setting-up exercise and frequently got in a five-mile or more walk, which he found the best method of relieving pent-up emotions as well as an inducement to sleep. As he walked around the prison yard with erect carriage at the pace of a mile per 15 minutes, he was often struck by the dehumanizing effect of prison. Only a handful of men would be throwing a ball; the rest lounged immobile, devoid of hope or initiative.

He soon realized that instead of preparing inmates for citizenship, prison was a training school for criminals. Every aspect of prison life was degrading; its monotony past comprehension until experienced. There was no privacy at all from the guards or the other inmates. Yet there was no one, with the exception of Doctor Coleman, he could talk with, and no one in whom he could confide.

The high point of the day was the arrival of the mail, which was censored. Miss Percie and Luke, Jr., were wonderful about writing every day and sending telegrams on Saturday so he would hear from them on Sunday. He wished, however, they would tell him exactly what was happening as it increased the difficulty of making decisions when one did not have all the facts. Yet he was appreciative of their trying to save him from needless anxiety when his instructions ran into inevitable snags and delays. However, when they amended his instructions, he feared that they were losing confidence in his judgment.

The extent of his fall was sometimes hard even for him to believe. Once he could originate policies for the state of Tennessee and influence decisions on the national level, yet he could not at that time even direct his own affairs. Nevertheless, he knew better than to give way to self-pity. He must face the future: only the tired gazed at the past. The question was, at his age without a penny in the world, how far could he come back when he was released?

The absolute conviction of his innocence rather than make him bitter—he could not afford the luxury of such an emotion—made him determined to obtain his freedom. Only by a well-organized campaign could he hope for an early release. But before an application for a pardon was filed certain matters must be accomplished.

His political enemies in Tennessee had been instrumental, he believed, in having the federal indictment in connection with the Holston-Union Bank returned against him, as well as the case in the criminal court of Davidson County, so that should he win one, he could be brought to trial on the others. Their determined purpose, he believed, was to get him out of the way, but it was really immaterial in which prison he was confined. Since he had been convicted at his trial at Asheville, prospects looked brighter for achieving that goal in North Carolina than in either of the other two cases, so those had been continued pending the outcome of his fight for extradition.

The month after Lea was imprisoned, the conspiracy charges in the Davidson County criminal court growing out of the failure of the Liberty Bank and Trust Company had been dropped. Attorney General pro-tem Seth Walker, who had been appointed by Judge Charles Gilbert to bring the charges, admitted the relative insignificance of the most serious charges that were brought against the Leas in their home town by remarking: "Any attempt to prosecute the case would be comparable to taking a man convicted of murder out of the penitentiary to prosecute him on a charge of carrying a pistol" (*The Nashville Tennessean* 16 June 1934).

The government brought J.B. Ramsey, president of the defunct Holston-Union Bank in Knoxville, to trial the latter part of January 1935. Of all the bank's transactions, it was only on those with which Lea was connected that the indictment had been drawn.[4] The trial lasted six weeks, but it only took the jury an hour and a half to find Ramsey not guilty. The verdict was also an automatic acquittal for Lea. There was no way he could be convicted of aiding and abetting the president of the bank in misapplication of funds when the president had been found innocent of that allegation. United States District Attorney James B. Frazier, Jr., stated the case against Lea would be retired, but no formal decree to that effect was entered in the court records.

On the day of the hearing on Lea's application for a pardon, a federal warrant and detainer in that case would be filed requesting North Carolina authorities, should his pardon be granted, immediately to turn him over to the federal government (Raleigh, *News and Observer* 16 June 1935). However, Lea's attorneys finally succeeded in having the charges formally dismissed later that month.

Before plans got underway to secure his pardon, it was also of vital importance he thought to have his income tax matter settled. The same persons who had been instrumental in bringing about the indictments against him had also instigated, Lea was convinced, efforts to have him prosecuted on his income tax returns for 1929.[5] One of the items under investigation was the sum he had paid his sister, Laura Robertson, which he had deducted as an interest charge due her for that year. Ever since she had turned over her inheritance to him to manage at the death of their father, Lea had sent her in monthly checks a handsome yield on her investment, never deducting that amount from the principal. However, the government had arbitrarily taken the position that all or part of the payment made to her in 1929 represented a return of capital.[6]

Another item under investigation was the profit realized by Bank Securities Corporation, which had been incorporated February 25, 1929, by a small group of which Lea was a member to reorganize and consolidate the Union and Planters Bank and Trust Company and the Manhattan Savings Bank and Trust Company, both of Memphis, into the Union and Planters Bank and Trust Company. Bank Securities Corporation, in its return for 1929, reported the profit it had gained from the transaction. However, the government contended that Lea and the other organizers of Bank Securities were individually responsible for the profit that had accrued to the corporation.[7]

Lea had filed an appeal from that ruling with the United States Board of Tax Appeals and did not pay the assessed tax on the disputed items. No action was taken on his appeal, but while fighting to have his conviction at Asheville reversed, Lea was assured by the commissioner of Internal Revenue that in the event he went to prison, the matter could be compromised for a nominal amount.[8] Still no action was taken.

Eventually after the expenditure of a great deal of time and effort over a period of years, the matter would be settled in December 1937 without the formality of a hearing. The amount of Lea's income for 1929 was finally agreed upon at $247,797 instead of $1,151,417 as the government had contended, and because of the settlement no penalty was imposed (Memphis, *Commercial Appeal* 19 December 1937).

Several days before his mother's death on February 10, 1935, Lea for no apparent reason had been thinking a great deal about her. He realized his difficulties had been to her as a running sore, yet he had at all times tried to be a good son. This time the temporary parole granted a prisoner to attend the funeral of his mother was handled in a routine manner with none of the elaborate precautions taken when he was permitted to go to his son's funeral. Services were at Christ Church in Nashville, and burial at Mount Olivet cemetery.

After the funeral, Fred Seely, who again was Lea's surety, went to Saint Louis, and Lea's guard, Oscar Pitts, confident that his presence was unnecessary, stayed at the Noel Hotel to allow Colonel Lea privacy during his three-day furlough.

Lea was informed that because the Henderson County bonds had turned out to be forgeries, Life and Casualty Insurance Company, which had accepted them as payment on the mortgage it held on Boxwood, was going to foreclose unless a substantial payment was made promptly. Lea was also notified by the Canal Bank in New Orleans on March 30 of the forthcoming sale of the debenture bonds of the Tennessee Publishing Company. There of course was no possibility of raising the funds to make a bid on either his home or the newspaper.

After the foreclosure of Boxwood, April 27, 1935, Mrs. Lea in September sold approximately half of their furniture from the warehouse where it had been stored. The sale ran for several days and it attracted large crowds, but many were there out of curiosity and did not bid. Even though most of the items brought low prices, a little money in addition to that required to clear the mortgage on the furniture and storage charges was realized.

The premiums on approximately $100,000 of insurance on Lea's life—all that remained of the more than $2 million that he had once carried—were due in September. The colonel appealed to six intimate friends and to six persons who because of him had made many times the amount he was asking them to lend, the repayment of which would be guaranteed by the assignment of a corresponding portion of his remaining insurance. Several did not even acknowledge his urgent plea, but through the generosity of a few the necessary money was raised. He was keenly aware that Miss Percie's mother, who was providing a home for her and the children, was getting along in years and that her sole source of income was an annuity. It was painfully evident that should Mrs. Warner die while he was in prison or should he die without insurance, his wife and children would become the objects of public or private charity.

Lea's only possibility of earning money while he was incarcerated was from his pen, so he kept writing, but none of his stories and articles sold.

The first step toward obtaining the colonel's release was the letter written to Governor Ehringhaus on September 7, 1934, by W.S. Coursey, chief witness for the prosecution at the Leas' trial in which he stated:

...The testimony upon which Luke Lea and his son was convicted was based entirely upon his indebtedness to the bank ....

Many months before any note had been discounted for him, he had purchased, without recourse, several hundred thousands of dollars in notes receivable from the Central Bank and Trust Company, and had also purchased a large amount of bonds of the Central Securities Company, a subsidiary of the bank—in all the total amount being nearly $800,000.... None of these facts were known or came out at the trial of the case. So that, as the matter stood at the time of the trial, Colonel Lea and his interests were carrying worthless notes and bonds, to the extent of something like $800,000, and the bank was carrying obligations of Lea and his interests of about the same amount.[9]

Criticism of Coursey's having been employed by the Leas weakened the impact of his statements. Hence it was considered essential, even though the findings would corroborate his report, to have an audit made of all of Lea's transactions with the defunct Central Bank, the accuracy and objectivity of which audit could not be questioned. In his desperate need for funds Lea turned to the men he had led in battle. A.M. Pullen and Company, a highly regarded public accounting firm with which Lea had no previous connection, was selected.

While the audit was being made, it was advised that letters requesting his pardon must be secured in such numbers and from such persons that they would be impossible to ignore. The North Carolina press, uniformly hostile in the past, must be contacted and convinced of his innocence, then prevailed upon to print the facts about the transactions on which he had been convicted, thereby creating a climate favorable for his release. The Asheville newspapers, presumably to divert attention form their heavy indebtedness to the Central Bank, had been vehement in demanding the prosecution of Lea who they claimed had wrecked the bank, and their hostile tone had been followed by the majority of the state's press.

Mrs. Lea was in Raleigh most of the autumn of 1934, laboring tirelessly to execute the plans the colonel had formulated. The ongoing correspondence seeking to interest persons in his behalf required much secretarial work. His former private secretary, Ted Hagerty, because of her closeness to the Lea family had been unable to secure a good position, so she went to Raleigh in the autumn of 1934 to help. She stayed at the home of Mrs. Park Matthewson, where Mrs. Lea boarded when she was in Raleigh. Later Mrs. Lea and Miss Hagerty secured a room at the more convenient Bland Hotel downtown for the same price they had been paying Mrs. Matthewson.

The Leas believed that the Pullen Report which substantiated, as they were confident it would, the statements in Coursey's letter to the governor, could not fail to obtain the colonel's immediate release. However, all hopes of his being freed before Christmas were dashed on December 3. After having under advisement for nearly three months Wallace B. Davis' application for a pardon, Governor Ehringhaus decided not to grant clemency to the former president of the defunct Central Bank. This action would make Lea's bid for freedom infinitely more difficult. He was in an awkward position as far as the audit was concerned. Since it was generally known that the audit had been prepared, not to present it would be interpreted as a confession that it was not satisfactory. However, a request for clemency at that time was doomed to failure.

Shortly after the first of the year while cleaning out the hospital files to make room for the 1935 records, Lea found three hack saws and a small bottle of oil. He was uncertain whether they had been put there for a break-out attempt or as a plant in an effort to have him removed from the drug room. He immediately turned them over to the night guard on duty even though he realized that by doing so he might become implicated. However, Doctor Coleman after a short association knew the calibre of man Lea was. The doctor's respect for Lea and admiration for the manner in which he conducted himself in prison deepened into genuine interest and real friendship. The doctor's long discussions with him on a wide range of subjects provided the intellectual stimulation Lea sorely missed, and he was actually treated quite well while he was in prison due in no small measure to Doctor Coleman's watchful eye.

It was extremely difficult to get the effort for Lea's release under way. Everything depended on something else and at every step snags and interminable delays were encountered.

Through the good offices of James Hammond, publisher of the Memphis *Commercial Appeal*, Mrs. Lea was able to interest the Hearst publications in her husband's predicament. That organization agreed to assign to the case for five or six weeks Earl Shaub, the reporter who had covered for those papers the Leas' fight for extradition. Perhaps finally some good publicity would be forthcoming. Then would be the time to act.

Forsaken by so many, it was hard to turn down any proffered

aid. Lea's friends sometimes pursued courses of action that were at cross purposes with what other friends were trying to achieve. Nashvillians Dick Atkinson and Joe Williams, who had spearheaded a drive among Lea's friends to raise the funds needed to employ an attorney to try to secure his release, arrived in Raleigh in April for the purpose of securing letters and obtaining favorable publicity in his behalf. Their request for clemency was based on Lea's outstanding military record, their belief that he had served enough of his prison term, and that he was desperately needed by his wife and three young children.

In Raleigh at the same time was Lea's life-long friend David Shepherd of Sewanee. Never doubting Lea's innocence, Shepherd had made a detailed study of the case and had compiled a short but cogent brief, which showed Lea was not guilty on the counts on which he had been convicted. Shepherd's purpose was to get the facts into the hands of persons in positions that could obtain Lea's freedom, which he deserved not as an act of mercy, but as an act of justice.

It was essential that the attorney who represented Lea be of the highest standing. After going over the brief for several days, J. Melville Broughton, who later would serve as governor of North Carolina, was convinced the case had merit. He agreed the latter part of April to represent Lea and to present his application for a pardon.

The long planned for day finally arrived—June 1, 1935—the application was filed. A pardon was asked as a matter of justice on the grounds that the recently completed audit and newly discovered evidence proved that Lea was innocent of the banking law violations on which he had been convicted and for which he had served thirteen months of the six to ten years that he had been sentenced.

Corroborating Lea's contentions, Coursey's statements and Caldwell's affidavit, the Pullen Report pointed out that the first transaction with Lea interests was on May 12, 1930; therefore, the precarious condition of the Central Bank as reflected by the examiner's reports of 1928 and 1929 could not have been influenced by the Lea transactions. On July 3, 1930, the date of the examiner's last report, the bank had received $428,480.99 more credit accommodation from the Lea interests than it had rendered to them, so instead of hurting the bank as of that date, the Lea interests had substantially benefitted it.[10]

W.T. Lee, chairman of the Corporation Commission at the time bank examiner D.M. Darden's reports were made, wrote Pullen and Company on December 1, 1934, that the reason the Corporation Commission allowed the Central Bank to remain open, knowing its condition was increasingly precarious since the bank examiner's 1928 report, was that it hoped economic conditions would improve and that the bank thereby would be able to survive its difficulties and regain its solvency.[11]

At the time of the Leas' trial it was generally believed, and it was on that basis that the prosecution proceeded, that the Lea interests and Caldwell and Company and the Bank of Tennessee were one and the same. Lea's decision, on the emphatic but disastrous advice of his lead attorney, North Carolinian Albert Cox, not to put on proof, caused that erroneous assumption to be continued.

New evidence filed with the application for a pardon included photostatic copies of letters and records not available at the time of the trial because the records of the defunct Caldwell and Company were locked up in receivership. Those documents substantiated the claims of Lea that he was not a party to the $300,000 certificate of deposit transaction for which he was convicted in the first count, nor the $45,000 city of Asheville notes in count seven.

It was also generally believed, and the prosecution proceeded on that assumption, that the ten cashier's checks amounting to $100,000, the subject of count five, were sent in blank to Nashville for the benefit of Luke Lea. The Pullen audit showed, however, as Lea had maintained, that every cashier's check of the Central Bank handled by him or his interests was either paid for or promptly returned unused, and that neither he nor any of his interests profited one cent by any cashier's check transaction nor did the bank suffer any loss thereon. Moreover, the Pullen report showed that without the funds made available by Lea the bank could not have paid its clearings on October 10 and 11, 1930—the days on which he was convicted of defrauding the bank.

Lea in count seven was charged with the substantive crime of misapplication, which by statute applies only to bank directors, officers, employees, and agents, none of which Lea was.

In spite of the regularity of the handling of the items cited in count seven—the fact that the Central Bank, in failing and insolvent condition, lent over $800,000 to the Lea interests created great suspicion in the minds of the public and the prosecution at the time of the trail. However, the Pullen audit established from the records of the bank that Lea and the Lea interests rendered accommodations to the Central Bank in an amount almost equal to that rendered by the Central Bank to Lea and the Lea interests. Rather than the Central Bank, in an insolvent condition, lending money to the Leas, that bank exchanged securities in its portfolios for securities of various of Lea's interests which the bank then used to secure additional deposits from other customers.

In its various proceedings North Carolina never seriously attempted to hold Lea's conviction on count seven valid. The trial court ordered Lea's sentence under the seventh count to run concurrently with the sentence under the first and fifth counts. Hence, should Lea's sentence under count seven be held invalid, he would still have to serve the same length of time on the sentences imposed under the other two counts.[12]

The new evidence fully supported by documentary records clearly showed that the circumstantial evidence at the trial led to erroneous conclusions that resulted in Lea's conviction.

Filed also with the application were scores of letters from a wide cross-section of persons in North Carolina and Tennessee to indicate that a pardon for Lea would be well received.

When the application was filed on June 1, the hearing was set for June 12. As was customary the parole commissioner then contacted the trial judge and prosecutors of the case for their recommendations.

T.L. Johnson, recommended clemency; L.P. McLendon, the

other prosecutor, and Zeb Nettles, solicitor of Buncombe County made no recommendation; but the trial judge, M.V. Barnhill, expressed his "positive and unequivocal opposition to a pardon" due to his belief that Lea was "clearly guilty," not only as charged but in many other instances (Raleigh *News and Observer* 13 June 1935). The parole commissioner had invited anyone opposed to the application to appear at the hearing, which lasted six hours. No one came. Only two letters, both anonymous, had been received expressing opposition to the pardon.

J.A. Rennie, who made the audit on which the application for pardon was based, was present at the hearing to answer Judge Barnhill's criticism of the audit and to explain any portion of it to the parole commissioner. The costly error of Lea's not having taken the stand in his defense at the trial was demonstrated again. Barnhill termed that decision a refusal by Lea to subject himself to cross examination, and several times during the hearing Gill referred to the fact that Lea had not gone on the stand when he had the opportunity.

Broughton stressed the fact that North Carolina through its civil action in federal court against the receivers of Caldwell and Company had recognized that two of the transactions on which Lea was serving time in the penitentiary, the $300,000 certificates of deposit, the subject of count one, and the $45,000 city of Asheville notes, an item in count seven, were transactions solely between the Central Bank and Caldwell and Company and the Bank of Tennessee. Hence, the state was in the position of holding Rogers Caldwell liable civilly for transactions he admitted he had and to which the records of Caldwell and Company, the Bank of Tennessee, and the Central Bank established he was a party, while at the same time holding Luke Lea liable criminally for the same transactions with which he had no connection or interest.[13]

Then began the wait.

Governor Ehringhaus, stating he had been unable to discover any new evidence in the application that warranted a pardon, on July 13 denied the petition.

The bottom again fell out of the Leas' world. They had

presented evidence irrefutable to them, which established that:

Count one involved a transaction solely between the Bank of Tennessee, and Caldwell and Company, and the Central Bank.

Count five consisted of a transaction undertaken by Lea solely for the benefit of the Central Bank which temporarily saved the bank rather than defrauding it.

Count seven charged Lea with misapplication which by statute applied to only bank directors, officers, employees or agents, none of which he ever was of the Central Bank.

Yet the governor had termed that evidence inconclusive.

They knew it would be fatal to despair, but they dared not think how long the colonel could remain imprisoned. However, no further action could be taken at that time, and the money raised by their friends to try to secure his release had been exhausted.

The months following Governor Ehringhaus' refusal to grant him a pardon were Luke Lea's Gethsemane. Every day was a struggle not to be broken by the deadly routine of prison life. At times he feared its dehumanizing effect would dull his initiative and will. He tried to keep his attention riveted to his own matters: what he could contribute while imprisoned to the well-being of his family, how he could secure his freedom, how best to preserve his health and morale, what he could accomplish when he was released. He determined that during his confinement to try to better himself spiritually, mentally, and physically so that at the end of each day he could feel he had gained and not lost.

He was determined to be of as little burden to the family as possible, and the recurring battles he had to maintain "the will to win" were seldom apparent.

The one bright spot in the dismal situation was Ted Hagerty's remaining in Raleigh. Sometime previously the colonel had gotten her a job with his friend, North Carolina state senator Lunsford Long. She was Lea's link with the outside world. Every Wednesday she took him fruit along with typed copies of the work he had given her the preceding week, and he would give her instructions to communicate to Miss Percie and Luke, Jr.

Strong letters favoring clemency were finally received in December from Zeb Nettles, Buncombe County solicitor, and L.P. McLendon and Thomas L. Johnson, special prosecutors at the trial, together with a letter from Judge Barnhill stating he would no longer oppose clemency. The governor declined to act at that time.

Lea's deteriorating health was of much concern to his family. He continued to lose weight at an alarming rate. He had considerable pain from the ligaments torn in his ankle the preceding November, and on Thanksgiving he had suffered a mild heart attack. The previous spring his sinuses became so infected that he had to be sent into town repeatedly for treatment, and Doctor L.N. West would have operated at once was not warm weather just beginning. Then during the chill winter Lea had become quite ill with abscessed tonsils.

The middle of January, Larry MacPhail, a captain in the 114th Field Artillery who had accompanied Lea on his trip to Holland to try to kidnap the kaiser and who was then general manager of the Cincinnati Reds, offered the colonel a position with the baseball club and wanted him to accompany the team to Puerto Rico for spring training. Lea was deeply touched by MacPhail's gracious offer, which did not entail a long-term commitment to the baseball club but would provide him with immediate employment. Broughton requested Ehringhaus to parole Lea so he could accept MacPhail's offer. The governor refused. However, he spoke well of Lea, his work in the hospital, his prison record, and said the time was rapidly approaching when he would give him relief.

More than six weeks passed. Wednesday, April 1, began uneventfully, but late that afternoon Lea was summoned to the warden's office. He was informed that he would be paroled the following morning. His parole, as the parole of his son, was conditioned upon good behavior, and until further notice he was to report monthly to Judge W. W. Faw of the Tennessee court of appeals.

Governor Ehringhaus, in a prepared statement, said:

In the discharge of his duties as an honor grade prisoner, he has gone beyond the mere requirements and appears to have been animated by a desire to be of service to those unfortunate prisoners afflicted with disease....

Taking into consideration this exemplary conduct and the length of time served, it appears the ends of justice have been met.... I reserve the right to revoke this parole at will, for any cause satisfactory to myself and without evidence. (Raleigh, *News and Observer* 2 April 1936)

After being handed his parole, Lea returned to the hospital to complete the monthly report so as to leave his work at the prison finished up to the minute. Then he changed into his clothes that he had worn back to Raleigh from his mother's funeral 14 months before. The blue suit hung loosely, and the collar of the white shirt was too large. When Lea was dressed, the prison physician, under whom he had worked for a year and a half, presented him with a new gray hat. There were tears in Doctor Coleman's eyes as he watched Lea gather up his few personal belongings. As the two men shook hands, Lea said, "I'm leaving all this behind, but I won't forget you, Doctor."

Coleman replied in a voice choked with emotion, "I don't know what I'm going to do without you, Colonel."[14]

Luke Lea went through the prison gates a free man shortly after 11 o'clock. The moment toward which all his energies had been bent for the past nearly two years had come at last. He was a great deal thinner than when he had entered prison, and his hair was not as thick and was beginning to gray slightly, but his bearing was still erect and his presence commanding. Smiling broadly, he inhaled the air of freedom as his heart overflowed with happiness and gratitude that he had been victorious in the greatest battle of his life—the constant struggle not to be broken by imprisonment. He knew he faced an up-hill fight to reestablish himself, and he prayed "the will to win" would sustain him in whatever adversities lay ahead.

After going to see several persons including Governor Ehringhaus to express his appreciation for his parole, Lea started motoring for home accompanied by Luke, Jr., Luke, Jr.'s wife, Sara, and Ted Hagerty. They reached Asheville a little after midnight, and to his great joy Miss Percie and Mary Louise had driven there from Nashville to meet him.

When he reached the outskirts of Lebanon about 5:30 the following afternoon, he was met by an honorary escort of motorcycle patrolmen led by Davidson County Sheriff L.A. Bauman. As the colonel's car neared the public square, several hundred people, gathered there to welcome him home, surged up the street to greet him personally.

Smiling broadly, Lea got out of the car and was immediately surrounded by friends jostling to reach him. He shook the hands of those he could reach and called greetings to others. The excitement became electric as Lea moved through the crowd to stirring tunes played by the American Legion band under the direction of Sidney Groom, who had led the band attached to Lea's regiment during its service in France.

When Lea after nearly an hour had made his way through the welcoming throng to the other side of the Lebanon square, he was persuaded to mount to the top of a bus to say a few words.

Visibly touched by the outpouring of affection at this tumultuous welcome, he said:

I would not be human if I did not appreciate the friendship which has been shown to me here today. What I have been through makes me know as nothing else could that friendship is what makes life worth while. (*The Evening Tennessean* 4 April 1936)

He next paid tribute to his wife for having stood by him and having worked untiringly in his behalf. The colonel's words were interrupted by a cheer that went up from the crowd, who then called for Mrs. Lea. The throng parted so she could be escorted to her husband's side.

As Lea climbed down from the bus, the automobile of Hilary Howse, mayor of Nashville, had been eased through the crowd. The exuberant gathering became quiet as they watched Mayor Howse, who had always opposed Lea politically, extend the official welcome of Nashville to the colonel on his return home.

The procession then formed. To call as much attention to his return home as the machine guns and police cars with sirens blaring had given to his departure for prison, the motorcade of more than a hundred cars accompanied by a motorcycle escort bore Lea and his family triumphantly to Nashville (*The Evening Tennessean* 4 April 1936). They went through the heart of the city then out West End Avenue to Royal Oaks, where waiting on the porch were Laura and Overton who raced into their father's arms as he got out of the car.

He and Miss Percie went into town the following morning to buy a suit that fit. The heart-warming reception of yesterday continued. As he strode down the sidewalk, he was stopped by friends and strangers. It was the tonic he needed.[15]

No sooner had he returned to Royal Oaks than a stream of visitors began. The deluge of long distance calls, telegrams, and letters continued.

Erstwhile both friend and foe, former governor Ben W. Hooper wrote:

...I was awfully glad when I learned from the press of your release. I have always felt that your conviction was a tragic mistake and injustice. I have sometimes thought that you would do some pretty mean things in politics, but I have always known darn well that you would not defraud anybody or any institution of a red cent....

That evening friends hosted a banquet in Lea's honor at the Noel Hotel. The lobby resounded with strains of martial music by the American Legion band as the more than 300 persons, who had come from all parts of Tennessee to welcome him, assembled in the ballroom.

Lea received a standing ovation as he was called upon by toastmaster, Judge J.D.B. DeBow, and the flag bedecked room echoed with long rounds of applause. He bowed several times and waved as his friends continued to cheer. Then he signaled for silence. His voice was firm, but he was obviously striving not to succumb to deep emotion as he began to speak:

My beloved friends-

There is no bitterness of any kind in my heart. If there was, the joy of this meeting would drive it away.

I have been through my garden of Gethsemane. I have been confronted with the problem of whether to live, to go on, and I have decided to have the courage to face life. You have given me a fresh courage and opened a new page of life. And I feel it my greatest ambition that I may walk worthily in the faith and confidence you have shown me....

Turning to his wife, he voiced his undying gratitude to the woman who had stood by him through all adversity, whose words and deeds had never been of reproach but of encouragement. He continued:

There comes a time when everyone must take an inventory, and that is what I am doing. I am now penniless and 57 years old. I know my life's expectancy is not great, but I have the faith and confidence of thousands of my friends who have sustained me and wealth overflowing from the love of my family.

After speaking hopefully of the future, he concluded softly:

I will always try to govern myself so that you, like I, will look back upon this occasion with greatest pleasure. (*The Nashville Tennessean* 5 April 1936)

The following morning the Leas attended the 7:30 celebration of the Holy Eucharist, which was the first time Lea had received the sacrament in a church since before he went to prison. Immediately after Mary Louise's confirmation that morning, the colonel enplaned for Washington to begin his climb back into the world.

Chapter Seventeen
Promises Fulfilled

Less than a month after Luke Lea was paroled, James Hammond, publisher of the Memphis *Commercial Appeal*, presented to him the intriguing proposition of running for governor of Tennessee. The group Hammond represented would finance Lea's campaign, take care of his household expenses, and provide a fund for him to live on after the election as they knew he could not live on the governor's salary. Hammond assured Lea that he could be elected.[1] Lea agreed to consider this gratifying offer but quickly came to the conclusion that it was not feasible. Were he to accept, he would be beholden to the persons who provided his financial backing. Moreover, were he elected, the governorship would delay his reentry into the publishing field on which he had his heart set.

Staying out of politics, however, was not possible for Lea. Early that summer Speaker of the United States House of Representatives Jo Byrns died suddenly. Richard M. Atkinson, former Attorney General of Davidson County and a political friend of Lea's, was one of three aspirants for the House seat thus vacated. When Atkinson was painfully injured in an automobile accident the end of of July, Lea, at the candidate's request, took charge of his campaign. Atkinson emerged the victor by a scant thirteen votes.[2]

Although Lea had been stripped of his one-time power, he knew whom to contact in various counties to turn out the vote, so his advice was sought again during the summer of 1936 by the strategists of Gordon Browning's gubernatorial campaign. Boss Crump of Memphis announced a couple of weeks before the primary that he was supporting Browning, an endorsement which assured his nomination. Two years later, however, Browning was defeated by Prentice Cooper, who was backed by Crump. From that incoming administration, Lea knew he could expect only hostility. Hence, with the power structure in Nashville still aligned against him, most doors in his native city remained closed to the colonel. Consequently he had to continue to seek employment elsewhere and would be away from home much of the time.

His myriad activities after his release from prison could roughly be divided into three categories. First was his dream of establishing a magazine supplement to the country weekly newspapers. Second, while always working on that plan, he had to seek whatever employment he could find to support his family. Finally, because of his deep commitment to the commonweal and his crusading spirit, he always gave careful thought to current problems facing the country. Frequently he prepared detailed memoranda on pertinent issues that he tried to get to persons in decision-making positions. His three primary purposes were usually intertwined in whatever he was working on at the moment, and it was often difficult to determine which was paramount.

Once Lea had thought a plan through to conclusion, the challenge lay in its implementation. He enjoyed fitting the various possibilities together in different combinations, but chafed at the delay occasioned by waiting until one step was concluded before he could proceed to the next. He had the vision to see what needed to be done, and the means he worked out to accomplish his plans were logical and beautifully simple in that each piece neatly dovetailed into the others. The trouble lay in the concept they embraced being larger than the terms in which the average person was accustomed to thinking, and often in being ahead of his time in formulating a solution to a problem before that situation was widely perceived as requiring change.

A different type of mind would have concentrated to the exclusion of everything else on accomplishing the first phase of the plan. Then consideration would be given to expanding to the second phase. Not being a methodical plodder, the tedious was irksome to Lea. After working out various means of implementation, his mind turned to other matters.

Lea never discarded what he considered a good idea such as the development of a network of super highways. He had been scheduled to present his plan to Herbert Hoover on October 29, 1929, but because of the stock market crash that day all of the president's appointments had been canceled.

Aiding Lea on this project and a variety of other matters through the coming years and with whom he shared an office in Washington from 1937 until his death was General R.C. Marshall, Jr. A widely respected business broker, Marshall was highly successful, had formerly been secretary-manager of the General Contractors Association and was associated in several enterprises with G. Hall Roosevelt, brother-in-law of the president.

Lea drafted his ideas into what became known as the Super-Highway Bill, S. 3428. Introduced in the Senate by Ohio Senator Robert J. Buckley in February 1938, it provided that the federal government charter a corporation for the construction of at least three transcontinental super-highways east and west and six north and south. Bonds issued by the corporation and guaranteed by the United States would provide funds for their construction, but tolls paid by motorists would make the project self-liquidating within a short time.[3] White House endorsement was quick and enthusiastic.

Bill H.R. 9478, similar to Senator Buckley's super-highway bill, was introduced in the House by Congressman Henry Steagall of Ozark, Alabama. The plan received such overwhelming support that Lea was elated and confidently expected the measure would be enacted into law at that session of Congress. At last one of his big plans was about to click. His expertise in working the matter out not only would insure his future financial security but would also give him the satisfaction of knowing that he had made a real contribution to the welfare of his country.

Of course in due time super-highways would span the country, but not then. K.D. McKellar, senior senator from Tennessee and a long-time foe of Lea's, was not in favor of the Buckley bill and kept it bottled up in committee. Meanwhile Buckley was defeated for reelection.

Lea considered the fate of the bill only a temporary setback, but the delay was fatal to any immediate financial benefit to him. He immediately requested Congressman Cartwright of Oklahoma to push through the House the bill introduced in the previous Congress. Next he secured the agreement of another senator to introduce a similar super-highways bill in the Senate early in 1939, McKellar's promise to support the measure having first been obtained.

While the bill was proceeding through the slow parliamentary steps, Lea was considering the feasibility of constructing a super-highway from the Texas border to the Panama Canal.[4] His mind raced forward. The ultimate objective of this program should include super-highways down each coast of South America connecting with the highway to the Panama Canal, thereby making the Americas real neighbors and opening the United States as the marketplace of the Western Hemisphere.

Lea's long cherished plan for a national weekly would fill an unoccupied field in journalism and start from its first issue with a large prepaid circulation established through a contest giving to subscribers the most valuable prizes ever offered in a newspaper promotional campaign. With its progressive editorial policy, its emphasis on Americanism, and being financially self-sustaining, the magazine would be influential in molding public opinion. Almost half of the modest annual subscription rate would be used to purchase the securities of the holding company that would be formed to acquire leading daily newspapers throughout the country.

The beauty of Lea's plan was twofold. It could be put into operation with any of several newsprint companies, motor corporations that would supply the prize automobiles, securities underwriters, and newspapers, and would be quickly financially advantageous to each participant.[5]

The difficulty was that the participation of several groups was necessary, and once any committed to that large an undertaking, it was important to move ahead immediately. It would be hard, he knew, to sustain the enthusiasm of one group while trying to interest other necessary parties. Delay was the danger.

Time and again he came within a hair's breath of putting through this plan. One of Lea's greatest attributes was his refusal to accept no. When his proposal was turned down, he reworked it and presented it to yet another group.

Lea effected a consolidation in 1939 of the *Dixie Farm and Poultry Journal* with the *Tennessee Valley Farmer*. The new publication, *Dixie Farmer*, had a circulation of approximately 150,000, much of which lay in the rich Tennessee valley.

The Parthenon Publishing Company was formed to publish the farm journal. It would be extremely difficult to secure the cash with which to print the first few issues, but Lea knew it had the potential for making money, and a good farm paper could be gotten out with a minimum of time and effort. The colonel would sell national advertising while he was in the East working on his larger plans; Luke, Jr. would actually get out the paper, simultaneously investigating which county papers in Tennessee could be bought; and Ted Hagerty would do the secretarial work. At last a concrete step had been taken toward getting back into the publishing field.

The *Dixie Farmer* limped along but because of lack of capital never realized its potential. Due to newsprint shortage during World War II, the eight-page paper was reduced to a bimonthly tabloid of four smaller pages with subscriptions at $.60 for three years.[6] Finally it suspended publication in 1944.

Lea was increasingly drawn into public relations work, as his legislative expertise was valuable in assisting clients get bills through Congress. Beginning in 1942, he represented the Tri-State Independent Oil Association, Victory Oil Lines, Texas Pre-fabricated House and Tent Company, and the Nashville Auto-Diesel College.

Firmly convinced of the importance of understanding and friendship among the nations of the Americas, Lea drafted a bill to be introduced in Congress in 1944 that authorized the formation of the Pan-American Foundation, which in cooperation with the state and federal governments, would establish scholarships in the

United States for students from Canada, Mexico, Central, and South America. Those countries would be benefited by the knowledge their students acquired in the United States, which in turn would gain from the good will of the men and women it educated.[7]

Lea's prison experience undoubtedly developed his compassion. Yet his sympathies had always been with the little man. A business and political progressive, many of his views in his later years were considered liberal, yet he believed that the liberty Americans had always enjoyed was based on the fiscal responsibility of the government. He advocated a reduction of taxes, affordable housing, self-liquidating public projects, aid to education, collection of the multibillion dollar international debt, and prison reform.

While on one level his incarceration was put behind him, on another, the horrors of prison life, its cruelties and inhumanities, were seared into his soul. He was convinced the penal system neither protected society, deterred crime, nor rehabilitated the convict. He prepared a resolution in 1937 for Senator George L. Berry of Tennessee to submit to the president establishing a commission, of which Lea would be a member, that he envisioned would ameliorate the condition of prisoners and also prevent an ever-increasing economic waste.[8] His plan was not implemented, but his interest and efforts continued. Neither was Lea able to interest a publisher in assigning someone to work with him in bringing to the attention of the public existing penal conditions, which, if properly done, he was confident would arouse mass indignation for reform.

In Lea's opinion the day was not far distant when common sense would dictate that persons convicted of nonviolent crimes would not be confined but would be punished by having to contribute to the injured party the amount of the injury, plus a penal fine, and the cost of the trial. Hence, the guilty person would not become a financial burden to the taxpayers. Until the prison system could be completely revised, Lea advocated that its emphasis be changed from punishment to rehabilitation. Inmates should be taught reading, writing, simple arithmetic, and a trade, so upon release they could become self-supporting.[9]

The colonel continued trying to regain *The Tennessean*.[10] Unable while he was in prison to raise the funds with which to bid on the 250 bonds of the Tennessee Publishing Company that the Canal Bank held, he managed nevertheless to hold up sale of the newspaper.

E.W. Carmack, Jr., son of the late Senator Carmack, who at the time he was slain in 1908 was editor of *The Tennessean*, acquired on June 4, 1935, from Mrs. Lea all of the common stock of the Tennessee Publishing Company (except approximately five shares) under an agreement that he would pay to her its value at the expiration of one year as determined by arbitration.[11] The day set for the petition asking for the sale of newspaper to be heard, June 6, Carmack filed before Judge John J. Gore a petition under 77-B of the Federal Bankruptcy Statutes to reorganize the property. Litigation continued until the paper was purchased at public auction on January 7, 1937 by Silliman Evans for $850,000[12] even though the court's attention had been called to the property's questionable title which inhibited bidding.[13]

Lea believed that Paul Davis did not care who got *The Tennessean* as long as it was not the Leas and was someone who would operate the newspaper in a manner that was friendly to the American National Bank. Lea also believed that R.F.C. Chairman Jesse Jones allowed Paul Davis to buy the $250,000 of debenture bonds of the Tennessee Publishing Company from the Canal Bank without putting up any money and to force the sale of the newspaper on the condition that Jones' friend, newsman Evans of Texas, be allowed to purchase it at the court-ordered sale. The Tennessee Publishing Company was unable to stay the confirmation of the sale, but continued to keep the litigation open.

With the passage of years, the political climate and personalities changed. By early 1945 Jesse Jones was no longer head of the R.F.C., hence Paul Davis and Silliman Evans could no longer count on the favored treatment they had reputedly received from that powerful quarter in the past. Senator K.D. McKellar was reportedly fearful that he was about to lose the formidable support of Boss Ed Crump of Memphis.[14]

It was in that atmosphere that Lea and McKellar made up their long standing bitter political differences. By virtue of seniority, McKellar had become one of the most powerful men in the United States Senate. Persuaded that a great wrong had been done, he determined to use his considerable influence to have the 1937 sale of *The Tennessean* set aside.

Lea provided him with the facts and figures and on February 26, 1945, McKellar introduced Resolution 87 calling for an investigation of the disposal of the government's interest in that newspaper. The committee to which it was referred reported it favorably, and it was then considered by the Senate and passed as amended.[15]

The first step of the judiciary subcommittee empowered to investigate all phases of the sale of the Tennessee Publishing Company properties would be to investigate the action of the R.F.C. in acquiring and selling the $250,000 of bonds of the Tennessee Publishing Company, pledged to the Canal Bank and Trust Company, and of the $210,000 of bonds that came into possession of the American National Bank among the assets of the Fourth and First National Bank when those two institutions were merged in 1930.[16]

At long last the regaining of his property seemed almost within Lea's grasp. He advised that the investigation be conducted on the solid foundation that the sale had destroyed the freedom of the press. The investigation moved slower than he had hoped, but progress was being made.

With the $15,000 life insurance Percy had left to the three younger children, the Leas had purchased in the autumn of 1936 a lovely residence of white stone, designed similar to Monticello, at the corner of Craighead and Whitland. Lea enjoyed being able again to have close friends in his home. Informal Sunday night suppers of soup, salad, and dessert quickly became an established weekly custom, which always included the Starnes and frequently the Fensterwalds and Derivauxs, Luke and Sara, and later the Mallisons when they moved back to Nashville. Often other intimate friends—the Henry Dickinsons, Tom Hendersons, Allen Browns, and Stutson Smiths—were guests, and it was not uncommon for there to be one or more extra persons for dinner during the week. Ted Hagerty was again the colonel's secretary and frequently was an overnight guest. Even though he no longer took an active role, he always retained an intense interest in Tennessee politics, and the conversation usually centered on political events throughout the world.

When he was in Nashville, he conferred almost daily with his lawyer, J.G. Lackey, with whom he discussed fully all aspects of his business. There was one matter, however, on which Lea would never take his attorney's advice although he realized its soundness. Repeatedly Lackey tried to persuade him not to attempt to repay the more than a million dollars that he was indebted personally and through his companies. However, considering those debts a moral obligation, Lea refused to avail himself of the bankruptcy law.[17]

Luke Lea was pardoned on June 15, 1937, 14 and a half months after he had been paroled, by the newly elected governor of North Carolina, Clyde R. Hoey, who promptly carried out that previously announced intention. It was particularly gratifying that Hoey granted a full pardon on the merits of the case without a hearing, and his action met with widespread approval.[18] To their great relief Luke, Jr.'s, parole had already been terminated in the autumn of 1936 through commutation of his sentence.

Lea's post-prison diaries indicate that he had known after his release life would be difficult, but that he had underestimated the apparent viciousness of his enemies who continued to try to block his every endeavor to get back on his feet. He was grateful, however, that the bitterness toward him did not extend to the three younger children. His occasional despondency he kept to himself, while his natural optimism enabled him to look to the future and redouble his efforts.

Without magnificent health and incredible energy, Lea could

not have survived the fast pace on which he thrived. His body, however, sent him repeated signals in the autumn of 1944 that would have been imprudent to ignore. After an appointment at Johns Hopkins Hospital he agreed to go back for a cardiogram and laboratory tests.[19]

There was no way he could slow down. For the present he must continue to travel and spend most of his time in Washington. It was important that he prosecute his business as forcibly as possible. It would only worry his family to admit some health problems, so he would just take as good care of himself as he could.

Home for the weekend the middle of November 1945, he postponed his return to Washington because he was not feeling well. The pain continued intermittently Tuesday, and on Wednesday no longer was there any doubt that he was having an attack of something. Although he could ill afford the time and money it would cost, he knew he had no alternative but to go into the hospital.

At first it was thought the problem was the colonel's heart, but an electrocardiogram was normal. Spasms of excruciating pain continued, so the gall bladder was suspected. Other doctors were called into consultation, and additional tests were run. There was talk of operating, but a leading surgeon ruled out that option as he did not know for what he would be operating.

The colonel began vomiting dark blood. The doctors were doing all they could, but he was steadily getting worse. Miss Percie and the children maintained their composure so as not to alarm him. He was acutely aware, however, that he was gravely ill. A skilled nurse was desperately needed, but not even a sitter could be secured during the wartime shortage, so his wife, relieved occasionally by one of their daughters, sat beside his bed. By promising to stay at the hospital himself, Doctor R.C. Derivaux finally persuaded Miss Percie to go home Sunday afternoon and try to sleep for a few hours.

The colonel was asleep. His two daughters were sitting on either side of the bed, each holding one of his hands. His breathing was harsh and rasping but it was regular. Doctor Derivaux stepped out into the hall to talk with an intern.

Suddenly Laura was aware that the rasping sound had stopped. "He's not breathing," she said as she called Doctor Derivaux.

He dashed into the room, followed by the intern. The girls were sent outside. The physicians did what they could, but Colonel Lea was dead.

So some patient might be helped in the future, Mrs. Lea consented to an autopsy. It was determined that the colonel had been stricken with pancreatitis, the symptoms of which attacks were often confused with heart and gall bladder malfunction, and which at that time was inoperable.

Luke Lea's death at age 66 was a great shock. It seemed impossible that a man so vibrant and robust could be dead. Stunned as his family was, it was, nevertheless, a consolation that his illness had lasted only a few days and that he had been spared the last ignominy of lingering, incurable suffering.

The newspaper account of Lea's death said he had been living quietly since his release from prison. Those who knew him well smiled at the ineptness of that statement. He had withdrawn from the limelight, but he remained the man about whom Governor Gordon Browning once remarked: "...had so much activity about him that you never could tell which direction he was going until he was there" (Lee, *Tennessee in Turmoil* 12).

Born to wealth and position, he could have led a life of ease, but such an existence had no appeal. He believed he had an obligation to serve his fellow men. His vision of what could be and his unquenchable desire to bring about improvements compelled him to battle unceasingly for what he was absolutely certain was the common good.

How had it all happened? those gathered that chill November afternoon around his grave mused. How could Luke Lea have lost his newspapers, his realty holdings, his political influence?

If only he had not continued to be involved in Tennessee politics after his election in 1911 to the United States Senate, it all might have been different. However, it was unrealistic to expect him to terminate his interest in the issues that affected the lives of all Tennesseans and to remain aloof from the uneasy coalitions that had evolved.

If only he had not antagonized the railroads and the liquor interests, he would not have incurred the undying opposition of those powerful groups. But he believed the influence they had on Tennessee along with other southern states was corrupt and stultifying and must therefore be overthrown.

If only he had not become so immersed in the day-to-day affairs of state government in the latter 1920s, he would not have made so many additional political enemies and also alienated those who were opposed to any person's having so much power. It had never been his intention to become involved on that level, but Governor Horton, being inexperienced, leaned upon him heavily for counsel, and in Lea's desire for the progress of the state to be continued, he had allowed himself to be drawn in ever deeper.

If only he had accepted the appointment to the United States Senate in 1929, he could have participated in directing the policies of this nation through a perilous period of history. Yet his belief that he could serve his state best as a private citizen coupled with the attention demanded by his many business enterprises compelled him to decline.

If only he had not become associated with Rogers Caldwell in various business ventures, he would not have become so linked with him in the public mind that he would be jointly blamed for the loss of funds in the collapse of Caldwell and Company and other Caldwell enterprises with which he had no connection.

If only he had paid more attention to details and not left matters hanging, or had been able to delegate authority, his affairs would not have been so jumbled. If only he had not been so overextended, he would not have been so vulnerable to the depression.

If only he had not been so audaciously sure of himself, it might not have been so difficult for his friends to disagree with him and he might have listened to their advice.

If only he had not gone voluntarily to North Carolina to stand trial when passions were so inflamed, he would in all probability never have been convicted. But knowing he had committed no crime, not to go was to him unthinkable.

If only he had set up a trust fund for his family while he was able and had not gone deeply into debt fighting to maintain his freedom, he could have had financial security in his later years. But how could anything be held back when that amount might tip the scales in his favor?

If only his energies had not been so widely scattered or his plans so ambitious, perhaps after his release from prison one of his major projects could have been pushed to resolution. Even if in the beginning it were on a small scale, in time it could possibly have grown to his envisioned proportions. But it was not his nature to concentrate on one matter to the exclusion of all others or to think in small terms.

If only, if only….

But if he could have done any of those things, he would not have been Luke Lea. Being the person he was combined with the conditions that existed and the people who opposed him, each major decision he made led inexorably to the next event.

Lea never dwelt on "what if's," but in retrospect, he made several misjudgments that proved costly in the extreme. He thought the Federal Reserve would not permit the large numbers of banks to fail during the 1930s and the country to slide into the terrible depression. He did not realize at first that his lines of credit had been destroyed when the banks with which he did business failed. He did not foresee the consequences of waiving extradition and voluntarily going to North Carolina to stand trial, and of not taking the stand in his own defense. Not being vindictive himself, he never dreamed that his political foes would go to such lengths to try to destroy him.[20]

The fact that Luke Lea went to prison was proof to many of his guilt. He did not live to see his name vindicated, but he was confident that in time he would be exonerated. Through all his vicissitudes he was sustained by the knowledge that he was innocent, the trust of his wife, his children, his close friends, and his faith in God.

What was this man really like whom his enemies despised with implacable fury, yet who inspired in his friends absolute trust? Some thought him arrogant and ruthless but most of the employees of *The Tennessean* and the men he led in battle had an unshakable devotion and loyalty to him. Some thought he wanted power, others believed he strove for the betterment of his fellow men, but most agreed he had the courage of his convictions. To most people Luke Lea revealed only small facets of himself. To many he will always be an enigma, even though he left an indelible impression on most with whom he had contact. He is remembered by some for his zest for living, his ready smile, the confidence and energy he radiated. Most acknowledged his wide range of interests, his quick mind, his devotion to his family. Despite the many accusations hurled at him, there was never a whisper of marital discord. Few were immune to his compelling charm. He was credited by columnist Joe Hatcher with being able to walk into a room filled with his enemies and in five minutes, through the sheer force of his personality, be in command of the situation. No announcement was made of his visit one day to Senator W.E. Brock in his glass-enclosed office overlooking the plant of his Chattanooga candy factory, yet the men and women left the machines and were drawn as if by a magnet to the windows of the office to get a look at Luke Lea.[21]

The physical bravery Luke Lea exhibited on the battlefields of France paled in comparison to his raw courage in not allowing his proud and sensitive spirit to be crushed by the degradation of prison. In spite of continued rebuffs after his release, he built a new life with his mind and his determination his only tools.

Luke Lea did not accomplish everything he set out to do upon his release. Many of his hopes and dreams were interred with him. Although he had made substantial payment on his mammoth debts, he had not succeeded in liquidating them. He had not been able to set aside money for his family's future. He had not regained *The Tennessean*, and his demise was also the death knell of the Senate investigation of its sale. He had not brought about needed reforms in the penal system.

What he did, however, in those nine years was considerable. His refusal to be defeated by reversal of fortune and his joy in living created a happy, secure, stimulating life for his family. He was too busy enjoying the limited time he could share with them to pass on old bitternesses. Rather his thoughts turned toward the future.

Although he died impoverished as wealth is counted in coin, Luke Lea had the satisfaction of knowing that he had left the world a little better than he found it. He had a part in shaping the course of events in Tennessee in the first third of the 20th century in which much progress had accrued.

To have shared intimately in Luke Lea's life was a rare privilege. To me he left joyous memories, the example of a life victorious in the triumph of the human spirit, and an abiding pride that this man was my father.

Notes

Chapter One
A Life Bright with Promise

[1]Her obituary in the Nashville newspaper, the Daily American, said she died suddenly with her husband and Mr. and Mrs. Overton Lea at her bedside and listed marasmus as the immediate cause of death. Partly because of her naturally retiring disposition, the article stated, but mainly because of her continuing ill health, she was known to perhaps fewer people in Nashville personally than any other lady of her station. "Her life has been passed practically in seclusion for many years, as she rarely appeared in public except on fine days, at certain times of the year, driving in her carriage." The obituary further surmised that "she has always been perhaps the richest woman in Tennessee."

[2]John M. Lea to his sister, Margaret Henegar, August 23, 1887, Lea Papers.

[3]According to an unidentified Nashville newspaper dated September 28, 1869, Colonel John Overton, one day prior to the Civil War, was riding his horse to the courthouse and passed an auction in progress. The officer of the law who was conducting the sale called to him that a good bargain was being offered. A cow was tied under a tree nearby, and assuming it was the cow that was being auctioned, Colonel Overton entered a bid of a dollar more and proceeded on to court. Much to his surprise he discovered a few days later that he had bought a lot instead of a cow. After he recovered from his amazement, he determined to build a hotel on the lot, which he did with bricks made on his farm, Travellers Rest. He named the palatial structure the Maxwell House in honor of his wife, Harriet Maxwell Overton. Though incomplete, the structure was used as a hospital during the Civil War. Completed following the war, it was the last word in elegance and was for many years the leading hotel in the city, before it was gutted by fire on Christmas night, 1964.

[4]Conversation with Mrs. James O. Murdock, 1954.

[5]Conversation with Mrs. George A. Frazer, February 25, 1970.

[6]Luke Lea, "A Living Death" (unpublished sketch, 1934-1936), pp. 7-8, handwritten draft, Lea Papers.

[7]Overton Lea, Jr., New York, to his mother, Lealand, October 25, 1901.

[8]Overton Lea, Jr., New York, to his mother, Lealand, June 10, 1903.

Chapter Two
Publisher and Politician
[1]B.L. Wiggins to Luke Lea, August 8, 1903, Lea Papers.
[2]B.L. Wiggins to Luke Lea, February 7, 1905, Lea Papers.
[3]Interview with Walter Seigenthaler, July 18, 1972.
[4]Memorandum, Lea Papers.
[5]Home Telegraph Company of Nashville v. The Mayor and City Council of Nashville, February 22, 1907.
[6]Interview with Judge Albert Williams, Murfreesboro, July 10, 1978.
[7]This summary of the prohibition movement relies heavily on Paul E. Isaac, *Prohibition and Politics, Turbulent Decades in Tennessee, 1885-1920* (Knoxville: University of Tennessee Press, 1965).
[8]Account of the convention reported in *Nashville American* and *Nashville Banner*, 29 May-2 June 1906.
[9]Interview with Walter Seigenthaler, July 18, 1972.
[10]Overton Lea to Percy Warner, July 12, 1908, unposted letter, Lea Papers.
[11]For this account of the Carmack-Patterson campaign and its aftermath, I am indebted to Isaac, *Prohibition and Politics*, pp. 137-169.
[12]Conversation with Luke Lea.
[13]Luke Lea, "The American Dreyfus Case" (unpublished manuscript, 1934-1936), p. 18, Lea Papers.
[14]Luke Lea, "The American Dreyfus Case" (unpublished manuscript, 1934-1936), p. 17, Lea Papers.
[15]Indebted for information concerning the development of Belle Meade to Oscar Cromwell Tidwell, Jr., *Belle Meade Park* (Nashville, 1983).
[16]Luke Lea to Nashville Railway and Light Company, December 5, 1910, Lea Papers.
[17]Bradley Walker, secretary-treasurer of the Nashville Golf and Country Club, to Luke Lea, September 1, 1911.

Chapter Three
The Youngest Member of the Club
[1]Luke Lea to L.V. Woodlee, April 7, 1910, Lea Papers.
[2]Luke Lea to Charles T. Cates, Jr., October 21, 1910, Lea Papers, detailed the financial arrangements in purchase of *The American*.

The Tennessee Publishing Company was organized to take over both of the newspaper properties, and it first purchased the property of The Tennessean Company and assumed the payment of the bonds of The Tennessean Company, amounting to $125,000.

It purchased the property of *The American* from the American Company, and assumed the first mortgage bonds of The American Company to the amount of $110,000, and the second mortgage bonds of The American Company amounting to $150,000.

It then issued a consolidation bond issue in the amount of $460,000, and placed $125,000 of this in escrow to provide for the payment of bonds of The Tennessean Company. It then placed $110,000 in escrow to provide for the payment of the first mortgage bonds of The American Company, and $150,000 in escrow to provide for the payment of the second mortgage bonds of The American Company.

[3]Account of deadlock taken from daily issues of *The Nashville Tennessean and the Nashville American* and *Nashville Banner* published during the convention.

[4]Undated and unidentified newspaper clipping, Lea Papers.

[5]Associated Press dispatch, datelined Washington, July 13, 1911, Lea Papers.

[6]W.P. Dillingham to Luke Lea, January 6, 1912, Lea Papers.

[7]Unidentified newspaper clipping datelined Washington, July 11, 1912, Lea Papers.

[8]September 13, 1915, tabloid, Lea campaign literature, p. 2.

[9]Luke Lea to D.H. Belcher, January 4, 1912, Lea Papers.

[10]Unidentified newspaper clipping datelined Washington, March 19, 1912, Lea scrapbook, Lea Papers.

[11]Undated memorandum on Senate record, Lea Papers.

[12]Account of transfusion taken from unidentified newspaper clipping datelined Washington, June 19 and published in papers across the nation; and Luke Lea, "The American Dreyfus Case" (unpublished manuscript, 1934-1936), pp. 19-20, Lea Papers.

Chapter Four
A Progressive in State and National Politics, 1911-1914

[1]For additional information concerning the attempt to repeal the 1909 election laws, and about Fusion and the harmony movement, see Paul E. Isaac, *Prohibition and Politics, Turbulent Decades in Tennessee, 1885-1920* (Knoxville: University of Tennessee Press, 1965), pp. 196ff. Behind the scenes activity taken from correspondence of Luke Lea with Herman Suter, Percy Warner, A.M. Shook, Stanley Trezevant, Governor John I. Cox, and others, Lea Papers.

[2]Luke Lea to former Governor John I. Cox, April 26, 1911, Lea Papers, detailed the basis on which he thought a settlement could be achieved.

...It is to be understood, from your conversation that, you, and the faction of the Democratic Party to which you belong, are ready and willing to signify publicly your purpose to leave the present temperance laws untouched by any amendment, modification, or repeal at the present legislature, so that this assurance being given, the only difference remaining would be the election law.

It is insisted by your faction that the proposed amendment to the election law does not change the principle of the election law, and, while many may and do not agree to this construction of this amendment, yet, your construction of it furnishes a basis for settlement. For if the amendment makes no change in the principle of the election law, then it must inevitably follow that it will be satisfactory to you and your associates if the old law should be left in full force and effect, provided the personnel of the State Election Board is satisfactory to you and your associates ....

[3]Luke Lea to Chester C. Platt, May 30, 1912, Lea Papers.

[4]Lee Douglas to Luke Lea, May 17, 1912, Lea Papers.

[5]Unless otherwise noted account of Baltimore convention taken from Arthur S. Link, *Wilson: The Road to the White House* (Princeton: Princeton University Press, 1947), pp. 434-51, and daily Associated Press dispatches from Baltimore published in the *Nashville Banner*.

[6]Luke Lea to Jim Deming, August 5, 1912, Lea Papers.

[7]Luke Lea to Edwin Leham Johnson, September 15, 1912, Lea Papers.

[8]Luke Lea to E.H. Crump, August 9, 1912, Lea Papers.

[9]David A. Shepherd to Luke Lea, November 13, 1912, Lea Papers.

[10]Memorandum, Lea Papers.

[11]Conversation with Luke Lea, Jr., April 18, 1983.

[12]Typed analysis of Underwood-Simmons bill marked Speech of Senator Lea, Lea Papers.

[13]Campaign for reelection pamphlet, 1915, Lea Papers.

[14]Memorandum, Lea Papers.

[15]Luke Lea to Arthur P. Oakes, October 12, 1914, Lea Papers.

[16]September 1914 memorandum on handling the state's October maturities, written by Luke Lea, Lea Papers.

[17]The account of L & N's efforts to get Lea to drop the investigation he instigated into the railroad's activities, unless otherwise noted, was taken from a copy of a memorandum written by Lea and filed with the Interstate Commerce Commission making the investigation in 1916, Lea Papers.

[18]The account of hearings, unless otherwise noted, was taken from Document 461, Louisville & Nashville Railroad Company, hearings before the Interstate Commerce Commission, relative to the financial relations, rates, and practices of the Louisville & Nashville Railroad Company, the Nashville, Chattanooga & St. Louis Railway, and other carriers; Washington, Government Printing Office, 1916.

[19]Interview with John D. Erwin, July 23-25, 1973.

[20]December 23, 1936, memorandum on *The Tennessean* written by Luke Lea, Lea Papers.

[21]Luke Lea to W.M. Clemens, March 25, 1911, Lea Papers.

[22]Interview with John D. Erwin, July 23-25, 1973.

[23]Excerpt of report, Lea Papers.

[24]Luke Lea to Frank Earl Parham, September 12, 1931, Lea Papers.

[25]Luke Lea to A.B. Ransom and William R. Manier, August 6, 1914, Lea Papers.

Chapter Five
Politics in Tennessee and the Bid for Reelection

[1]John D. Erwin of Chattanooga had become Lea's secretary in the summer of 1913. They would be connected for many years through a variety of matters, and the friendship thereby formed would last throughout their lives. After Lea left the Senate, Erwin became the Washington correspondent at various times for several newspapers including *The Nashville Tennessean*, the *New York Evening World*, the *Philadelphia Record*, *Chattanooga News*, *Commercial Appeal*, and the *Knoxville Journal*. He played a prominent role in exposing the Teapot Dome scandal. He was Ambassador to Honduras from 1937 to 1947, and even though it is unusual for a person to be reappointed ambassador to the same country after an interval of time, he again served for three or four years in that position beginning in 1951.

[2]Unidentified Bristol newspaper, May 29, 1914, Lea scrapbook.

[3]John D. Erwin to Luke Lea, September 3, 1914, Lea Papers.

[4]John D. Erwin to Henry Morrow, November 4, 1914, Lea Papers.

[5]Luke Lea to Governor Thomas C. Rye, February 18, 1915.

[6]Interview with John D. Erwin, July 23-25, 1973.

[7]Marshall Morgan to Luke Lea, August 2, 1915, Lea Papers.

[8]Interview with John D. Erwin, July 23-25, 1973.

[9]Luke Lea and John L. Parham correspondence, August 9-September 13, 1915, Lea Papers.

[10]Reelection campaign tabloid containing speech and commentary, Lea Papers.

[11]Luke Lea to H.L. Johnston, president Knoxville Clearing House, August 14, 1915, Lea Papers.

[12]Frank Avent to George L. Berry, October 2, 1915, and Lea campaign speeches, Lea Papers.

[13]Lea's campaign speeches, Lea Papers.

[14]Frank Avent to I.B. Stevens, Dyersburg, October 19, 1915, Lea Papers.

[15]*The Tennessean*, 6 October 1974, article by Joe Hatcher, and interview with Joe Hatcher, March 16, 1971.

[16]Frank Avent to A.H. Wiggs, Linden, October 14, 1915, Lea Papers.

[17]Luke Lea to J.W. Holt, Wartrace, November 2, 1915, Lea Papers.

[18]Reelection campaign literature, Lea Papers.

[19]J.F. House to Luke Lea, April 1, 1919, Lea Papers.

[20]Henry E. Graper, Lexington, to Luke Lea, November 25, 1915, Lea Papers.

[21]Interview with John D. Erwin, July 23-25, 1973.

[22]A.M. Gaines to Frank Avent, November 4, 1915, Lea Papers.

[23]Interview with John D. Erwin, July 23-25, 1973.

[24]Luke Lea to George L. Berry, September 2, 1916, Lea Papers.

[25]Luke Lea to the National Council for Industrial Defense, September 3, 1916, Lea Papers.

[26]Luke Lea to Mitchell Long, February 7, 1917, Lea Papers.

[27]Luke Lea to John H. Noyes, August 19, 1916, Lea Papers.

[28]Copy of Resolution, Lea Papers.

[29]Undated and unidentified newspaper clipping, Lea Papers.

[30]Luke Lea to Senator John W. Kern, March 27, 1915, Lea Papers.

[31]Luke Lea to Mrs. Overton Lea, September 27, 1916, Lea Papers.

[32]P.M. Burdette to Luke Lea, June 2, 1916, Lea Papers.

[33]Luke Lea to J. H. Allison, May 23, 1916, Lea Papers.

[34]Luke Lea speech, Lea Papers.

[35]Luke Lea, "If" (unpublished article, 1934-1936), p. 6, Lea Papers.

[36]Luke Lea to Mitchell Long, February 7, 1917, Lea Papers.

Chapter Six
Colonel of the 114th Field Artillery

[1]Opinions of Luke Lea expressed in his letters and various other writings.

[2]Unless otherwise noted, the organization and record of the regiment is taken from the official history; Reese Amis, captain, battery C, *History of the 114th Field Artillery* (Nashville, 1920). Sidelights and anecdotes are taken from Luke Lea, "The American Dreyfus Case" (unpublished manuscript, 1934-1936), pp. 10-12, 16-17, 20-32, Lea Papers.

[3]Unidentified newspaper, Lea Papers.

[4]Undated editorial, Columbia *Daily Herald*, Lea Papers.

[5]Interview with P.R. Dinwiddie, soldier in 114th Field Artillery, July 11, 1979.

[6]Unless otherwise noted, personal recollections of Luke Lea are taken from his 1918 diary in possession of the author.

[7]Luke Lea to Luke Lea, Jr., December 17, 1943.

[8]Luke Lea to Percy Warner, July 10, 1918, Lea Papers.

[9]Luke Lea, "The American Dreyfus Case," 21-22, Lea Papers.

[10]Luke Lea to Percy Warner, September 3, 1918, Lea Papers.

[11]Luke Lea, "The American Dreyfus Case," 31, Lea Papers.

[12]Luke Lea, "The American Dreyfus Case," 24-25, Lea Papers.

[13]Luke Lea, "The American Dreyfus Case," 25-26, Lea Papers.

[14]Interviews with Joe Hatcher, April 11, 1973, and E.P. Charlet, May 3, 1973.

[15]Luke Lea, statement concerning his military service, Lea Papers.

Chapter Seven
Attempt to Capture the Kaiser

[1]Account of the trip into Holland edited from Luke Lea, "The Kaiser Story" (unpublished manuscript, 1934-1936), Lea Papers, which is a more detailed account than that published in the *Tennessee Historical Quarterly* 20, No. 3 (September 1961).

[2]Luke Lea, "The Kaiser Story," p. 3, Lea Papers.

[3]Luke Lea, "The Kaiser Story," p. 14, Lea Papers.

[4]Luke Lea, "The Kaiser Story," pp. 14-15, Lea Papers.

[5]Luke Lea, Diary, December 24-26, 1918, in possession of author.

[6]Luke Lea, "The Kaiser Story," p. 24.

[7]Luke Lea, "The Kaiser Story," pp. 33-34.

[8]Luke Lea, "The Kaiser Story," p. 34.

[9]Luke Lea, "The Kaiser Story," p. 35.

[10]Luke Lea, "The Kaiser Story," pp. 36-37.

[11]Luke Lea, "The Kaiser Story," p. 38.

[12]Luke Lea, "The Kaiser Story," p. 39.

[13]Luke Lea, "The Kaiser Story," pp. 40-42.

[14]The letter to Colonel House read as follows:

A leave just concluded, and a trip to the 89th Division to recover personal baggage...permit the acquisition of certain important and accurate information.

This information includes the close and intimate relations of England and Belgium to the exclusion of other nations, the plans of Belgium to acquire part of Holland, and the bad blood between Belgium and Holland, facts relative to the Dutch Army and radio communications, the military status of the former Kaiser in Holland, the inefficiency of the Belgium Army of Occupation in Germany, the love and devotion of the former Kaiser and Field Marshal Hindenburg by practically all Germany, the food situation in Belgium, Holland, Luxembourg and Germany, and the wish among part, at least, of Germans and Holland merchants for an entente of Holland, Germany, Russia, and Japan that could combat any alliance of England, France, Italy and the United States.

If you would desire a more detailed report upon any of these subjects, the General commanding the Brigade will give permission for a personal visit to you at any time you might suggest....

[15]Transcript of sworn testimony of Colonel Lea taken at G.H.Q., A.E.F., January 26, 1919, by Colonel J.C. Johnson, Inspector General, First Army, American Expedition Forces, p. 4, Lea Papers.

[16]Luke Lea, "The Kaiser Story," pp. 62-63.

[17]Luke Lea, "The Kaiser Story," p. 63

[18]Luke Lea, "The Kaiser Story," pp. 64-65.

[19]Luke Lea, "The Kaiser Story," p. 66

[20]Luke Lea, "The Kaiser Story," p. 66

[21]Luke Lea, "The Kaiser Story," p. 66.

[22]Luke Lea, "The Kaiser Story," p. 69.

GENERAL HEADQUARTERS
AMERICAN EXPEDITIONARY FORCES

France, 17 February, 1919

FROM: The Adjutant General, A.E.F.

TO: Colonel Luke Lea, 114th Field Artillery

SUBJECT: Entry of Holland and visit to the ex-Emperor of Germany

1. The Commander-in-chief directs me to inform you that a report of the investigation of your entry of Holland and visit to the ex-Emperor of Germany, in the early part of January, has been laid before him and has received his careful consideration, and that while he is pleased to find that your actions are free from deception, he nevertheless views them as amazingly indiscreet. You should not have entered Holland at all without the authority of your *military* superiors. Paragraph 7 of G.O. No.6, G.H.Q., 1918, clearly intends that leaves to visit neutral countries will only be granted in exceptional cases and by authority of these Headquarters. This, however, is not *the* serious part of the affair. As an officer of the American Army you had no right whatsoever to present yourself at the chateau of the ex-emperor of Germany without the authority of the President of the United States first obtained. Furthermore, it should have been apparent to you that the meaning and purpose of your visit might well have been misunderstood, as indeed it was in some quarters, and might have entailed the most disastrous consequences, both political and military.

[23]Luke Lea, "The Kaiser Story," p. 69.

[24]Interview with Reese Amis, 1953.

Chapter Eight
A Power to be Reckoned With

[1]Undated and untitled newspaper article, Lea Papers.

[2]For a detailed account of the part Colonel Lea played in the organization of the American Legion, see article by Cromwell Tidwell, "Luke Lea and the American Legion," *Tennessee Historical Quarterly*, 28, No. 1 (Spring 1969): 70-83.

[3]Luke Lea to Mrs. Overton Lea, May 4, 1922, Lea Papers.

[4]Memorandum, Lea Papers.

[5]Conversation with Mrs. Luke Lea, February 15, 1973.

[6]Luke Lea to E.B. Jeffers, managing editor of the Greensboro *Daily News*, November 19, 1919, Lea Papers.

[7]J. M. Broughton, unsigned copy of letter, May 21, 1935, Lea Papers.

[8]Interview with E.P. Charlet at his home in Nashville, May 3, 1973.

[9]Information concerning Percie Warner Lea obtained from innumerable conversations with her.

[10]Memorandum, Lea Papers.

[11]Luke Lea to Mrs. Overton Lea, May 9, 1922, Lea Papers.

[12]Luke Lea to Luke Lea, Jr., July 31, 1942, Lea Papers.

[13]Conversation with Luke Lea, Jr., June 2, 1979.

[14]Interview with Governor Gordon Browning, March 6, 1969, at his home in Huntingdon, Tennessee.

[15]Austin Peay to Luke Lea, July 27, 1925, Lea Papers.

[16]Interview with Governor Gordon Browning, March 6, 1969.

Chapter Nine
The Dream Expands

[1]Memorandum, Lea Papers.

[2]Memorandum on proposed memorial, Lea Papers.

[3]Luke Lea to Congressman Finnis J. Garrett, December 10, 1921, Lea Papers.

[4]Undated and unidentified newspaper clipping, Lea Papers.

[5]Copy of citation, Lea Papers.

[6]Memorandum, Lea Papers.

[7]Conversation with Mrs. Luke Lea, September 13, 1973.

[8]Memorandum, Re: Tennessee Publishing Company, Lea Papers.

[9]Luke Lea to Giles Barksdale, Bank of America, New York City, November 30, 1927, Lea Papers.

[10]*A.B.C. Records*, analysis of *The Tennessean* papers by newspaper analyst T.F. McPherson, Tampa, Florida, Lea Papers.

[11]Lovick P. Miles to Luke Lea, April 4, 1927, Lea Papers.

[12]Conversation with Mrs. Luke Lea, September 13, 1973.

[13]Memorandum, Lea Papers.

[14]A.F. Sanford to Luke Lea, February 16, 1927, Lea Papers.

[15]The author is indebted to J. Basil Ramsey for the following information concerning Luke Lea's relationship with him and the Holston-Union National Bank; interview at his office in New York City, November 6, 1967.

[16]Telephone interview with Mrs. Reba Harris, Federal Reserve Bank of Nashville, February 5, 1979.

[17]Memorandum, September 23, 1927, Lea Papers.

[18]Conversation with Mrs. Luke Lea, September 13, 1973.

[19]Luke Lea to Henry Ford, July 9, 1921, Lea Papers.

[20]Luke Lea to James H. Allison, December 13, 1913, Lea Papers.

[21]Luke Lea to Mrs. Overton Lea, November 27, 1926, Lea Papers.

[22]Deed recorded one year later, January 10, 1928, Deed Book 805, p. 181,

Davidson County Courthouse.

[23]Park Board Minutes, June 22, 1927.

Chapter Ten
Zenith of Political Influence

[1]Conversation with Ted Hagerty, July 4, 1975.
[2]Luke Lea to Henry H. Horton, undated memorandum, Lea Papers.
[3]Luke Lea to Bob Claggett, July 19, 1930, Lea Papers.
[4]Luke Lea to George Morris, November 5, 1930, telegram, Lea Papers.
[5]Interview with J.B. Ramsey, November 6, 1967.
[6]Conversation with Mrs. Luke Lea, September 13, 1973.
[7]Conversation with Ted Hagerty, September 13, 1973.
[8]Information concerning Ted Hagerty and her viewpoint on various matters secured from innumerable conversations with her.
[9]Luke Lea to Henry H. Horton, September 1, 1929, Lea Papers.
[10]Undated newspaper clipping, "Day by Day with Governor Patterson," Lea Papers.

Chapter Eleven
The Bubble Bursts

[1]Account of Luke Lea's relationship with Wallace B. Davis taken from Luke Lea, "The American Dreyfus Case" (unpublished manuscript, 1934-1936), pp. 33-56, Lea Papers.
[2]Account of Luke Lea's involvement with the Central Bank taken from Luke Lea, "The American Dreyfus Case," pp. 57-69, Lea Papers.
[3]Conversation with Luke Lea, Jr., July 21, 1978.
[4]W.S. Coursey to Governor J.C.B. Ehringhaus, September 7, 1934, Lea Papers.
[5]Photostatic copy of Luke Lea's bank statements from the Central Bank and Trust Company for those dates, Lea Papers.
[6]Luke Lea's conversations with James E. Caldwell and James B. Brown recounted by Luke Lea, Jr., July 21, 1978.
[7]Conversation with Mrs. Luke Lea, February 15, 1973.
[8]Howard White, former assistant cashier of the Liberty Bank and Trust Company, to author, February 24, 1986, Lea Papers.
[9]Interview with E.P. Charlet, May 3, 1973.
[10]Account of closing of Holston Union National Bank, interview with J.B. Ramsey, November 6, 1967.
[11]Conversation with Luke Lea, Jr., July 21, 1978.
[12]Conversation with Luke Lea, Jr., September 15, 1979.
[13]Conversation with Luke Lea, Jr., September 15, 1979.

Chapter Twelve
Ensnared

[1]Luke Lea, "The American Dreyfus Case" (unpublished manuscript, 1934-1936), p. 73, Lea Papers.

[2]Answer of Tennessee Publishing Company to Bill of Complaint filed by C.O. Carpenter, receiver for the Holston-Union National Bank, March 3, 1933, in the district court for the middle district of Tennessee, pp. 16, 22, copy, Lea Papers.

[3]Luke Lea, "Essay on Y" (memorandum concerning Paul M. Davis, 1934-1936), p. 3, Lea Papers.

[4]Account of Frank Rice's visit to Luke Lea, conversation with Mrs. Luke Lea, October 24, 1966.

[5]Conversation with Luke Lea, Jr., September 15, 1979.

[6]Luke Lea, "The American Dreyfus Case," p. 74, Lea Papers.

[7]Luke Lea to Edward L. Donhey, Los Angeles, October 19, 1931, Lea Papers.

[8]Answer of Tennessee Publishing Company to Bill of Complaint, p. 12, Lea Papers.

[9]Answer of Tennessee Publishing Company to Bill of Complaint, p. 12, Lea Papers.

[10]Answer of Tennessee Publishing Company to Bill of Complaint p.13, Lea Papers.

[11]Frank Lander to Cobey Carmack (Mrs. E.W.), July 26, 1931, Edward Ward Carmack Papers, Tennessee State Library and Archives, original in Southern Historical Collection, University of North Carolina at Chapel Hill.

[12]Interview with Wallace Edwards, July 13, 1979. Edwards was Governor Horton's secretary at the time of the impeachment effort and later served as Governor Gordon Browning's administrative assistant.

[13]Interview with Wallace Edwards, July 13, 1979.

[14]Interview with Joe Hatcher, January 29, 1971.

[15]Memorandum written by Luke Lea, Lea Papers.

[16]Lea, "Essay on Y," p. 4, Lea Papers.

[17]Lea, "Essay on Y," p. 4, Lea Papers.

[18]Luke Lea to Mrs. Overton Lea, March 9, 1931, Lea Papers.

[19]Luke Lea to Mrs. Overton Lea, March 9, 1931, Lea Papers.

[20]Conversation with Mrs. Luke Lea, October 24, 1966.

Chapter Thirteen
The Law's Disgrace

[1]Luke Lea, "Essay on Y" (memorandum concerning Paul M. Davis, 1934-1936), p. 4, Lea Papers.

[2]Luke Lea, "Essay on Y," p. 4, Lea Papers.

[3]Luke Lea, article, 1934-1936, Lea Papers.

[4]E.J. Clode, Jr., affidavit, Lea Papers.

[5]Shortly before the Leas went to prison in 1934, John Thrash, a deputy sheriff of Buncombe County, who had been one of the jury guards during the trial, made an affidavit that Judge Barnhill before the trial began repeatedly expressed the opinion that the Leas and Davis were guilty and stressed the future importance to all persons connected with the prosecution in their being convicted, especially the elder Lea, because of his prominence and because of the wealth and influence of his enemies in Tennessee. Copy of affidavit, Lea Papers.

[6]Interview with Brainard Cheney, June 6, 1979. Cheney, a noted Southern writer, was a political reporter on the *Nashville Banner* for many years.

[7]Luke Lea, "In Re: Lea Case" (signed statement believed by Lea to be true and accurate account of case as developed at trial in superior court of Buncombe County, in the Supreme Court of North Carolina, and upon petitions for certiorari in the United States Supreme Court), p. 1, Lea Papers.

[8]Lea, "In Re: Lea Case," p. 2, Lea Papers.

[9]Memorandum, Lea Papers.

[10]The author being of the opinion that the press associations' coverage was more accurate and objective than the partisan *Nashville Banner* or Asheville newspapers, the account of the trial, unless otherwise stated, is taken from the daily Associated Press reports published on page one of *The Nashville Tennessean.*

[11]Answer of the Tennessee Publishing Company to Bill of Complaint filed against it by C.O. Carpenter, Receiver for the Holston-Union National Bank, March 3, 1933, in the district court for the middle district of Tennessee, p. 13, copy, Lea Papers.

[12]Answer of the Tennessee Publishing Company to Bill of Complaint, p.13, Lea Papers.

[13]Answer of the Tennessee Publishing Company to Bill of Complaint, p.14-15, Lea Papers..

[14]Brief in Support of Application for Pardon, compiled by J.M. Broughton and filed with North Carolina Parole Commissioner, June 1, 1935.

[15]Conversation with Mrs. Luke Lea, October 24, 1966.

[16]Lea, "In Re: Lea Case," p. 3, Lea Papers.

[17]Conversation with Mrs. Luke Lea, October 24, 1966.

[18]Conversation with Mrs. Luke Lea, October 24, 1966.

[19]Lea, "In Re: Lea Case," p. 3, Lea Papers.

20Conversation with Mrs. Luke Lea, October 24, 1966.
21Copy of John Thrash's affidavit, 1934, Lea Papers.
22Lea, "In Re: Lea Case," pp. 6-7, Lea Papers.

Chapter Fourteen
In Search of Justice

1Luke Lea to Mrs. W.C. Robertson, September 12, 1931, Lea Papers.

2Medical information re: Luke Lea, Jr., taken from his patient record at Memorial Hospital, New York, May 13-30, 1932, copy, Lea Papers.

3In 1934, shortly before the Leas went to prison, John Thrash, a deputy sheriff of Buncombe County, made an affidavit in which he stated that about ten days before the trial ended Solicitor Nettles called him (Thrash) into the solicitor's office and said that when they took the jury home, to let the members of the jury be alone with their wives and families, provided no outsiders were present; that when the wives of the jurors came to visit them, to allow them to talk alone with their husbands, but not to let the jurors leave the jury room; that Nettles also stated he had been told there was trouble in the Justice family, and if Mrs. Justice came to see her husband to let her have an opportunity to tell her husband what the trouble was, but not to let him leave the jury room. Copies of all affidavits cited in Lea Papers.

4Affidavit of LeRoy M. Carmichael stated he was requested by Nettles to make an affidavit that he had seen Luke Lea and Wiley Noland together, even though to his (Carmichael's) knowledge he had never seen Noland in his life.

Affidavit of H.L. Justice stated that Nettles tried to get him to make an affidavit that Luke Lea was with Wiley Noland when Noland called upon him (Justice), although Lea had not been present; Nettles even threatening to send him (Justice) to the penitentiary if he did not make such an affidavit.

Affidavit of Mrs. Lyda Justice stated that Nettles repeatedly tried to get her to swear that she had been visited not only by her father-in-law, H.L. Justice, but by Wiley Noland and Luke Lea when such was not the case.

5W.S. Coursey, star witness for the state during their trial, made an affidavit shortly before the Leas went to prison in 1934, that prior to the trial Nettles had told him repeatedly that the weakness in the joint cases against Davis, the Leas, and Charlet was the lack of proof that any of the Tennessee parties had been in Buncombe County at or about the time charged in the proposed indictments, but the grand jury would return any indictment on a bank case against any defendant he (Nettles) requested without even reading the indictment. Coursey further stated that Nettles repeatedly stated to him (Coursey) and in his presence, that he (Nettles) knew neither of the Leas were in Buncombe County at or about the date of the charges made in the indictment, but that he (Nettles) would get by with it as the grand jury would return the indictment and the indictment, when returned, established venue.

308   Luke Lea of Tennessee

[6]"In Re: Lea Case," footnote cited fully—note 7 ch. 13.

[7]For disposition of criminal indictments returned against Rogers Caldwell see McFerrin, *Caldwell and Company*, pp. 206-17.

[8]Lea, "In Re: Lea Case," p. 11, Lea Papers.

[9]J.R. Byers, T.M. Cogburn, and W.C. Flynn, jurors at the trial, each later would make an affidavit stating that Claude Gilbert, deputy sheriff who guarded the jury, was frequently absent when on duty at night, leaving the jury unguarded sometimes for hours, and that on several occasions while the jury was left unguarded, different jurors would leave the room where they slept.

Cogburn also stated visitors were admitted to the jury room.

Flynn stated he had made a separate affidavit July 21, 1932, at the direction of Solicitor Nettles, at whose office were nearly all members of the jury in the Lea, Davis, Charlet case, on that date assembled for the purpose of making affidavit on the request of the solicitor. On that occasion Flynn was told by Nettles that it was not necessary for him (Flynn) to say anything in his affidavit about Gilbert leaving the jury unguarded, because he (Nettles) had talked with other members of the jury and none of them had left the courthouse or talked with anyone about the case.

Nettles also stated to Flynn, on July 21, 1932, that any juror who made an affidavit that any way helped the Leas and Davis in their motion for a new trial would be guilty of a felony, and that Nettles would prosecute any juror who was guilty of violating the law. Nettles stated that if any juror had expressed an opinion of the case prior to its trial and his becoming a juror, he would have committed perjury, and that if any juror had discussed the case with any of the officers in charge of the jury during the trial, that juror would have committed a felony.

Flynn asked Nettles whether in his (Flynn's) affidavit, he should mention the conversation he (Flynn) had had with Nettles during the trial in which Nettles told him that the defendants had stolen all the money there was in western North Carolina and hidden it in Tennessee; and that Nettles had replied that was not necessary to mention as the solicitor was a representative of the state government, and any conversation with him was proper.

[10]Lea, "In Re: Lea Case," pp. 11-12, Lea Papers.

[11]Lea, "In Re: Lea Case," p. 11, Lea Papers.

[12]Lea, "In Re: Lea Case," pp. 9-10, Lea Papers.

[13]L.E. Gwinn, J.G. Lackey, H.E. Colton, and J.M. Dickinson to Governor Hill McAlister, January 19, 1933, Lea Papers.

[14]Luke Lea to W.C. Robertson, March 31, 1933, Lea Papers.

[15]Interview with Maxey Hewitt, August 24, 1973. Hewitt stated this interview was the first time he had ever discussed fully with anyone his experiences in Jamestown.

[16]Unidentified newspaper clipping, 18 February 1933, Lea Papers.

Chapter Fifteen
The End of the Legal Battles

[1]Answer of the Tennessee Publishing Company to the Bill of Complaint filed against it by C.O. Carpenter, Receiver for the Holston-Union National Bank, March 3, 1933, in the district court for the middle district of Tennessee, p. 15, copy, Lea Papers.

[2]Answer of the Tennessee Publishing Company to Bill of Complaint, p. 22, Lea Papers.

[3]Answer of the Tennessee Publishing Company to Bill of Complaint, p. 22, Lea Papers.

[4]Answer of the Tennessee Publishing Company to Bill of Complaint, p. 4, Lea Papers.

[5]*Our first century of growth with Nashville,* First American pamphlet, highlights of history of First American National Bank, undated, p. 3, Lea Papers.

[6]Luke Lea to Ferdinand Pecora, May 29, 1933, Lea Papers.

[7]Luke Lea to Ferdinand Pecora, May 29, 1933, Lea Papers.

[8]Luke Lea to Charles Melvin Neff, July 25, 1933, Lea Papers.

[9]C.O. Carpenter to Luke Lea, Jr., June 28, 1932, September 29, 1932, Lea Papers.

[10]Luke Lea, "Essay on Y" (memorandum concerning Paul M. Davis, 1934-1936), p. 5, Lea Papers.

[11]Luke Lea, "Essay on Y" (memorandum concerning Paul M. Davis, 1934-1936), p. 5, Lea Papers.

[12]Answer of the Tennessee Publishing Company to Bill of Complaint, p. 1, Lea Papers.

[13]Answer of the Tennessee Publishing Company to Bill of Complaint, p. 3, Lea Papers.

[14]Answer of the Tennessee Publishing Company to Bill of Complaint, p. 12, Lea Papers.

[15]Answer of the Tennessee Publishing Company to Bill of Complaint, pp. 40-41, Lea Papers.

[16]Answer of the Tennessee Publishing Company to Bill of Complaint, p. 42, Lea Papers.

[17]Signed copy of F.D. Ferguson's November 17, 1932, and April 24, 1934, affidavits; and signed copy of John S. Mitchell's and R.V. Welch's affidavits, Lea Papers.

[18]Luke Lea to J.G. Lackey, October 13, 1933, memorandum, Lea Papers.

[19]Unless otherwise noted, account of this day and the next taken from Luke Lea's diary in possession of the author.

[20]Conversation with Mrs. Luke Lea, September 30, 1969.

Chapter Sixteen
Prison

[1]Unless otherwise noted, material for this chapter taken from Luke Lea's diary, 1934-1936, in possession of the author.

[2]Interview with Edwin M. Gill, May 6, 1977.

[3]Interview with Edwin M. Gill, May 6, 1977.

[4]Interview with J. B. Ramsey, November 6, 1967.

[5]Luke Lea to Edward Finlay, January 5, 1934, and Charles M. McCabe, collector, Internal Revenue Service, Nashville, to Enoch Brown, August 8, 1935, Lea Papers.

[6]Luke Lea to John S. Glenn, Jr., undated memorandum, Lea Papers.

[7]Protest of Rogers Caldwell vs. Commissioner of Internal Revenue, September 30, 1932, Lea Papers.

[8]Luke Lea to Luke Lea, Jr., August 28, 1934, Lea Papers.

[9]W.S. Coursey to Governor J.C.B. Ehringhaus, September 7, 1934, copy, Lea Papers.

[10]Report on Investigation of Transactions between Central Bank and Trust Company, Asheville, North Carolina, and Colonel Luke Lea and His Interests, prepared by A.M. Pullen and Company, Certified Public Accountants, 1934, p. 7, Lea Papers.

[11]W.T. Lee to A.M. Pullen and Company, December 1, 1934, copy, Lea Papers.

[12]Facts concerning transactions in the three counts on which Lea was convicted taken from Brief in Support of the Application for Pardon, compiled by J.M. Broughton and filed with Parole Commissioner, June 1, 1935, Lea Papers.

[13]Broughton, Brief in Support of Application for Pardon, p. 9, Lea Papers.

[14]United Press dispatch by John A. Parris, datelined Raleigh, April 2, 1936, Lea Papers.

[15]Luke Lea's diary, April 4, 1936.

Chapter Seventeen
Promises Fulfilled

[1]Luke Lea to Luke Lea, Jr., April 17, 1936, Lea Papers.

[2]Luke Lea's diary, August 12, 1936, in possession of author.

[3]Memorandum re: Super-Highways, Lea Papers.

[4]Memorandum, January 13, 1939, Lea Papers.

[5]Memorandum re: National Weekly, Lea Papers.

[6]Issues of *Dixie Farmer*, Lea Papers.

[7]Memorandum re: Foundation, Lea Papers.

[8]Memorandum re: Prison Reform, Lea Papers.

[9]Memorandum re: Prison Reform, Lea Papers..

[10]Various memoranda, 1933-1944, Lea Papers.

[11]Mrs. Luke Lea, affidavit (copy, unsigned and undated), Lea Papers.

[12]*Eleven Hundred Broadway*, tabloid published by employees of Newspaper Printing Corp., 2, No 7 (June-July-August, 1971).

[13]Tennessee Publishing Company, Complainant vs. C.O. Carpenter, Receiver of Holston-Union National Bank, The American National Bank, Paul M. Davis, J.C. Bradford, Cecil Sims, Frank M. Bass, Frank A. Berry, K.T. McConnico, Lit J. Pardue, Harley Fowler, and divers other parties unknown to complainant, Defendants: January 1937 in the United States district court of the middle district of Tennessee, p. 18, copy, Lea Papers.

[14]Conversation with Luke Lea, Jr., December 13, 1982.

[15]*Congressional Record.* Senate, 79th Congress, pp. 376-79:

Resolved, that the committee on the Judiciary or any duly authorized sub-committee thereof is authorized and directed to make a full and complete investigation of the circumstances surrounding the disposal of the Government's interest in *The Nashville Tennessean*, a newspaper published in Nashville, Tenn., with particular regard to the part played in such transaction by employees or former employees of the Government, and to report thereon to the Senate at the earliest practical date, together with its recommendations, including recommendations for necessary legislation in connection with such transactions. If in the course of the investigation facts are disclosed which indicate that the interests of the United States were not properly protected or that any violation of any law may have occurred, and the committee is of the opinion that the sale should be set aside or other legal proceedings instituted, it shall transmit its findings to the Attorney General with such recommendations for action as it deems advisable.

For the purpose of this investigation, the committee or any duly authorized sub-committee thereof, is authorized to hold such hearings, to sit and act at such times and places during the sessions, recesses, and adjourned periods of the Seventy-ninth Congress, to employ such clerical and other assistants, to require by subpoena or otherwise the attendance of such witnesses and the production of such correspondence, books, papers, and documents, to administer such oaths, to take such testimony, and to make such expenditures, as it deems advisable. The cost of stenographic services to report such hearings shall not be in excess of 25 cents per hundred words. The expenses of the committee under this resolution, which shall not exceed $3,000, shall be paid from the contingent fund of the Senate upon vouchers approved by the chairman of the Committee.

[16]Memorandum, 1945, Lea Papers.

[17]J.G. Lackey to R.C. Marshall, Jr., December 7, 1945, Lea Papers.

[18]J.M. Broughton to Luke Lea, July 1, 1937, Lea Papers.

[19]Luke Lea-J.E. Howard correspondence, November 13, December 9, 1944, Lea Papers.

[20]Conversation with Luke Lea, Jr., December 13, 1982.

[21]Interview with Joe Jatcher January 29, 1971; Conversation with Mrs. William Brock, Chattanooga, August 16, 1973.

A Note on Sources

Mention should be made of the volume and condition of Luke Lea's papers. From the day he graduated from law school in 1903 until his death in 1945, he kept every letter he received and a copy of every letter he wrote. During the Senate years countless letters soliciting his vote for and reams urging his vote against every bill under consideration were first acknowledged and then filed. Inter-office memos of *The Tennessean* papers during the years he was publisher were kept as were envelopes on which he had scribbled figures and notes. He was always working on several matters simultaneously. Copies, usually in triplicate, of each draft of a project as it developed, were corrected, retyped and filed. Memoranda other persons sent to him for his opinion were frequently retained and filed. He seemed constitutionally unable to throw away any scrap of paper on which was writing. The fact that he saved all records tends to indicate that, at least in his own eyes, he committed no illegalities.

Having the intimate knowledge of Luke Lea that I as a daughter possess, I am satisfied that what he wrote is, at least according to his knowledge of the situation, absolutely accurate. There would have been no point in his writing to his attorney a detailed memorandum of a transaction unless he stated the facts as they were, or as he remembered them, and his memory was usually correct.

After the Tennessee Publishing Company was placed in receivership in 1933, storage of Lea's files became a problem. Moves to the several offices he was to have at various times, to home, to basement, to garage, with some containers overturned, and papers stuffed back wherever they would fit, destroyed any semblance of the order in which they had originally been filed. Through the years dust, leaking roofs, and silver-fish took their toll.

When my father died money could not be spared to have current files at his office moved to our home, and there was the pressure of time to vacate the office so an additional month's rent would not have to be paid. My mother and I sorted through his papers and took home those that looked as if they might be important. The rest were burned in the office fireplace.

Soon thereafter my father's filing room in the basement at home, together with the recreation room, was converted into an apartment to bring in sorely needed income, so those files were stacked in a dark corner.

Shortly, the roof of the little garage at our home began literally to fall in. There was no money with which to have it repaired and it could not be left as an eyesore to the neighborhood, so it had to be torn down. It was crammed with old files. My mother believed the easiest solution of what to do with those papers was to burn them. I strongly believed, however, that if my father had saved them all those years, they could not be destroyed without first going through them. Consequently she and I looked through each manila folder. If it appeared to contain correspondence relating to only one matter and that matter was of little or no interest, such as requests from constituents when he was in the Senate for packages of flower seeds available at no cost from the government, those letters were burned. If, however, the contents of a folder seemed interesting, or if it was a day-to-day file containing an assortment of matters, it was stacked in the basement for me to go through later.

Even though I had gone through literally hundreds of folders, destroying what appeared to be of little interest, putting the rest aside to be read later, when my mother sold the house on Whitland Avenue in 1952, a mammoth quantity still remained to be sorted through, all of which I moved to my home.

I have outlined at some length the difficulties involved in

preserving my father's papers because I realize certain important documents must inevitably have been destroyed. The contents of a large number of folders, having succumbed to the ravages of bugs or being water soaked, had literally disintegrated before I tried to look through them. Not being a trained historian or librarian, I further acknowledge my lack of ability, especially in the beginning, to recognize that valuable information could be gleaned from almost any written material, although the document itself is of little or no interest.

For years I felt inundated by the sheer mass of disorganized papers. For the dual purpose of preserving them and getting them in a manageable form so I could begin to write, I first looked through the contents of each folder, dusted, relabeled, and filed according to year. This required many hundreds of hours of laborious sorting.

Mention should be made of three further difficulties inherent in these papers. First, my father's handwriting is extremely difficult to read and even after long familiarity with it, a word or phrase is frequently impossible for me to decipher. Fortunately, many years ago my husband insisted that two expert stenographers, who had long experience with Lea's handwriting, type the dairies he kept during World War I and while he was in prison.

Second, many of his routine business letters are disappointing. He relied a great deal on the telephone, but in the main he handled important affairs personally. His letters record with whom he was in contact at a given period, but the nature of the matter and its disposition often have to be pieced together from other papers or a general knowledge of his affairs.

Third, in the files that remain, papers relating to certain events seem intact, whereas material concerning others is sketchy or nonexistent. However, having access to a relatively large volume of papers, I concluded it was not necessary to attempt to locate additional correspondence nor to interview any more persons. Rather my problem has been to weed out, to select the typical to portray a true picture of the whole. Otherwise the man himself would not be seen clearly through the cloud of varying perspectives and mass of detail.

I have always believed that the privilege of telling Luke Lea's story belonged first to his family. Therefore I have retained his papers until my family responsibilities permitted me to research and write this book. However, during the years I have given several scholars permission to go through his papers for the particular period on which they were writing, and it has always been my intent that when I had finished with them, the bulk would be deposited in a library to be available for future research.

Selected Bibliography

Amis, Reese. *History of the 114th Field Artillery*. Nashville, 1920.

Bowers, Claude G. *The Life of John Worth Kearn*. Indianapolis: The Hollenback Press, 1918.

Cain, Byrd D. "Those Long Hot Days in Baltimore." *The Nashville Tennessean Magazine* (August 24, 1968).

Folmsbee, Stanley J., Corlew, Robert E., and Mitchell, Enoch L. *Tennessee—A Short History*. Knoxville: University of Tennessee Press, 1969.

Halley, R.A. "John McCormick Lea: The Ideal Citizen." *American Historical Magazine* (January 1904); 20-21.

Hayes, Arthur Garfield. *Trial by Prejudice*. New York: Covic, Friede Publishers, 1933.

Holt, James Laurence. *Congressional Insurgents and the Party System, 1909-1916*. Cambridge: Harvard University Press, 1967.

Hooper, Ben W. *The Unwanted Boy, the Autobiography of Governor Ben W. Hooper*. Edited by Everett Robert Boyce. Knoxville: University of Tennessee Press, 1963.

Hull, Cordell. *The Memoirs of Cordell Hull*. Vol. 1. New York: The Macmillan Company, 1948.

Illich, Mary Virginia. "The Case of Colonel Luke Lea." M.A. thesis, Duke University, 1935.

Issac, Paul E. *Prohibition and Politics, Turbulent Decades in Tennessee, 1885-1920*. Knoxville: University of Tennessee Press: 1965.

Lee, David B. *Tennessee in Turmoil: Politics in the Volunteer State, 1920-1932*. Memphis: Memphis State University Press, 1979.

Link, Arthur S. "Democratic Politics and the Presidential Campaign in Tennessee." *The East Tennessee Historical Society Publications*, 18 (1946): 109.

_____. *The Road to the White House*. Princeton: Princeton University Press, 1947.

_____. *Wilson and the New Freedom*. Princeton: Princeton University Press, 1956.

_____. *Woodrow Wilson and the Progressive Era*. New York: Harper, 1954.

Macpherson, Joseph. "Democratic Progressivism in Tennessee: The Administration of Governor Austin Peay." Ph.D. dissertation, Vanderbilt University, 1969.

McCombs, William Frank. *Making Woodrow Wilson President*. New York: Fairview Publishing Company, 1921.

McFerrin, John Berry. *Caldwell and Company*. Chapel Hill: University of North Carolina Press, 1939; reissued Nashville: Vanderbilt University Press, 1969.

McGill, Ralph. *The South and the Southerner*. Boston, Toronto: Little, Brown and Company, 1959.

Mowry, George E. *The Era of Theodore Roosevelt, 1910-1912*. New York: Harper & Brothers, 1958.

Qualls, J. Winfield. "The Fusion Victory and the Tennessee Senatorship." *The West Tennessee Historical Society Papers* 15 (1961): 90.

Shahan, Joe Michael. "Reform and Politics in Tennessee: 1906-1914." Ph.D. dissertation, Vanderbilt University, 1981.

Tidwell, Oscar Cromwell, Jr. "Luke Lea and the American Legion." *Tennessee Historical Quarterly* 28, No. 1 (Spring 1969): 70-83.

_____. *Belle Meade Park*. Nashville, 1983.

Tindall, George B. "Business Progressivism: Southern Politics in the 1920's." *South Atlantic Quarterly* 62 (1963): 92-106.

Lea Papers

Nashville, Tennessee. Mary Louise Lea Tidwell. Papers of Colonel Luke Lea.

Lea, Luke. Diary, 1918. Diary, 1934-1936.

_____. "The American Dreyfus Case." Manuscript. 1934-1936.

_____. "Essay on Y." Memorandum. 1934-1936.

_____. "If." Manuscript. 1934-1936.

_____. "The Kaiser Story." Manuscript. 1934-1936.

_____. "A Living Death." Sketch. 1934-1936.

_____. "In Re: Lea Case." Statement. 1934-1936.

_____. "Re: Foundation." Memorandum.

_____. "Re: National Weekly." Memorandum.

_____. "Re: Prison Reform." Memorandum.

_____. "Re: Super-Highways." Memorandum.

_____. Various memoranda. 1933-1944.

Letters, 1903-1945.

Memoranda, articles and stories, unpublished.

Document 461, Louisville & Nashville Railroad Co., hearings before the Interstate Commerce Commission, relative to the financial relations, rates, and practices of the Louisville & Nashville Railroad Co., the Nashville, Chattanooga & St. Louis Railway, and other carriers. Washington: Government Printing Office, 1916.

Transcript of trial. State vs. Luke Lea, et al., North Carolina, Buncomb County. In the Superior Court, July-August 1931, Special Term.

Briefs supporting appeals of verdict and habeas corpus proceedings, 1932-1934.

Copies of Affidavits Cited

Report on Investigation of Transactions between Central Bank and Trust Company, Asheville, NC, and Colonel Luke Lea and His Interests, Prepared by A M. Pullen & Company, Certified Public Accountants, 1934.

Answer of Tennessee Publishing Company to Bill of Complaint by C.O. Carpenter, Receiver of the Holston-Union National Bank, March 3, 1933, in the District Court of the Middle District of Tennessee.

Brief in support of application for pardon, compiled by J.M. Broughton and filed with the North Carolina Parole Commissioner, June 1, 1935.

Interviews

Browning, Governor Gordon. March 6. 1969.

Charlet, E.P. May 3, 1973.

Cheney, Brainard. June 6. 1979.

Dinwiddie, P.R. July 11, 1979.

Dobson, Sophie Ezzell (Mrs. Matthew H.). December 3, 1979.

Edwards, Wallace. July 13, 1979.

Erwin, John D. July 23-24, 1973.

Evers, F. Bernard. August 21, 1978.

Frazer, Sadie Warner (Mrs. George A.). February 25, May 4, 27, 1970.

Gill, Edwin M. May 6, 1977.

Hagerty, Winifred [Ted]. Innumerable conversations.

Harris, Reba. Telephone conversation, February 5, 1979.

Hatcher, Joe. January 29, March 16, 1971; April 11, 1973.

Hewitt, Maxey. August 24, 1973.

Holt, W. Wythe, Jr. July 23, 1971.

Lea, Luke. Innumerable conversations.

Lea, Luke, Jr. Innumerable conversations.

Lea, Percie Warner (Mrs. Luke). Innumerable conversations.

Little, Lewie. October 17, November 29, 1973.

Murdock, Elizabeth Lea (Mrs. James O.). Several conversations.

Ramsey, J.B. November 6, 1967.

Seigenthaler, Walter. July 18, 1972.

Shaub, Earl. Summer 1969.

Shepherd, David A. Innumerable conversations.

Williams, Judge Albert. July 10, 1978.

Newspapers and Periodicals

American Press, January 1928.

Asheville Citizen, 28, 29 July 1931.

Asheville Times, 27, 28, 29 July 1931.

The Atlanta Constitution, 28 September 1927.

Chattanooga News, 16 August 1913.

Chattanooga Times, 14 September 1913.

Chicago *Inter Ocean,* 20 August 1913.

Columbia Herald, 23 August, 20 September 1913.

Editor and Publisher, September 1928.

The Evening Tennessean, 4 August 1934; 4 April 1936.

Denver Post, 6 December 1932.

Dixie Farmer, several issues, 1939-1944. Lea Papers.

Eleven Hundred Broadway (tabloid published by employees of Newspaper Printing Corp.), June-July-August, 1971.

Globe Democrat, 16 May 1927.

Kentucky Messenger, 19 May 1927.

Knoxville *Journal and Tribune,* 30 November 1902.

The Linotype South, May 1916.

Memphis *Commercial Appeal,* 10 May 1934; 19 December 1937.

Montgomery Adviser, 13 December 1916.

Nashville American, 29 May-2 June 1906; Anniversary Edition 1910.

Nashville Banner, 29 May-2 June 1906; 16, 27 May 1912; 16 December 1915; 3 February 1918; 15 February 1928; 1, 28, 29 January, 7 February, 1 March, 1 May, 25 July, 26, 27 August 1931; 11 February, 2, 14, 21 March 1933; 5 April 1936.

The Nashville Tennessean, 10 November 1908; 24 March, 1 April 1919; 4 August 1922; 24, 25, 28 February 1928; 15 June, 13 August, 9, 14, 16 November, 11, 13, 17, 24, 31 December 1930; 7, 9, 17, 21, 30 January, 24, 30 May, 3, 10 June, 26 July, 11, 23 August 1931; 16 June, 20, 25 October 1932; 25 January, 3, 8, 13, 15, 20 February, 12 April 1933; 11 May, 10, 11, 16 June, 4 August 1934; 5 April 1936; 10 January 1971 (article by Joe Hatcher).

The Nashville Tennessean and the Nashville American, 24 January 1911; 19 May, 3 July 1912; 3 March, 26 July 1913; 16, 20, 22 March 1914; 11 July, 5, 21 November 1915; 5, 6 May 1916.

New York Times, 29 May 1913; 3 February, 10 December 1933.

Publishers Service Magazine, vol. 3, nos. 19 - 6 October 1932; 21 - 3 November 1932; 22 - 17 November 1932.

Raleigh *News and Observer,* 23 December 1932; 13, 16 June, 1935.

The Raleigh Times, 25 August 1931.

Sewanee Cap and Gown, 1900.

Sports Illustrated, 16 October 1961.

The Tennessean, 8 September 1974 (article by John Tyree Fain); 6 October 1974 (article by Joe Hatcher); 30 March 1975 (article by Joe Hatcher); 21 August 1977 (article by Louise Davis); 16 May 1978 (article by Joe Hatcher).

Time Magazine, 23 January 1928.

U.S. Congress. *Congressional Record*. 62nd Congress, 2nd Session, 1912, pp. 4574, 6790; 63rd Congress, 1st Session, 1913, pp. 20, 25; 64th Congress, 1st Session, December 6, 1915-September 8, 1916, pp. 9032, 12825, 13873.

Washington Post, 1 July 1912 (article by Frank Whitehead).

The World, 26 September 1914.

Index

Abernathy, William K., 20-21
Allison, J.H., 77, 88; *pictured, 159*
American, Nashville, 22, 59, 62. See also *Tennessean, Nashville*
Amis, Jonas, 50
Amis, Reese, 121, 126, 186
Anti-Saloon League, 17-18, 23
Arledge, A. Yates, 218
Atkinson, Richard M., 212-13, 270, 280

Baird, Winston, 59
Bank of Tennessee: formed by Caldwell and Company, 247-48; refused credit by Bank of Kentucky, 195-96; placed in receivership, 197. *See also* Caldwell and Company
Banner, Nashville, 22, 62, 67, 71, 181-82; in "Kyrock" controversy, 176-77
Barnhill, M.V., 218, 226, 273, 275
Bass, C. Neil, 176
Bate, William B., 18
Bauman, L.A., 260
Beeler, Roy, 242
Belle Meade: Lea's role in development of, 25-26, 76-77; threat to Lea holdings in, by L&N, 60-61

Bentinck, Count Godard, 110-13, passim; 117
Berry, George L., 71, 285
Berry, Harry S., 82, 176, 211
Bourne, Louis M., 218
Bradford, J. Charles, 218, 219
Broughton, J. Melville, 270, 273
Brown, Elsworth, 107, 115; *pictured, 166*
Brown, Henry D., 241, 242
Brown, James B., 195
Brown, Laurence, 251
Brown, Nuch, 126, 186
Browning, Gordon, 135, 142, 280-81; describes Luke Lea, 290
Bryan, E.W., 199, 200
Bryan, William Jennings, 65
Bullard, R.L., 100, 120
Bullock, Edward L., 29
Burdette, P.M., 189

Caldwell and Company, 147-48, 151; and 1929 banking transactions, 189-98; collapse of, 195-98; role of, in Lea case, 273
Caldwell, James E., 195
Caldwell, Rogers, 147-48, 152, 235-36
Carmack, Edward Ward, 18, 23; killing of, 24

321

seeks Luke, Jr.'s liberty, 258-59; and death of son Percy, 259-60; learns of forged bonds, 261; effects of incarceration on family of, 261-62, 263, 266-67, 274; Davidson County indictment against, dropped, 264; federal banking charge dismissed, 264-65; personal financial affairs of, investigated, 265-66; mortgage on home of, foreclosed, 266-67; takes steps to obtain release, 267-73, 275-76; exonerated by audit, 268, 270-72; obtains interest of Hearst newspapers in case, 269; files pardon application, 270-72; denied, 273; paroled, 275-76; hometown reception for, 277-79; declines to make governor's race, 280; role in campaign of Richard Atkinson, 280; supports Gordon Browning for governor, 281; post-release work of, 281-82, 284; conceives interstate highway system, 282-83; plans national magazine, 283-84; publishes *Dixie Farmer*, 284; proposes Pan-American Foundation, 284-85; urges prison reform, 285-86; public policy views of, 285; attempts to regain *Tennessean*, 286-87; persuades Senator McKellar to investigate 1937 *Tennessean* sale, 287; home life of, 288; vows to repay indebtedness, 288; pardoned, 288;

last illness of, 288-89; dies, 289-90; achievements of, assessed, 290-94.
Lea, Luke (great-grandfather), 6-7
Lea, Luke, Jr., 27, 186, 200, 210, 213, 218, 230-31, 233, 254-55, 258, 288; *pictured, 167; 168, 171*
Lea, Mary Louise Warner, family background of, 26; children born to, 27, 28; health crises of, 28, 40-41, 75-76; dies, 121; *pictured, 161*
Lea, Overton, Jr. (brother), 9, 11, 13-14, 15
Lea, Overton (father), 6, 8; as cattle breeder, 8-9, 10; financially backs *Tennessean*, 21, 22; dies, 41; *pictured, 155*
Lea, Overton (son), 184
Lea, Percie Warner, 27, 128-29; *pictured, 167, 171*
Lea, Percy (son), 233, 259; *pictured, 167, 171*
Leake, J.O., 26
Lewis, E.C., 22, 59
Lealand, 6, 7, 8; rebuilding of, 9-10; *pictured, 157*
Liberty Bank and Trust Company, 198, 204, 212-13, 219
Little, Tom, 127
Long, Huey, 215
Louisville and Nashville (L&N) Railroad: ICC investigation of, 58-63; opposes Lea's reelection, 68; role in Lea's 1915 defeat, 73